When is the Nation?

This new collection of the key authors on nationalism delivers the latest thinking on the fundamental aspect of politics, sociology and international relations – nations and nationalism.

John Breuilly, Walker Connor, Steven Grosby, Eric Hobsbawm, Anthony D. Smith and Pierre L. van den Berghe comprehensively explain the key theoretical question in nationalism studies of 'when is the nation?', that is, 'in what point of history is a nation born?' In a world still imbued with the language and practices of nationalism, this is a pertinent question, to which main theories give different answers. The comparison and contrast of these main approaches in the volume not only offers an overview of the state of theoretical debates but also reveals their strengths and weaknesses. This new text:

- introduces the main schools of thought with clarity and concision
- tackles the most pertinent questions in nationalism
- delivers both theoretical and empirical perspectives
- uses an innovative new interactive debate format with questions and answers
- presents key case studies bringing theory to life

The inclusion of case studies gives the reader fresh insights into specific nations and national groups, including the USA, Greece, England and Fiji. The accessible debate format puts main theories and thinkers to the test, enabling the reader to interact with the issues directly.

This unique volume is an invaluable resource for students and scholars of nationalism, ethnicity and global conflict.

Atsuko Ichijo is Research Fellow in European Studies at Kingston University, London. She has recently published *Scottish Nationalism and the Idea of Europe* (Routledge, 2004).

Gordana Uzelac is Senior Lecturer in Quantitative Sociology, London Metropolitan University. Her main research areas include the formation of ethnic and national identities and the process of nation-formation in Eastern Europe (especially former Yugoslavia) and western societies.

When is the Nation?

Towards an understanding of
theories of nationalism

**Edited by Atsuko Ichijo and
Gordana Uzelac**

Routledge
Taylor & Francis Group

LONDON AND NEW YORK

First published 2005
by Routledge
2 Park Square, Milton Park, Abingdon, Oxon OX14 4RN

Simultaneously published in the USA and Canada
by Routledge
270 Madison Avenue, New York, NY 10016

Routledge is an imprint of the Taylor & Francis Group

Typeset in Baskerville
by RefineCatch Ltd, Bungay, Suffolk
Printed and bound in Great Britain
by TJ International, Padstow, Cornwall

British Library Cataloguing in Publication Data
A catalogue record for this book is available from the British Library

Library of Congress Cataloging in Publication Data
When is the nation?: towards an understanding of theories of nationalism/
    edited by Atsuko Ichijo and Gordana Uzelac.
        p.   cm.
    Includes bibliographical references and index.
    1. Nationalism.   I. Ichijo, Atsuko, 1967–   .   II. Uzelac, Gordana, 1966–
JC311.W455 2005
320.54′01 – dc22   2005001997

ISBN 0–415–35493–5 (hbk)
ISBN 0–415–36121–4 (pbk)

Contents

Ethno-symbolism

Contributors

John Breuilly is Professor of Ethnicity and Nationalism at the London School of Economics and Political Science. His recent publications include: *Austria, Prussia and Germany 1806–1871* (2002); *Nationalismus und moderner Staat. Deutschland und Europa* (1999); as co-editor, *Germany's Two Unifications: Anticipations, Experiences, Responses* (2004), and as editor, *19th Century Germany: Politics, Culture and Society 1780–1918* (2001). His current research projects include the modernisation of the German lands; a comparative cultural history of nineteenth-century Hamburg, Lyon and Manchester; and a collaborative project comparing the first and second German unifications.

Walker Connor is Distinguished Visiting Professor of Political Science at Middlebury College. He has held resident appointments at, *inter alia*, Harvard, Dartmouth, the Woodrow Wilson International Center for Scholars, Oxford, Cambridge, Bellagio, Warsaw, Singapore and Budapest. The University of Nevada named him Distinguished Humanist of 1991 to 1992 and the University of Vermont named him the Distinguished Political Scientist of 1997. He has published over fifty articles and five books dealing with the comparative study of nationalism.

Susan-Mary Grant is Reader in American History, University of Newcastle-upon-Tyne. Her publications include: *North Over South: Northern Nationalism and American Identity in the Antebellum Era* (2000); *Legacy of Disunion: The Enduring Significance of the American Civil War*, edited with Peter J. Parish (2003); *The American Civil War: Explorations and Reconsiderations*, edited with Brian Holden Reid (2000), and a number of articles on American nationalism and on the Civil War. The *American Civil War* was shortlisted for the Lincoln Prize, 2001.

Steven Grosby, Professor of Philosophy and Religion, Clemson University, is the author of *Biblical Ideas of Nationality, Ancient and Modern* (2003); editor and translator of *Hans Freyer, Theory of Objective Mind* (1998); and editor of *The Calling of Education* (1997) and *The Virtue of Civility* (1997). His numerous articles have appeared in such journals as *European Journal of Sociology, Journal of the Economic and Social History of the Orient, History of Religions, Zeitschrift für die alttestamentliche Wissenschaft, Social Compass, Nations and Nationalism*, and *Ethnic and*

Racial Studies. He is also co-editor of the four-volume reader *Nationality and Nationalism* (2004) and is author of the forthcoming *Nationalism: A Very Short Introduction* (Oxford University Press).

Eric Hobsbawm is Emeritus Professor of History, Birkbeck College, University of London. He is the author of a number of books including *The Age of Capital* (1975), *The Age of Empire* (1987), *Nations and Nationalism* (1990), *The Age of Extremes* (1994), *Interesting Times* (2002), and he co-edited *The Invention of Tradition* (1982).

Atsuko Ichijo is Research Fellow in European Studies at Kingston University, London. Her main research interests are nationalism and its relationship to 'Europe' and 'Eastern' and 'Western' nationalism. Her recent publications include *Scottish Nationalism and the Idea of Europe* (2004), 'The scope of theories of nationalism: comments on Scottish and Japanese experiences', *Geopolitics*, 7(2), 2002, pp. 53–74, 'The uses of history: Anglo-British and Scottish views of Europe', *Regional and Federal Studies*, 13(3), 2003, pp. 23–43. She is a member of the editorial team of *Nations and Nationalism*.

Krishan Kumar is William R. Kenan, Jr., Professor of Sociology at the University of Virginia. He was previously Professor of Social and Political Thought at the University of Kent at Canterbury, England. He received his undergraduate education at the University of Cambridge and his postgraduate education at the London School of Economics. Among his publications are *Prophecy and Progress: The Sociology of Industrial and Post-Industrial Society* (1978); *Utopia and Anti-Utopia in Modern Times* (1987); *The Rise of Modern Society; From Post-Industrial to Post-Modern Society* 2nd ed. (2005); *1989: Revolutionary Ideas and Ideals* (2001); *The Making of English National Identity* (2003).

Stephanie Lawson is Professor of International Relations and Director of European and International Studies at the University of East Anglia. She is a graduate of the University of New England and former Fellow in the Research School of Pacific and Asian Studies at the Australian National University. Her books include *The Failure of Democratic Politics in Fiji* (1991), *Tradition Versus Democracy in the South Pacific: Fiji, Tonga and Western Samoa* (1996), *Europe and the Asia-Pacific: Culture, Identity and Representations of Regions* (2003) and *International Relations* (2003). In addition, she has published over fifty book chapters and articles on issues concerning democracy, human rights, nationalism, ethnicity and the politics of culture.

Anthony D. Smith is Emeritus Professor of Ethnicity and Nationalism in the Department of Government at the London School of Economics. His books include *The Ethnic Origins of Nations* (1986), *National Identity* (1991), *Nationalism and Modernism* (1998), *The Nation in History* (2000), *Nationalism* (2001), *Chosen Peoples* (2003) and *The Antiquity of Nations* (2004). He is Editor-in-Chief of *Nations and Nationalism* as well as Vice-President of ASEN.

Anna Triandafyllidou is Senior Research Fellow at ELIAMEP, Athens, and Fellow of the Robert Schuman Centre of Advanced Studies, European University Institute in Florence. She teaches as Visiting Professor at the College of Europe in Bruges and works occasionally as an expert for the European Commission and the Greek government. She has held teaching and research positions at the University of Surrey, London School of Economics, CNR in Rome, New York University, University of Athens and EUI in Florence. Her recent publications include: *Immigrants and National Identity in Europe* (2001), *Negotiating Nationhood in a Changing Europe: Views from the Press* (2002), *Europeanisation, National Identities and Migration* (2003, co-editor), and *Multiculturalism, Muslims and Citizenship: A European Approach* (forthcoming in 2005, co-editor).

Gordana Uzelac is Senior Lecturer in Quantitative Sociology at the London Metropolitan University. Her main research areas include the formation of ethnic and national identities and the process of nation-formation in Eastern Europe (especially former Yugoslavia) and Western societies. She is a member of the Editorial Board of *Nations and Nationalism*. Her recent publications include 'Morphogenesis of nation', in S. Malesevic and M. Haugaard (eds) *Making Sense of Collectivity* (2002, London: Pluto Press, pp. 138–166), and 'When is the nation? Constituent elements and processes', *Geopolitics*, 7(2), 2002, pp. 33–52.

Pierre L. van den Berghe is Professor Emeritus of Sociology and Anthropology at the University of Washington, where he has taught since 1965. A specialist in race and ethnic relations, family and kinship, and human sociobiology, he has extensive teaching and research experience in Nigeria, Kenya, South Africa, Peru, Mexico, Guatemala, Germany, France and Israel, and is the author or editor of twenty-two books. Among them are *Race and Racism* (1967), *South Africa: A Case Study in Conflict* (1980), *The Ethnic Phenomenon* (1981) and *Stranger in their Midst* (1989).

Acknowledgements

This volume is based on the fourteenth annual conference of the Association for the Study of Ethnicity and Nationalism (ASEN) entitled 'When is the nation: the debate' that was held on 23–24 April 2004 at the London School of Economics and Political Science. The editors would like to thank the ASEN for providing the opportunity to bring these scholars together and therefore kick-starting the compilation of the volume. We would particularly like to thank the members of the 2004 conference committee who worked tirelessly for the conference: Daphne Halikiopoulou, John Hutchinson, Caroline Kisiel, Athena Leoussi, Lucian Leustean, Mansoor Mirsa, Steve Mock, Nino Nanava, Seeta Persaud, John Simpson, Anthony D. Smith, John Webster and Mitchell Young.

Special thanks are due for the British Academy whose generous funding made the conference possible.

Atsuko Ichijo and Gordana Uzelac

Introduction

Atsuko Ichijo and Gordana Uzelac

Nations and nationalism are among the forces that shape the contemporary world. Despite the 'end of history' thesis, the collapse of communist states and globalisation, our world is still deeply embedded in the language and practice of nations and nationalism – broadly defined – and they continue to puzzle and fascinate those want to understand the state of our society and the direction in which it is heading.

The surge of interest in nationalism studies is a relatively recent phenomenon. Although some of the classics (such as works by Edward H. Carr, Hans Kohn, Elie Kedourie and Karl Deutsch) were produced in the 1950s and 1960s, and scholars such as Ernest Gellner, Walker Connor, Tom Nairn and Anthony D. Smith started publishing on the theme in the 1970s, many of the key texts have been produced since the 1980s. There has been an even greater rush of publication in response to the collapse of the Soviet Union and the dissolution of Yugoslavia, the events whose effects were felt keenly in the 1990s.

The foci of the ever-expanding body of literature on nations and nationalism are on the four basic questions: 'what', 'when', 'why' and 'how'. The exact wording may vary, but these themes may be translated into the following questions: What is a nation?; When have nation and nationalism come into being?; Why are there nations and nationalism?; How are nations and nationalism formed? While the degree of importance attributed to each question differs from scholar to scholar, as demonstrated in Eric Hobsbawm's assertion in this volume that 'why' is not an issue that merits investigation (p. 128), it is quite fair to say that these are the four *basso continuos* of the study of nations and nationalism. Among the four, we have chosen to focus on 'when' in this volume. In order to explain why we have come to this decision, we need to look back to the genesis of the present volume, which reflects, incidentally, a history of nationalism studies in the English-speaking world.

The genesis of the book

This volume is based on the fourteenth annual conference of the Association for the Study of Ethnicity and Nationalism (ASEN) in April 2004 which was organised to mark the retirement of Professor Anthony D. Smith, one of the leading scholars of nations and nationalism, from the London School of Economics and Political Science in September the same year. It was quickly decided that the theme of the conference should be 'When is the nation?', since this is one of the issues Anthony D. Smith has been focusing on, and his writing on it has kept the momentum going in the debate about nations and nationalism by challenging some of the established views, especially the modernist accounts. The organisers felt that it was therefore entirely appropriate to focus on the 'when' question in this conference.

The question was first raised in writing by Walker Connor in his article, 'When is a nation?' which appeared in *Ethnic and Racial Studies* in 1990. In this, Connor challenged the received wisdom of the time that the French nation was one of the very oldest nations of Europe by referring Eugene Weber's *Peasants into Frenchmen: The Modernization of Rural France, 1870–1914* (London, 1979). Connor holds that nations are mass phenomena and that nations do not exist unless the masses acquire national consciousness. Since Weber's work demonstrated convincingly that many of the ordinary French were not aware of their being French as late as the First World War, Connor argued that the French nation did not exist until well into the twentieth century. And if one of the supposedly oldest nations was in fact not that old, how old could any other nation be? He then challenged other scholars to investigate 'when is a nation?', since this would reveal even more about nations and nationalism than the customary examination of 'what is a nation?' (Connor 1990).

Connor's article arguably embodied a widely held concern in nationalism studies. The issue of whether or not nations and nationalism are modern phenomena had already become one of the hotly contested points with the publication of major works such as Benedict Anderson's *Imagined Communities: Reflections on the Origins and Spread of Nationalism* (1983), John Armstrong's *Nations before Nationalism* (1982), John Breuilly's *Nationalism and the State* (1982), Ernest Gellner's *Nations and Nationalism* (1983), Anthony Giddens' *The Nation-state and Violence* (1985), *The Invention of Tradition* (edited by Eric Hobsbawm and Terrance Ranger, 1983), and Anthony D. Smith's *The Ethnic Origins of Nations* (1986). The publication of Connor's article coincided with another major study by Eric Hobsbawm (*Nations and Nationalism since 1780*, 1990) and was followed by such works as Liah Greenfeld's *Nationalism: Five Roads to Modernity* (1992). All of these works have invariably touched upon the issue of 'when' and they have appeared to reach a consensus that, as far as nationalism is concerned, it is a modern phenomenon which has accompanied, among other things, the processes of industrialisation, the spread of capitalism and the establishment of the modern state. As for the nations – as a human group, not as a state – opinion remains divided. Most of these theorists have taken the modernist stance that nations and nationalism are indeed modern, while others, including Smith and Armstrong, have maintained that there could be pre-modern nations, if not pre-modern nationalism.

In the following years, the scope of discussion about nationalism has vastly expanded to include normative issues as well as postmodern concerns. The issue of 'when' has, however, never been settled. The debate has continued partly because the participants have failed to engage with one another for the lack of a common framework. When the editors of this volume set out to organise the above-mentioned conference, we realised this could be made into an occasion to facilitate a truly engaged debate. In order to have such a discussion on the 'when' question, three paradigms – primordialism, modernism and ethno-symbolism – were identified as the key approaches to the question. Briefly, in the primordialist explanation, nations are seen as something intrinsic to human nature, as a type of social organisation that human beings need to form in order to survive in this world. Nations are therefore timeless – they may be found in antiquity as well as in modern times. Modernists, on the other hand, place nations firmly in the modern era. Unlike primordialists who tend to see nationalism as a product of nations, modernists believe, in Gellner's celebrated phrase, that 'it is nationalism that engenders nations, not the other way round' (Gellner 1983: 55). Since nationalism is a modern phenomenon, nations that are created by nationalism can only be modern. The third approach, ethno-symbolism, attempts to combine the strengths of both approaches. According to ethno-symbolists, although nationalism is a modern ideology, successful nations are built upon pre-modern heritage and it is possible to recognise a nation before the onset of modernity.

Six leading scholars in the field – John Breuilly, Walker Connor, Steven Grosby, Eric Hobsbawm, Anthony D. Smith and Pierre L. van den Berghe – were then asked to present their views along one of these three schools of thought. Breuilly was asked to present his view with regard to the 'when' question from the modernist stance, and Connor was given the task of replying to it from the ethno-symbolic point of view. Grosby was to present the primordialist case which Hobsbawm agreed to address from the modernist stance. We asked Smith to spell out the answer to the 'when' question from the ethno-symbolic perspective, on which van den Berghe was invited to comment from the primordialist viewpoint. The conference was successful in involving these scholars as well as the audience in the discussion of the question, and this volume is a product of our efforts to bring the debate forward. The editors approached other scholars to contribute case studies as a basis to examine the strengths and weaknesses of these three paradigms, and wide-ranging cases from England (by Krishan Kumar) to Fiji (by Stephanie Lawson), Greece (by Anna Triandafylliou) to the USA (by Susan-Mary Grant) are now assembled in this volume.

Why 'when is the nation?'

As the following chapters demonstrate, discussing the 'when' question inevitably leads to the 'what' question. The contributors agree that to be preoccupied with fixing a date of the birth of a specific nation does not help us to further our understanding of nations and nationalism. This could be an important topic for historians of a certain nation or for those who are active in pursuing nationalist politics, but examining a single case without placing it in a wider context does not aid our endeavour to understand what nations and nationalism are. Since there is a consensus that nationalism itself is a modern product, any study on nationalism should deal with the nature of modern society in which we live. Likewise, the discussion of nations has some significance from this point of view, insofar as it addresses the issues of modernity and more broadly what society is. After all, nations and nationalism are social phenomena, not an article of faith.

In the context of the current volume, what matters is the sociological implication of the answer to the 'when is the nation?' question. As Smith argues elsewhere, the orthodoxy in nationalism studies at present is that nations and nationalism are modern products, something that has emerged in response to a series of revolutions – political, industrial and scientific – since the eighteenth century (Smith 1998). Most of the literature cited above is broadly modernist in that the authors basically hold this line of thinking. If there was indeed a pre-modern nation as primordialists and perennialists would argue, our understanding of a nation, nationalism and, consequently, modern society would need to be adjusted accordingly. The 'when' question is in fact a sociological question disguised as a historical one.

In addition, the 'when' question raises a fundamental methodological question, a question that lies at the heart of the dispute about whether or not there was a nation before the rise of modernity. How can we certify the existence of a pre-modern nation beyond doubt? Here, the point made, perhaps the sharpest ever, by John Goldthorp is relevant. As a sociologist, Goldthorpe questioned the wisdom of using historical data by his fellow sociologists since history was, after all, about those records that happened to have survived until today. Sociology as a discipline, on the other hand, is equipped with methods to create new sets of data about the present; it did not have to be constrained by what happened to have survived (Goldthorpe 1991).

Goldthorpe's warning was not particularly concerned with the study of nations and nationalism, and it was directed towards other sociologists. The limitation of relying on history in discussing a sociological phenomenon including a nation that he pointed out is, none the less, a real issue for those who are interested in investigating the nature of nations and nationalism. When Connor called for more research on 'when' in his 1990 article, he was aware of this particular methodological problem (Connor 1990). In this volume, John Breuilly spells out in clear terms the problems we face in examining the possibility of existence of pre-modern nations. How much can we read into a fact that a particular name has survived, he asks (Chapter 1)? In a similar fashion, Eric Hobsbawm takes a sceptical view of using historical material as evidence of the pre-modern nation (Chapter 4). Of course, one of the reasons why these historians are sceptical about the uses of historical evidence in the discussion of what is essentially a sociological phenomenon derives from the unsettled nature of the 'what' question, which brings us back to the earlier point. However, if we recall Connor's plea for more research into 'when' and the vast amount of literature produced on this question, we may conclude that the 'when' question merits separate investigation. The ways in which we carry it out are hotly disputed. What can we do then? Anthony D. Smith's contribution to this volume addresses this dilemma and proposes to disentangle the sociological question ('when is *a* nation?') from the historical one ('when is *the* nation?') (Chapter 5). As we can see from Breuilly's response to Smith's attempt, this has not settled the dispute. Steven Grosby (Chapter 3) suggests a different approach – philosophical anthropology – and Pierre L. van den Berghe argues that the introduction of biological understanding in the form of Darwinism should help us out of this muddle (Chapter 6). What the volume highlights therefore is a need for further discussions of the methods scholars of nations and nationalism can employ in order to move the field forward.

The plan of the book

The aim of the book is, as discussed above, to move the debate forward. In order to achieve this, the structure of the book follows the format of the 'When is the nation?' conference which was designed to generate engaged debates. The conference was organised in four sessions; the first three sessions were devoted to a debate between two approaches out of the three – primordialism, modernism and ethno-symbolism – followed by a question-and-answer session. The fourth session brought all the speakers together to offer an overall evaluation of the scholarly discussions in the study of nations and nationalism. The first part of this volume follows the conference closely. John Breuilly first spells out his modernist understanding of nations and nationalism, to which Walker Connor replies from his distinctively non-modernist framework. Steven Grosby then takes up the case for primordialism developed along the line that was advocated by Edward Shills, to which Eric Hobsbawm responds from his clearly materialist and modernist stance. Anthony D. Smith, then, offers a redefined version of ethno-symbolism, to which Pierre L. van den Berghe adds a socio-biological aspect. Each set of debates is preceded by a short introduction to one of the approaches to highlight the main points for the benefit of the reader. Each debate is followed by a question-and-answer session in which some contentious points made in the chapters are further discussed. Part I concludes with a panel discussion on the points raised during the conference.

There are some recurring themes in Part I. The role of modernity in the formation of a social group called a nation has, of course, naturally attracted most attention. At the same time, an old problem of the terminology, especially the conflation of nation and state in both scholarly literature and everyday discussion, also surfaces repeatedly, which seemed to have led to a rather pessimistic assessment of the development of nationalism studies by Walker Connor. More fundamentally, the issue of epistemology emerges in an exchange between Steven Grosby and Eric Hobsbawm: Are there external facts that are independent from our mind or is everything an affair of the mind? Without settling this fundamental question, no meaningful discussion between two minds is possible. The debate between the two suggests that more work is required in order to prepare a common ground on which fruitful exchanges of ideas may take place. Another issue that is mentioned repeatedly is neo-Darwinism. The participants did not find it difficult to acknowledge the utility of biology in understanding nations and nationalism, but what has invited most attention is the role of neo-Darwinism in explaining gender relations, not its explanatory power in the issue of 'when is the nation?'

In Part II, four scholars examine a variety of cases in order to evaluate the three approaches. Krishan Kumar, in a similar vein to Breuilly in Part I, challenges the conventional view that the English nation is an old one (Chapter 7). He examines literature from the early modern period to argue that Englishness was suppressed under Britishness, and, with the development of all-Britain institutions such as the Union of Parliament and the British Empire, English national identity was prohibited from growing, and in fact the English national consciousness is a very recent phenomenon. If a supposedly old nation is in fact not so old, what can the primordial approach add to our understanding of nations and nationalism, Kumar asks. Susan-Mary Grant, unlike other historians in this volume, evaluates ethno-symbolism favourably in her study of the birth of the USA (Chapter 8). It allows her to evaluate the place of the Civil War in US history, and more importantly in American nationalism. This is important for Grant who, like other contributors, refuses to fix a birth date of the US nation but recognises the re-energising effect of 'old' ideas in the history of American nationalism. The point that a nation is always in a process, which was once taken up by Connor (Connor 1990) and developed by Grant in this volume, is then closely examined by Anna Triandafyllidou in the case of the Greek nation (Chapter 9). The Greek nation occupies a peculiar place in the study of nationalism since it can claim both old and new at the same time. Triandafyllidou illustrates the fact that the Greek nation is constantly in formation by examining two recent significant incidents: the 'Macedonian question' and immigration. Finally, Stephanie Lawson examines a lesser known case of Fiji, paying particular attention to the claim of 'being indigenous' by the ethnic Fijians (Chapter 10). All three approaches are considered in its explanatory power in the case of Fiji, and she concludes that the modernist approach is best placed to explain the emergence and development of the Fijian nation.

Evaluating which approach is more powerful than others in explaining nations and nationalism is a task left to the reader. We, the editors, are confident that this volume provides ample material for the reader to form his or her own opinion.

References

Connor, W. (1990) 'When is a nation', *Ethnic and Racial Studies*, 13(1), pp. 92–103.

Gellner, E. (1983) *Nations and Nationalism*, Oxford: Blackwell.

Goldthorpe, J. (1991) 'The uses of history in sociology: reflections on some recent tendencies', *British Journal of Sociology*, 42(2), pp. 211–230.

Smith, A.D. (1998) *Nationalism and Modernism*, London: Routledge.

Part I

Theoretical issues

Modernism

Introduction

Literature on nations and nationalism tends to label modernism as the most dominant approach to the study of these phenomena. This dominance is explained not only by the sheer number of theorists who call themselves modernists, but also by the apparent explanatory potency of these theories. In short, modernism claims that nations and nationalism have appeared as consequences of the processes that mark the modern period of social development. Nations and nationalism are epiphenomena, or even unintended consequences of processes of modernisation and industrialisation. Thus the question of 'When is the nation?' in these theories is translated into 'When is modernity?' The social conditions of societies in transition to modernity have, according to these theories, stipulated the emergence of nationalism, either as a political movement or a doctrine that then created nations. This is where all similarities between these theories end.

In order to provide a brief overview of modernist theories, it will be necessary to concentrate on themes that these theories have in common, rather than to attempt futilely to demonstrate the richness of each theoretical approach. Hence, in what follows, similarities between modernist theories will be sought out on several levels. We will analyse, on the one hand, conditions that are marked as necessary for the emergence of what we call modernity and, on the other, processes that have generated the emergence of nationalism and ultimately the formation of the nation. In each group of theories we will then examine how they define the nation and how they account for the emergence of the nation that has shaped modern societies.

Modernist theories could be crudely divided between, on the one hand, those who see the period of transition to modernity as a set of processes that led towards the system integration and, on the other, those that emphasise processes of socio-cultural integration. The former theories describe the process of modernity as erosion of the traditional structures that had to be replaced by new ones, which in turn would result into a new form of stability in now modern societies. The latter explains the transition 'from below' – as a set of social changes that would eventually substitute the broken social bonds of population dragged into modernity by redefining social relationships, and develop new forms of a now national culture.

The system integration theories are based on the notion that rapid industrialisation, urbanisation and technological advances in Western Europe disturbed the *system integration* of the traditional societies and hence initiated a restructuring of old and the emergence of new social institutions. Hence, for example, Ernest Gellner in his path-breaking *Nations and Nationalism* (1983) describes a modern industrialised society as based on the idea of perpetual growth. It demands a highly mobile, literate, specialised workforce. This demand reshapes the state institutions that now have as their task the transformation of a previously centralised, closed and fused society into a decentralised, open and specialised one (Gellner 1983: 14). Mainly by the means of centralised education, the existing 'low culture' is transformed into 'high culture'; that is, 'a culture characterised by standardisation, a literacy- and education-based system of communication' (Gellner 1983: 54). This new education system erases regional cultural differences, and moulds the population into a community of co-nationals. This period of transition is now labelled the age of nationalism. 'Nationalism is not the awakening of an old, latent, dormant force, though that is how it does indeed present itself. It is in reality the consequence of a new form of social organisation, based on deeply internalised, education-dependent high cultures, each protected by its own state' (Gellner 1983: 48). Nationalism makes nations.

Another group of modernist theories claim that the erosion of pre-modern structures cannot be seen only as a consequence of changes in economic spheres of society. Michael Mann (1995), Charles Tilly (1975), John Breuilly (1993) and Anthony Giddens (1985) are more inclined to emphasise the changes in the political structures as crucial for the emergence of the modern world. Transition to modernity according to these authors is characterised by military and administrative expansions, centralisation of government and a taxation system on the whole clearly bounded territory of the state. In modernity the state becomes the main (f)actor of social change. Hence, this group of theories hold that, in Mann's words, 'nations and nationalism have primarily developed in response to the development of the modern state' (1995: 45). The consolidation of the modern state and the rapid expansion of its functions – which occurs, according to these authors, mainly through unilinear historical stages – has several consequences for their societies. Breuilly emphasises emerging conflictual interests between civic society and the state, Giddens focuses on the alienation and ontological insecurity of the population that has lost its traditions, and Mann sees as the main consequence increasing political participation of the broader population. 'Self-conscious nations,' he claims, 'emerged from the struggle for representative government' (Mann 1995: 48).

Modernity is characterised not only by economic and political changes; it has also brought out a system of new ideas that radically oppose pre-modern conceptions. The notions of popular sovereignty, national self-determination, citizenship and democracy have soon taken roots among, at first, the urban middle class, and have then spread through to the working class and peasantry. Modernity, Breuilly and Mann would stress, is the age of political mass movements.

Nationalism as a mass political movement has developed its unique ideology that has served as justification for 'seeking or exercising state power' (Breuilly

1993: 2). Breuilly (ibid.) identifies three main assertions as the basis of nationalist argument:

1   There exists a nation with an explicit and peculiar character.
2   The interests and values of the nation take priority over all other interests and values.
3   The nation must be as independent as possible. This usually requires at least the attainment of political sovereignty.

It is nationalism, therefore, which serves as a means for reintegration of the society and the state. It creates a strong link between them – a community of co-nationals. Giddens can now define the nation as a 'collectivity existing within a clearly demarcated territory, which is subject to unitary administration, reflexively monitored both by the internal state apparatus and those of other states' (Giddens 1985: 116). While this state apparatus serves as a guardian of the community, the same community defined as the nation provides legitimation for these institutions. Hence the nation may be seen as an unintended consequence of the historical process of system integration.

The second group of modernist theories sees nations and nationalism as a vehicle of the process of *socio-cultural integration* of modern societies. This integration, depending on the author, occurs either on the level of ideas or through the means of communication.

The first group of authors, including Elie Kedourie (1960) and Eric Hobsbawm (1989) among others, examines the rise of nations and nationalism through the social and cultural reintegration of collapsed traditional society. The process of transition has to replace the lost traditions and create a new basis for solidarity of the population. From this point on Kedourie and Hobsbawm offer different explanations.

Kedourie is quite specific in defining the origins of nationalism. For him, nationalism as a doctrine was invented in Europe in the early nineteenth century. Kedourie does not see nations and nationalism originating from political or economic changes. Rather, he traces the origins of nationalism within the revolution of ideas that characterised the end of the eighteenth and the beginning of the nineteenth centuries known as the Enlightenment and German Romanticism. Kant's concept of self-determination, Herder's cultural populism, Fichte's linguistic and cultural exclusivism brought to the world the concept of nationalism that stole the position which tradition and religion had once occupied. In Durkheimian fashion, Kedourie sees nationalism as a self-worship of the community where nationalist doctrine becomes a 'political religion'. Nationalism here is an intellectual project, where the excluded and marginalised youth becomes a vehicle of mass mobilisation around the concept of the nation as a culturally homogenous community which offers the replacement of lost traditions and values.

Hobsbawm also sees nationalism occurring in the moment of rapid transformation in societies when older traditions cease to fulfil the task for which they were designed. Nationalism offers their replacement: 'New traditions simply resulted from the inability to use or adapt old ones' (Hobsbawm 1989: 5). This approach also considers the creation of the nation as a modern process, but its method is found in the so-called 'invention of traditions'. Eric Hobsbawm sees this set of practices as a method for the implementation of certain values and norms of behaviour simply by repetition (ibid.: 4). To create the cohesion and stability necessary in such a society, Hobsbawm lists 'three main modes of inclusion and control': (1) by establishing or legitimising institutions; (2) by the invention of new status systems and modes of socialisation, which will also provide modes for desirable beliefs, value systems and behaviour; and (3) through the formation of a community such as the nation, which can provoke a sense of identification either within that community or with the institutions representing, expressing or symbolising it (ibid.: 9). Put in this way, the nation becomes the perfect means for a new socio-cultural integration of modern societies, and it is constructed with that aim in mind.

Benedict Anderson (1983) shares many of the above-mentioned premises. He too tends to explain the rise of nations and nationalism as the instrument of a new socio-cultural integration of a society shattered by the rapid industrialisation, modernisation and advances in technology. However, Anderson does not find the explanation in the content of the ideas but in the means of their transmission. For him, nationalism is not about 'what' people think, but 'how'.

The transition from pre-modern to modern societies was characterised by the general process of secularisation, standardisation of the concept of time and the invention of commercial print. These processes, according to Anderson, made nationalism possible. The first process has transferred the loyalties from religious community to the community of destiny – the nation. The second process has opened up the space for imagining community in a 'homogenous, empty time' (Anderson 1983: 24) where an individual could identify with anonymous masses of co-nationals. Finally, the emergence of 'print-capitalism, and especially newspapers seen as "one-day best-sellers", besides standardising the vernacular, offer an image of the world "visibly rooted in everyday life" (ibid.: 36). These processes have resulted in the creation of the nation, 'an imagined political community – and imagined as both inherently limited and sovereign' (ibid.: 6).

After this brief overview of some of the more dominant modernist theories of nations and nationalism, one can only conclude that differences between them are such that their categorisation under the same label seems unfruitful. Nevertheless, since the purpose of this introduction is a general overview of a single category labelled the 'modernist perspective', an analysis of its critiques will, once again, have to be concentrated on their similarities rather than their differences.

The critics of modernist approaches have labelled these theories, among others, structuralist, functionalist, constructionist and instrumentalist. The first two terms indicate that the modernist approach is concerned mainly with structural changes in the transition to modernity and the influences of social institutions on social change. In a Parsonian manner this approach emphasises the reconstruction of old, disfunctional institutions and the formation of new ones that have brought about a new equilibrium in society. This equilibrium is achieved mainly at the level of the social system. In such an explanation social institutions themselves are seen as actors of social change. Hence the emergence of nations and nationalism are seen as unintended consequences of broader social processes. The nation is formed 'from above', the population is moulded into a new form of community, actors are constrained by dominant structures.

Those critics who see some of the modernist theories as constructionist or instrumentalist emphasise their so-called upward conflation, where the changes in social structure are explained by unconstrained actions of agency. The concepts of 'invention' and 'imagination', for example, only assume the role of a social actor that radically changes the social structure and culture of a society in transition. Socio-cultural integration is explained as a result of an agency's free will. Consequently, these theories explain the emergence of the nation as a result of agents' interests and agendas. The agency in these theories appears as unconstrained by previous social structures or cultures. It seems that the new community of the nation is created *ab ovo*.

In addition, it is important to note that unlike primordialists and ethno-symbolists, modernist theories are unavoidably Eurocentric. It was Europe, after all, that experienced changes at its political, economic and social levels around the end of the eighteenth and the beginning of the nineteenth century, changes so dramatic that they deserve a label as the beginning of a new era. Theories that offer some explanation of the rise of nations and nationalism in non-European societies (e.g. Kedourie (1971) or Anderson (1983)) are mainly engaged in applying the developed European model to these communities. Here, the explanation of the emergence of a phenomenon such as the nation is firmly grounded in one specific geo-political area in a specific historical period marked with an equally specific set of social processes known as modernity. Hence, the explanation of the same phenomena in different places and times requires a creation of different typologies. The modernist theories do not have to be concerned with the 'navels' (Gellner 1996) of the national phenomenon when dealing with the example of Western Europe. Yet, as soon as attention is turned to the non-European cases, they are compelled to either mark culture as unimportant for the explanation of nation formation, or introduce terms such as 'ethnic' or 'proto-' nationalism, where the 'navels issue' creeps back into the picture.

The modernist approaches offer numerous detailed historical and sociological analyses of case studies that have enabled us to observe more closely the important social processes of the formation of nations and nationalism at the levels of structure, culture and agency. It is also characterised by the insistence on more rigorous and narrow definitions of these phenomena and hence equips us with a basis for fruitful comparative analyses. However, one cannot but observe that modernists found themselves in a position where it is not possible just to crudely dismiss challenges from primordialist and ethno-symbolist perspectives. These challenges compel modernists to engage with questions of, first of all, the nature of social change, and hence, consequently, with an integrated explanation of the relevance of pre-modern structures, cultures and role of agency. One such an attempt is presented in the following pages.

References

On modernist approaches to nations and nationalism

Anderson, B. (1983) *Imagined Communities*. London and New York: Verso.

Breuilly, J. (1993) *Nationalism and the State* (2nd ed.). Manchester: Manchester University Press.

Gellner, E. (1983) *Nations and Nationalism*. London: Blackwell.

Gellner, E. (1996) 'Do nations have navels?', *Nations and Nationalism*, 2 (3), 366–370.

Giddens, A. (1985) *The Nation-state and Violence*. Cambridge: Polity Press.

Hobsbawm, E. (1989) Introduction: Inventing traditions. In E. Hobsbawm, and T. Ranger (eds) *The Invention of Tradition*. Cambridge: Cambridge University Press, pp. 1–14.

Hobsbawm, E. (1990) *Nations and Nationalism Since 1780: Programme, Myth, Reality*. Cambridge: Cambridge University Press.

Kedourie, E. (1960) *Nationalism*. London: Hutchinson.

Kedourie, E. (ed.) (1971) *Nationalism in Asia and Africa*. London: Weidenfeld & Nicolson.

Mann, M. (1995) A political theory of nationalism and its excessess. In S. Periwal (ed.) *Notions of Nationalism*. Budapest: Central European University Press, pp. 44–64.

Tilly, C. (ed.) (1975) *The Formation of National States in Western Europe*. Princeton, NJ: Princeton University Press.

Critique of modernism

Özkirimli, U. (2000) *Theories of Nationalism: A Critical Introduction*. Basingstoke: Macmillan.

Smith, A.D. (1998) *Nationalism and Modernism: A Critical Survey of Recent Theories of Nations and Nationalism*. London: Routledge.

1   Dating the nation

How old is an old nation?

John Breuilly

Introduction

I take a modernist position on nation and nationalism. I dispute the primordialist and perennialist claims that there are pre-modern nations and even nationalisms. I also dispute the ethno-symbolic argument that earlier ethnic histories constitute an essential or even significant foundation for modern nation-building.

The arguments involved are well known and often rehearsed.[1] I am sceptical of the validity of any of them when they take the form of general assertion accompanied by brief examples. The lack of context and detail for those examples enables one to construct a scissors-and-paste argument of any kind. Instead I will examine in detail one case where the perennialist interpretation appears strong: medieval and early modern England. If the perennialist argument can be refuted for this strong case, *a fortiori* the refutation may be assumed to work for weaker cases.

It is more difficult to refute ethno-symbolism than perennialism because its advocates agree on the modernity of nation and nationalism and focus instead on the more elusive question of the foundational role of pre-modern ethnic identity for the formation of modern nations and nationalisms. Instead of the empirical-chronological critique of perennialism, modernist critiques of ethno-symbolism must be framed in terms of method. I will dispute the validity of the way ethno-symbolists analyse long-run historical change and, consequently how they connect ethnic claims made by modern nationalism to notions of a longer ethnic past.

Smith distinguishes the sociological question: 'When is *a* nation?' from the historical question 'When is *the* nation?' As a sociologist he gives priority to the first question, considering what he regards as the key ethno-symbolic processes which combine to form nations, before considering the historical record for the formation of specific nations. As a historian I proceed in the opposite direction, asking whether Smith's way of framing the question about nation formation helps in the understanding of particular cases. If it does not help us to understand a particular historical case, I conclude it is generally not helpful.

I begin by considering definitions of nation, national identity and nationalism. Second, I outline a thought experiment designed to show how easy it is to reason wrongly about these concepts as applying to long-run historical phenomena.

Third, I scrutinise the claims that England provides us with a good example of a pre-modern nation and national identity, and even of nationalism. Fourth, I argue that it is not possible to construct a valid long-term historical account of ethnic groups understood as societies linked over time through a complex of ethnic symbols because there is no such past. I conclude that the evident centrality in modern nationalism of myths about ethnic pasts is best explained in modernist terms.

Defining the nation

I do not know what nations were before the era of modern nation-states during which large parts of the population subject to the rule of particular states have come to share common memories and institutions and to regard themselves as members of a nation, whether identified with or against the state. Prior to this era national terminology cannot be taken to refer to the generality of subjects and even less to be terms those subjects use to describe themselves. Rather it operates within elite discourses to underpin narratives of civilisations or to justify conflicting political claims. We encounter these discourses in fragments of evidence, mainly written texts, and must be cautious about attributing too much significance, coherence or continuity to such terminology, even at an elite level.

I disagree with Anthony D. Smith when he argues that the nation must not be defined in modernist terms because that means one cannot recognise pre-modern nations.[2] This implies that nations have a 'real' existence irrespective of definition. If one thinks that the modern nation is so radically different from and discontinuous with anything that went before it, one might take the view that a broader definition which obscured this point was not useful. However, to engage in an argument, one needs agreed as well as useful definitions and I accept those which Smith provides for nation, national identity and nationalism, with one significant alteration to the third of these. I think, incidentally, that most perennialists could accept these definitions as well, so at least we can argue on common ground.

I take these definitions from Smith's most recent book *Chosen Peoples*.

> NATION: 'a named human population occupying an historic territory and sharing common myths and memories, a public culture, and common laws and customs for all members.'
>
> (Smith 2003: 24–25 for these three definitions)

This differs from the definition Smith offers in his paper to the conference from which this book arose:

> a named and self-defined community whose members cultivate common myths, memories, symbols and values, possess and disseminate a distinctive public culture, reside in and identify with a historic homeland, and create and disseminate common laws and shared customs.

The term 'self-defined' is added while that of 'all members' is omitted, opening up the possibility of nations which are confined to a self-conscious elite and exclude the majority of the population, what Smith in an earlier book called an aristocratic as opposed to a demotic ethnic group (Smith 1986). Already there is a move from the nation as a group towards the nation as a term of elite discourse. This should not be a problem provided that we recognise when we are dealing with self-defined elites and when with 'whole populations' and do not imagine that the use of the same names in the two kinds of cases by itself indicates any other connection.

> NATIONAL IDENTITY: 'the maintenance and continual reinterpretation of the pattern of values, symbols, memories, myths and traditions that form the distinctive heritage of the nation, and the identification of individuals with that heritage and its pattern.'

It is difficult to see how there could be a nation without such a national identity process. It is easier to study these processes than their assumed outcome – a nation. In what follows I will therefore focus on the process and ask just what can be established about it historically.

> NATIONALISM: 'a political movement for the attainment and maintenance of autonomy, unity and identity on behalf of a population, some of whose members deem it to constitute an actual or potential "nation".'

Smith uses the term 'an ideological movement'. I replace 'ideological' with 'political' because I find it difficult to establish just what an ideological *movement* is as opposed to intellectuals arguing a national case. Even if the goal is not political self-determination, a *movement* must seek to alter power relationships – perhaps in relation to language or other cultural policies – and is perforce political.

To anticipate: I will argue that in the English case the terminology of nation does become important in the medieval and early modern periods but in two very distinct ways which do not really support Smith's definition of nation; that national identity was conceived in 'regnal' not cultural or social terms, and that nationalism is non-existent.[3] I will further argue that insofar as there is any significant continuity in the way specific national terms come to operate under modern conditions, these are better explained in terms of political arguments about institutions than as part of some ethno-symbolic reservoir of myths and memories. Before doing that, however, I will suggest how we can attribute too much or perhaps the wrong kind of significance to the way names for human groups are passed (or not passed) from generation to generation.

A thought experiment

Imagine a knock-out competition involving 128 competitors. Each competitor has a name and a distinctive marking. The competitors are divided into sixty-four pairs which decrease to thirty-two pairs in the second round and so on, until a winner is declared after seven rounds. The nature of the competition varies from round to round. Sometimes it is a contest of chance such as the tossing of a coin. Sometimes skill or strength determines the result.[4]

We know in advance that there can only be one winner. However, given that we know no more about the competitors at the outset than their name and marking and that the character of contests varies from round to round, we cannot predict who that winner will be.

Once the competition is finished and we look back over the successive rounds, the name that will stand out as it figures in every round will be that of the winner. So will the winner's marking. We will barely notice the names and markings of those who lost in the early rounds.

It would be easy, looking back after the final result and seeking to tell the story of this competition, to see the winner's name and marking as somehow the *cause* of the victory. This temptation will increase if someone claiming identity with the winner towards the latter stages of the competition has a vested interest in just such an explanation.

I have been describing a selection process. Selection processes always have a history and this history displays continuity. However, unless one can point to a specific causal mechanism of selection (such as the superior talent of a higher seeded player), continuity means nothing more than survival through random selection. Furthermore, unless one can show the same causal mechanisms at work in each and every generation, continuity cannot be related to one dominant factor.[5]

Debates about 'ethno-genesis' and the antiquity of nations relate to just such selection processes. Societies (more precisely, individual members and/or outsiders) give themselves names which they associate with distinctive characteristics (marks). Names and marks are selectively transmitted from one generation to another. Some names survive for a long time. However, to assume that this, by itself, tells us anything about the 'successful' names beyond survival is like assuming that the name and mark of the winner of a knock-out competition based on a combination of chance and constantly changing performance criteria contributed to that victory. To make this more than a story of random survival, we have to show that the names and marks of the winners promoted long-term survival and that successful performances operated according to similar rules from one generation to the next.

If one argues that modernity means that names and markings acquire new functions and that the rules of selection are altered (above all, by having to associate the names with democratic appeals to the will, interests and characteristics of the 'nation' as a large, inclusive society), then the focus will be less upon the continuity of names, which will be seen as lexical items that have fortuitously survived for a number of generations, and more upon the new ways in which such names are used.

To refute modernist objections to ethno-symbolic or perennialist ways of telling a long-run story of continuity, it is not enough to demonstrate a long and continual history of certain names. Rather, one must show that these names are used for the same purposes and in the same ways from generation to generation. Postmodernists never and ethno-symbolists rarely get beyond noting the existence of names and how they are used in texts, as if that explained anything much. Perennialists have argued persuasively that national names in earlier epochs have meanings and functions similar to those which they possess under modern conditions. Primordialists confuse the antiquity of certain names with a continuity of meaning attributed to those names. Socio-biologists confuse the kinship connotations of national names with the idea that kinship (real or fictive) is at the heart of human allegiance. Only the modernist approach, which understands how old names which have survived or been revived for many different reasons are appropriated for new purposes under modern conditions, can adequately explain why appeals to an ethnic or national past are central in modern nationalisms.

I have made a series of general assertions. The only way to sustain them is empirically. Many historians and others have argued that the case of England provides us with the best example of nation, national identity and even nationalism. It is therefore worth examining these arguments.

'Dating' the English nation[6]

Medieval England

The Anglo-Saxon period

Many accounts of the origins of Englishness begin with *Bede's Ecclesiastical History of the English People*, written *c.* AD 731, which argued for the existence, identity and mission of the English against other peoples on the island of Britain.[7] The text frequently furnishes its own context in historical accounts which can lead to circular reasoning. Non-textual sources which indicate the continuation of 'British' cultural traits after their supposed destruction by the 'English' suggest that the sharp distinctions Bede draws between peoples is problematic (Rollason 2002: 7).

At most, Bede should be read as a project, not a description.[8] Bede pressed the claims of Roman Christian rulers against Celtic Christian and pagan rulers; more specifically he supported Christian rulers of Northumbria against their enemies. His distinctions between Angles, Jutes and Saxons make little sense for the mixed tribal groupings which had settled in England since the collapse of Roman power. His choice of the term 'English people' (*gens Anglorum*) rather than 'Saxon people' relates to the centrality for Bede of Pope Gregory's mission to the English and the conversion work of St Augustine of Canterbury. It has no ethnic or linguistic meaning.[9]

Thus in Bede the term 'English' is subordinate to a primary Roman Christian and a secondary Northumbrian dynastic value. Roman Christianity spread by conquest (one ruler replacing another) and conversion (missionaries working on rulers). Much of *The Ecclesiastical History* is concerned with the conversion of pagans to Christianity and the acceptance by Celtic Christians of Roman Christian practices such as the dating of Easter.[10] Conversion was a top-down process of which Bede provides wonderfully vivid accounts. 'Anglicisation' meant the conquest and/or conversion of rulers.[11]

Given the political and cultural fragmentation of the time, Bede's assertion of an English identity is incredible. The fall-back position is that Bede's text was an agent in the *later* making of English national identity. As Brooks (1999: 5) puts it:

> *Bede's Ecclesiastical History of the English People* provides many of [the] crucial components necessary for ethnogenesis: it asserts a common history and origin myth for the English; it emphasises the enmity (both military and ecclesiastical) of the Britons and thus justifies their forfeiture of most of the island of *Britannia*; and it gives only the slightest glimpses of an earlier Roman and British Christian history – the minimum necessary to provide a credible context for the conversion of the pagan Anglo-Saxons.

Brooks, for example, traces Bedan influences in the use of the term 'English' upon Boniface and Alcuin writing later in the eighth century (Brooks, 2004). The argument acquires real force for the late ninth century, especially in relation to Alfred (ruled 871–899) who drew upon *The Ecclesiastical History* (which he had translated into English, thereby promoting its 'ethnogenesis' function) as well as the *Anglo-Saxon Chronicle*, and who framed justifications for his territorial claims in national terms. However, if we accept the point made by Susan Reynolds (1997: ch. 8)[12] that it was normal for regnal claims to be justified by claims of affinity with a territory or its inhabitants, one can see just why an 'English' argument made sense in Alfred's disputes with other Anglo-Saxon rulers as well as with Danish rulers.

Alfred shifted from projecting his realm as 'Saxon' to 'Anglo-Saxon' or even 'English' (*Angelcynn*), as he extended his power over Mercia and Kent. Later, in the 890s, Alfred's court stressed that the language into which Gregory, Boethius, Bede, parts of the Bible and other writings were translated was *English* (Foot 1996). Educating 'free-born' men in reading and writing English was an aristocratic project to construct cultural, linguistic and religious unity within the different territories brought under Alfred's rule. This territory was called 'Engla Land' (Wormald 1994). Alfred's challenge to Danish control in northern England was, in a way directly influenced by Bede, framed in terms not of conquest but of bringing the English back together. Selecting the names 'English' and 'England' to describe his realm and his subjects answered, therefore, to ambitious schemes to expand and unify disparate territories. Given that the name chosen survives to this day, one might plausibly claim this as the period in which national identity was founded.

Alfred's achievement lay in his realisation that by harnessing and focusing these three forms of identity (cultural, linguistic, legal) through an appeal to a common memory, and by imposing a cultural hegemony, he was able to provide a retrospective and self-consciously historical explanation for the creation of a fourth, national consciousness. In that sense, while Bede invented the English as a people in the sight of God, they were made one nation by 'Alfred of the English' (Bishop Wulfsige in Foot 1996: 49).

However, it is doubtful whether such a justification made sense beyond the claimant and members of the small elite Alfred tried to educate in being English.[13] Mid-ninth-century charters relating to lands in northern England refer to a plurality of identities: Anglo-Saxon, Northumbrian, pagan and Briton (Brooks 2004). 'England' and the English was a local Christianising (Bede) and then dynastic (Alfred) project. If, of course, that changing project was pursued energetically, consistently and successfully, it might produce an English nation. However, one must not confuse the project with one possible outcome.

In fact, in the short term Alfred's project failed. The Danish rulers who laid the foundation for political unity in early eleventh-century England used national terms to co-opt Saxon elites and to appeal against threats from Scandanavia and Normandy but did not deploy them in the same way as Alfred. This concern to defend a fragile polity based on bringing together Danish and Anglo-Saxon regions against outsiders was continued by the last Anglo-Saxon rulers. National terms before 1066 had little ethnic or cultural significance (Gillingham 2000). One does not find cultural stereotyping in Bede (e.g. Britons against English, pagans against Christians, civilised against barbarian) in contrast to many twelfth-century texts. Anglicisation was understood by Bede as a process of religious conversion, and by Alfred as the extension of his rule and the use of Old English as a written vernacular. Neither viewed it as ethnic transformation. They both use the term 'nation' in ways which make sense to a Biblical scholar and an ambitious king but they do not mean by this term a whole people with a common language, historic territory or shared culture.[14]

The construction of a political nation

Prior to the tenth century, England was divided into conflicting political units, some of which described themselves as 'English'. The term served specific church and monarchical projects aimed at extending uniformity of belief and rulership. By the late Anglo-Saxon period these projects had achieved some success. There was one kingship. Institutions such as shires and shire courts were established in much of the realm. Legal codes were proclaimed. Methods for raising taxes and armies were applied with a degree of uniformity. There was a particularly impressive capacity to issue, withdraw and reissue a common coinage. These elements of national government were built on by Norman rulers after 1066. The terms 'England' and 'English' served to describe this government, its ruling elite and even occasionally to appeal to the subjects of this rule.[15] The term 'English' continued but changed its meaning, and began to be accompanied by the term 'England' to describe the territory of the English.

If one assembles claims about the consolidation of shires and their courts, familial continuities within the landowners using such institutions, the national scope of parliaments from the thirteenth century and the consolidation of a national church system, one could argue that from the late Anglo-Saxon period there developed self-conscious elites with extensive and continuous institutions which embodied and reproduced ideas of the English nation.[16]

Well – *possibly*. There are important qualifications and counter-arguments. First, this is a process over time. What may have become the case by the fourteenth century cannot be read back into the tenth. The continuity of a term such as English does not automatically mean a continuity in the meaning of that term. Second, the existence of an institution does not automatically produce some determinant, 'matching' consciousness. Thus we may see the shire court as a 'national' institution because of its territorial reach and significance but that does not, in itself, tell us whether people using such courts thought of them as national. Combining these two points, the longevity of certain institutions does not imply some constant and matching group identity or consciousness over that whole period.

Take the example of shires and shire courts. As I understand it, these came to be established over much of England by the late Anglo-Saxon period. Presumably they took time to embed themselves in areas where they had been most recently established, and varied in how they functioned according to local circumstances.[17] They met only twice a year and, for most of those involved, were confined to adjudicating disputes within the county. Why should infrequent meetings of so many local institutions, even if all were organised along (roughly) similar lines and theoretically under one royal authority, be assumed to have induced a sense of national identity? In the absence of *direct* evidence of such a shared sense of identity I do not see how one is justified in making such a claim. Indeed, it would seem more plausible to assume the opposite; namely that most of the people using these institutions cared or thought little about their national significance and regarded them primarily as instruments for the resolution of local disputes.[18]

As for longevity, institutions change their purposes and the constituencies they serve. The 'thegns' using shire courts in late Anglo-Saxon England have no significant connections or affinities with the early modern gentry for whom we do have some evidence of a sense of national identity.[19] Neither am I persuaded – unless presented with good, direct evidence – that substantial landholders attending a court in Wiltshire once every six months had any sense of 'imagined community' with their counterparts doing the same in Cheshire. Such a capacity for imagination involves not just similarity but communication. Clearly there was some communication; shire courts were established by and answerable to royal authority. To that extent these were national institutions, but that might have an impact only on the consciousness of an extremely small elite consisting of the king and some of his officials.

Continuity in governmental institutions does not automatically mean continuity in names and cultural identity. The Normans were a conquest elite; perhaps 8,000 people imposed their rule on a population of 1.5 million.[20] This warrior class had a strong ethnic sense of itself as Norman, an identity which was proclaimed not only in England but also in Scotland, Ireland, Wales, Sicily and, of course, Normandy. The Normans may well have appropriated Anglo-Saxon institutions but equally they brought new patterns of landholding closely linked to military requirements and to which the term 'feudalism' is often applied. They took over the top ranks of the Church. They introduced Latin as the written language of government and a little later French became the written language of the educated. The Anglo-Saxons were a people under alien rule and culture; the word 'English' frequently meant the low-born who were ruled. Later, when national myths were being constructed, it was this discontinuity that was often emphasised. In the seventeenth century one finds critics of the monarchy employing a political rhetoric of the 'Norman yoke', seeing government and rule since 1066 as a break with Anglo-Saxon traditions, an alien imposition.

Since the advent of professional historiography in the Victorian period the continuity argument has come to prevail, and for good scholarly as well as other reasons. However, on closer inspection there are a number of different arguments. Generalists such as Hastings combine these in a 'pick-and-mix' fashion designed to produce the strongest impression of a continuous English national identity. It is important to prise these different arguments apart.

The first, and in my view most important argument concerns the system of rule and the notion of 'regnal identity'. Whatever one concludes about the degree of continuity and of change in modes of government, it is clear that the Normans developed a strong, national system of rule in England. It is also clear that this was specific to England and to a limited part of eastern Wales. There was Norman rule in Scotland and Ireland but it was either separate from (Scotland) or unlike (Ireland) the arrangements in England. At the same time the inheritance from the Anglo-Saxon period meant that it was unlike the system of rule prevailing in the Duchy of Normandy. Ironically, the very completeness and swiftness of the Norman conquest meant an acceptance of Anglo-Saxon political institutions. As a political system England was coherent and distinctive.

Furthermore, England soon became the most important territory under Norman rule. As Elton points out, just at the level of title, Duke William had now acquired a well-established title of kingship. More than this, England up to the early fourteeth century was a growing and increasingly prosperous kingdom.[21] Coupled with a strong system of government which could raise taxes and armies, this made it far more important than Normandy, even before her loss in 1204. Well before 1204 the Norman rulers of England were making claims on 'France' rather than regarding themselves as Normans who also ruled in England. This contrasts strongly with other imperial elites which continued to identify with the dominant centre from which they came and to which they aspired to return: Romans; sixteenth-century Spaniards; the British in nineteenth-century India. Rouen was not Rome or Madrid or London. Indeed, it was quickly displaced by London (or rather Westminster) as the 'imperial capital', and also second in wealth and population in northern Europe only to Paris. The shift of centrality from Normandy to England also explains why Normans in Wales and Ireland looked to England as the political centre, something which inhibited their assimilation into local culture.

However, even this on its own would not explain the Normans abandoning the name 'Norman' and taking that of 'English'. It could as easily have led to the transference of the name 'Norman' to the political elite of England. The term 'English' after 1066 had quickly come to mean the subject population of the country, distinct from the elite. Insofar as the notion of 'people' or 'nation' was a political or elite concept, it appeared that the English had ceased to exist. Henry of Huntingdon, son of a Norman, said as much around 1154:

> In . . . [1087], when the Normans had fulfilled the just will of the Lord upon the English people, and there was scarcely a noble of English descent in England, but all had been reduced to servitude and lamentation, *and it was even disgraceful to be called English*, William, the agent of this vengeance, ended his life. *For God had chosen the Normans to wipe out the English nation*, because he had seen that they surpassed all other people in their unparalleled savagery.
>
> (Greenaway 2002: 31; emphasis added)

One explanation stresses numbers and patterns of settlement.[22] The centralised nature of the Anglo-Saxon state meant that one decisive battle could deliver the whole kingdom to the Normans.[23] The brutal repression of rebellions in the two decades following 1066 ensured the effective imposition of Norman rule throughout the land. The Normans were a small elite distributed thinly across the country. Their empire took the form of what Kumar has called the 'Roman' model (a political-military elite) rather than the 'Greek' model (immigrant settlement in particular areas). The Greek model is more apparent in Ireland. In this model there remain geographically distinct 'native' and 'immigrant' societies with elites in the former and non-elites in the latter, even if not completely similar in social structure. Such a model encourages a polarisation of ethnic identities. Acceptance of 'native' names and customs amounts to assimilation into native society. Conversely, native elites may assimilate into the immigrant society, as arguably happened with the formation of an Anglo-Welsh gentry.

However, there was no question of Normans assimilating the customs of those whom they regarded as a subject people, nor of them having the demographic weight to impose their own customs upon even the middling ranks of English society, nor again of being able to construct two parallel if unequal societies of natives and immigrants. To rule the country Normans had to rely heavily upon Anglo-Saxons, even if the highest level of landowners and church leaders were almost entirely Norman imports. Within a generation or so English was being used as the everyday spoken language, even if it was marginalised as a written language. How far the Norman elite was a male one which had disproportionately to marry Anglo-Saxon women (rather than Norman women marrying Anglo-Saxon males) who in turn brought up their children in their language and customs is uncertain, but in any case everyday interactions such as dealing with peasants, merchants and relative priests would press towards the use of spoken English.

The absence of an imperial centre elsewhere, the very small number of Normans compared to the population they ruled and the identification with the kingship and governing institutions of England go a long way to explain the 'Englishing' of the Normans. However, to these political and demographic explanations one needs to add specifically cultural ones. These explanations also make it clear that we are *not* dealing with national identity in anything like the forms it came to assume in modern times.

By the mid-twelfth century various historians have claimed to discern the development of a positive view of English identity, expressed particularly by second and third generation Normans. In part this may be explained in narrow political terms. These Normans often resented 'foreigners' coming over from Normandy (before 1204) and from other parts of France thereafter, especially if they were seen as royal favourites, or deputies (*justiciars*) for absentee kings. It seems ironic that Simon de Montfort, by origin and clearly by name French, should use the rhetoric of Englishness in the resistance he led to Henry III in the mid-thirteenth century. But already a century earlier Henry of Huntingdon, William of Malmesbury, Gerald of Wales and others had expressed similar views. In Henry of Huntingdon's case it is clear that, having mourned the death of the English people as having taken place by 1087, he was able to celebrate their resurrection by the time of his death in 1154. What he meant of course was not the end of Norman rule but rather the shifting of the name 'English' to the second generation elite of great landowners and church leaders.[24]

Yet this celebration of the new English was expressed in Latin and French. Language, seen as standing at the heart of ethnic and national identity in modern times, was irrelevant to this understanding of national identity.[25] This is not to say that what one observes here is simply the transference of ruling elite values and customs from a box marked 'Norman' to one marked 'English'. It was important that some components of Anglo-Saxon culture were regarded as worthy of respect by the Norman newcomers. Thomas, for example, stresses the veneration paid to English saints by pious Normans (Thomas 2003: ch. 17). Old English was not regarded as a barbaric language. The adoption of Latin and French did not involve the elevation of Norman culture above that of Anglo-Saxons but rather expressed more general European assumptions about civilisation and culture. Elite Anglo-Saxons and Normans shared cultural values, above all embodied in their church and faith. Finally, and more speculatively, the 'wild' ethnic stereo-types associated with *Normanitas* were less suited to an age which by the twelfth century was coming to pride itself as chivalric and cultivated. There were no easy assumptions of Normans being civilised and Anglo-Saxons barbaric which could have impeded an assumption of 'Englishness' that was already favoured by institutional, settlement and demographic factors.

Yet the very attention to the question of the relationship of 'Anglo-Saxon' to 'Norman' in itself gives a sharpness and significance to concepts of 'ethnic' identity which is misleading, a product of our present-day preoccupations rather than a reflection of contemporary concerns.[26] Insofar as an 'ethnic' as distinct from a 'regnal' identity mattered in this time it took a very different form, namely the contrast between the civilised and the barbaric.

Inter-ethnic and inter-state conflicts

By the mid-twelfth century, writers had elaborated stereotypes of the Irish and Welsh (rather less of the Scots) as barbarians who lacked money, towns, arable farming, and whose manners and morals contrasted unfavourably to those of the civilised English.[27] Such discourse echoed Herotodus on Scythians or Tacitus on Germans. The implication is that assimilation is possible if the right ways of life are adopted.[28] The contrasts were usually confined to elites; the conduct of tribal chiefs, their retinues and their holy men are compared to that of the English king, landowners and clergy, as is clear when the comparison touches upon such matters as literacy or table manners.

Such ethnographic contrasts underpin what Gillingham has termed a project of 'English imperialism'.[29] It is distinct from the political language used in disputes with the Scottish and the French, the principal enemies of this period. The Scottish crown and the society it ruled in the lowlands was not dissimilar to that of England in language and customs.[30] These were disputes between Anglo-Norman and Scottish-Norman elites with close interconnections through marriage and similar upbringing. Ethnographic distinctions played little role in such disputes (except when Scottish Gaeldom was involved), any more than they did in Anglo–French conflicts. The formidable military threats to England came from the more prosperous, arable and commercial kingdoms of Scotland and France rather than the poorer, pastoral societies of the Welsh and the Irish. Therefore, the language of nationality used in disputes with the Scottish and the French shifted away from the ethnographic to the political.

The Hundred Years War is often cited as proof positive of the importance of national identity and consciousness, even of nationalism. French and the English kings appealed to the nation and depicted themselves as defending national terri- tory. However, this was but a continuation of the growth of centralised monar- chical power in the two countries. Just as in England, so by the end of the thirteenth century the French monarchy was no longer appealing to vassals to defend their lord, or subjects to defend their king, but instead for Frenchmen to defend their kingdom (Allmand 1988: 103). It is another example of the growing importance of *regnal* identity in the political language of rulers.

The increasing costs of war made the relationship of subjects to the crown rather than intermediate authorities more central (ibid.: 115). This was the reason for royal propaganda, exemplified through commands for the clergy to preach patriotic sermons (Jones 1979). These were occasional appeals, concentrated in the first decade of the Hundred Years War. We do not know if and how churches implemented such royal commands, let alone whether anyone was persuaded by such prayers and sermons as may have been delivered.

The crown justified its policies on two grounds: claims in France and defence of the realm. Learned treatises argued claims to France in terms of lineages. These were 'popularised' through the posting of royal genealogies on church doors. Myths of descent extending back to Brutus, grandson of the Trojan Aeneas, were aristocratic, even if the writers were clerics and lawyers, and in any case had declining significance with the rise of powerful and impersonal territorial polities. Language and custom did not figure in these myths, nor did claims about the nation as a large, inclusive group. There were celebrations of military successes and mourning for defeat but these focused entirely on the king and his nobility. (In France there is the notable exception of Joan of Arc.)

As for 'defence of the realm', this was only an appeal to the 'English nation' defined as the subjects of the English crown. There is arguably an ethnic component in the descent myths but these were confined to elites. There is no ethnic component to the appeal to the common interest.[31]

Other identities and interests were of greater importance. The English crown held on to lands in France not through 'English' appeals but through warfare conducted by paid soldiers and by incorporating elites in Aquitaine and the short-lived occupations in other parts of France.[32] When the French crown conquered these areas it maintained its authority by coming to an understanding with local elites, including recent immigrants from England. The crown might deploy a rhetoric of the national interest but local interests and identities bulked larger (Allmand, 1988: 109–110).

Given that the crown defined the national interest and that royal claims to territory were based on lineages, the 'English' king could claim the 'French' crown and vice versa. By the 1420 Treaty of Troyes Henry V was designated next king of France, an agreement which would have come into effect had Henry not died in 1422, shortly before Charles VI. Henry VI was crowned king of France, though he was unable to realise this claim in the way one may assume Henry V would have managed.

How can one reconcile such a treaty with the argument that national identity and nationalism was politically significant? Admittedly the treaty of 1420 worried 'English' elites but this was because of anxiety about Henry acquiring powers and commitments which conflicted with their own, not because of any feeling that 'their' king could not also be the ruler of another 'nation'. The elaborate promises monarchs involved in personal unions had to make that they would respect the customs and laws of their different kingdoms does indicate the capacity to separate 'kingdom' (country) from 'crown', even in the case of hereditary as opposed to elective monarchy. There is a realm of 'England' and of 'France' (i.e. a set of political institutions which, even if it cannot be imagined apart from *monarchy*, may be imagined as distinct from the *monarch*).[33] However, even if the monarch was not identified with the nation, the 'nation' cannot be seen as anything but a monarchical institution.

Ethnographic language was occasionally used in political arguments. The enemy was stereotyped: the French as effeminate, the Scottish as savage. French or Scottish was shorthand for French or Scottish elites, not whole peoples. This language does not have the depth of that applied to the Welsh and Irish because it was a matter of occasional political manipulation rather than related to a continuous process of comparing different ways of life.

Medieval England was precocious in constructing centralised legal, political and religious institutions focused on monarchy, and these exhibited great continuity from the late Anglo-Saxon period onwards. However, 'national' institutions do not automatically bear some matching sense of national identity. Ancient origins do not express ancient consciousness. Many historians read too much of the later story into the earlier phase, create an over-coherent picture on the basis of fragmentary evidence, and conflate ethnographic contrasts between civilised and barbarian with the political justifications of rulers for their claims over other peoples and territories.

Reformation England

Arguments about national identity take on a new intensity for this period.[34] These are based on a range of new developments: the establishment of a Church of England under royal control, the claims to an English empire in other parts of Britain and the start of English settlement in North America, the conversion to Protestantism and the conceit of a 'Protestant nation', the formation of zealous religious groupings, the use of the recent invention of printing to make available the Bible and other religious as well as secular works in the written vernacular, a flowering of English literature, crowned in the work of Shakespeare.

As usual, the myth-making accounts lump together these various features to produce the strongest possible case for the existence of nationalism and popular national identity. Very crudely we can unpick these myths by making distinctions between political, religious and cultural issues.

At the political level there is no doubt that the national state was made immeasurably stronger between the early sixteenth and late seventeenth centuries.[35] The process was mainly about increasing the strength of centralised monarchical government. Institutions such as Parliament were instruments of rather than hindrances to that process (Elton 1979). The 'national' arguments deployed in the early phase of the English Reformation come from the court and royal servants; for example, claims about a national church with a history pre-dating the connection to Rome.[36] Insofar as Members of Parliament pursued their own interests, these concerned local disputes over property and offices. It is vital to the precocious formation of a national state in England that local goals were pursued through a national institution rather than local institutions, but that is another matter.[37]

If this was all that was involved, such institutional change would only strengthen the 'regnal' character of national identity. If Henry VIII had been able to obtain Papal agreement to the annulment of his first marriage, matters might have stopped there. Henry may well have enforced much greater power over the Church but that would have been to do no more than other 'national' monarchies at this time. No one seriously argues that the Concordat of Bologna (1516) between Francis I and Pope Leo X expresses French nationalism.

It is the rise of Protestantism which arguably introduces something new. It is argued that the crown identifies itself with the cause of Protestantism, initially if half-heartedly with Henry himself, enthusiastically with Edward VI, pragmatically with Elizabeth. By the 1630s the fear that the monarch is a crypto-Catholic or at the very least seeking to move away from the Calvinist doctrines of the Church fuels much of the resentment which expresses itself as outright opposition in the following decade.

Furthermore, Protestantism is seen as having a special cultural and political resonance. The stress on experiencing the word of God as *written* leads to English translations of the Bible which are published and circulated in large numbers, along with many other religious tracts. Reading the Old Testament, especially through embattled Calvinist spectacles, sustains arguments about the English as an, even *the*, Elect Nation. Such considerations led Greenfeld to argue in a recent general study that authentic nationalism was born in sixteenth-century England (Greenfeld 1992).

The major flaws in Greenfeld's arguments have been exposed by Kumar and there is no need to repeat his arguments here (Kumar 2003: 95–116). To summarise the main points: the crown never identified itself unambiguously with Protestantism or with the 'people'; Protestants thought in international and/or subnational (sectarian) terms; it is doubtful if more than a small, though influential minority of English people were zealous Protestants by the early seventeenth century; Protestantism divided rather than unified the English people.[38]

Similar criticisms may be made about the construction of a national literary culture. In his chapter in this book Kumar points to the complexity of Shakespeare, for example, his British as well as his English plays. With the exception of Henry V there is no major English hero in Shakespeare's plays.[39] Insofar as he celebrates England it is a monarchical and aristocratic England; his 'people' are comic figures who mangle the English language.

One must not press these negative arguments too far. Clearly the monarchy, with more powerful institutions and a print culture, had greater 'reach' into the population from the late sixteenth century than before. That meant a more energetic and influential royal propaganda designed to appeal to the 'nation'. It meant more stereotyping: positive in relation to the English; negative in relation to foreign enemies. At times of crisis Protestant preachers would adopt the rhetoric of Old Testatment prophets (though more often to condemn than to praise). Most of this represents an intensification of the regnal arguments of earlier centuries rather than something different.

It is not the identification of Protestantism and nation with the monarchy which introduces something different but their deployment *against* the crown. There is a long history of using arguments about the 'nation' and the common interest to oppose a monarch, as in the turmoil of 1258 to 1264. Clearly, however, these were factional arguments conducted within the elite which did not challenge monarchical rule as such. They shared affinities with the ideas of aristocratic republicanism and elective monarchy one finds in parts of medieval and early modern Europe. On the other hand, there are more popular movements associated with dissident religion and often repressed as heresy which reject monarchical rule.

What is new with the Reformation is the way in which the high politics of factional opposition and popular religious dissent[40] can combine, if only in tense, fragile and occasional ways. The most explosive moment in English history, of course, came in the 1640s.[41] Elements of political action at this time may be described as 'proto-nationalism', for two reasons. First, some of the political rhetoric of the time sought to detach the 'nation' from the existing political system and use it as a popular category to propose radically different arrangements. The idea of the 'Norman yoke', for example, appealed to the idea of a subject Anglo-Saxon nation which should throw off alien rule. Such arguments were still tied to dominant institutions, in this case to the common law and Parliament seen as institutions with origins in pre-1066 England. It was still difficult for contemporaries to conceive of the nation as an inclusive category – the 'poorest he as well as the richest he'[42] – and certainly not as an ethnic or cultural category. It was difficult to make the nation the principle of sovereignty and impossible to figure out how that principle could be institutionally embodied. Nevertheless, one could argue that there were anticipations of such ideas. Of course, in the radical sects religion mattered much more than nation. Millenial sects gave little attention to the organisation of earthly affairs as these were transitory and expected to perish soon.[43]

In a more tentative way I would suggest that these oppositional movements resembled later nationalist movements in structure rather than content.[44] The leadership of such movements was usually located within the 'political nation', but at times of crisis and the breakdown of normal authority patterns such leaders uneasily called upon popular religious groups for support. Such groups were concentrated in more commercial and urban settings such as London, Paris (the Catholic League during the French religious wars), and the heavily urbanised zones of the Netherlands, the Baltic coast, Switzerland and south Germany.[45] There were areas of rural mobilisation as well, such as the Huguenot movement in south-west France, but these displayed more traditional patron–client features than did the urban movements. Most but by no means all of these politico-religious oppositions took up Calvinist notions of justified resistance by intermediate authorities to princes as well as devising methods for institutionalising novel sectarian movements. These flourished only in times of crisis such as the confessional divisions between 1525 and 1590 and the political breakdowns of the mid-seventeenth century. Inherent tensions between elite factionalism and religious zealotry soon undermined such movements with the latter being repressed or marginalised. By 1700 they are mainly an uneasy memory, a warning to establishment figures not to let conventional conflicts get out of hand. However, they are also an interesting anticipation of later oppositional politics which take shape from the late eighteenth century, though now preaching national sovereignty, democracy and social equality rather than true religion.

I will not take the English example any further. In the eighteenth and nineteenth centuries English political institutions were identified with wider ones, especially with the Union of 1707 with Scotland and the creation of successive overseas empires in North America and Asia. I agree substantially with Kumar's review of the literature on British identity.[46] Politically there was no point in any form of English nationalism which could threaten the British institutions constructed in

Britain and overseas, just as there was no point in Russian nationalism in the Romanov empire or Turkish nationalism in the Ottoman empire or German nationalism in the Habsburg empire.[47] It is difficult to give any specific cultural content to 'English' national identity because the name 'England' is interchangeable with the name 'Britain'. Kumar argues that only in the late nineteenth century is there a 'moment of Englishness' (Kumar 2003: ch. 7),[48] and even then it never took any strong political form.

Conclusion

I cannot think of a stronger case for perennialist arguments about the pre-modern existence of the nation and national identity than medieval and early modern England. Yet I think one is entitled to feel sceptical about those arguments. Given that, I conclude that nation, or rather national identity in the sense of certain processes for constructing national identity, existed only at the elite level, in discontinuous and fragmented forms, in two different worlds of meaning (the ethnographic and the political) which were connected only casually to each other, subordinate to Christian and dynastic principles, arguments and images, often marginalised when in conflict with Christian and dynastic concerns, and having little in the way of a 'public culture' which could maintain, reinterpret and transmit national identity.[49] The consequent regnal identity was important in elite politics because England had developed strong, centralised state institutions. However, one cannot jump from that achievement to any assumption about a strong and significant sense of national identity at popular level and certainly not to any kind of nationalism.

Briefly in the early modern period, especially during the Civil War, a political rhetoric which detached the nation from monarchy and the established Church and clothed it in qualities of inclusiveness and sovereignty, did acquire significance but was soon repressed as stability was restored. Thereafter even regnal identity took on a British form, although it was able to continue emphasising Protestantism, parliamentary monarchy, common law and the English language in ways which thoroughly confused or equated England and Britain with one another.

The problem with ethno-symbolism

First, let me repeat the points made in the refutation of perennialism. It is very easy to engage in a scissors-and-paste history which finds the same or cognate names occurring in a range of texts, often widely dispersed in time and space and produced for a variety of purposes, and to construct from this a continuous narrative in which a certain name has now been endowed with national or ethno-symbolic significance, producing the very process through which it has been rather contingently selected. I have attempted to refute such perennialist claims for the strong case of England.

There is another interesting question. Why do some names disappear?[50] In his chapter Smith mentions four tenth/eleventh-century ethnies: Franks, Saxons, Lombards and Visigoths. The latter two names have disappeared; no one takes seriously any mythic claim of connection that the Northern League might claim. Saxon has given way to English, even though it was undoubtedly a name of greater significance for much of the medieval period. Indeed, that is arguably why Bede preferred the name English in preference to Saxon. It continues to have some resonance to this day in Germany, and is even used to signify affinities across the divided German states of the 1949 to 1990 period. Frank has survived as a name, although for those who used the name in the tenth century it certainly did not mean the Romanised, Romance-language-speaking elites of what was later to become the heartland of France.[51] Norman, as we have seen, was a name that was swiftly marginalised in post-Conquest England. Yet, as we have also seen, Henry of Huntingdon suggested that by 1087 the name of English was disappearing in favour of that of Norman. So why do some names disappear, some sink and then rise again, some continue uninterrupted, and yet others are devised in very recent times?[52] A focus on continually recurring names – the tendency in scissors-and-paste narratives – cannot address that question.

Was there some ethno-symbolic deficiency in the myths and memories associated with the name Norman compared to the name English, Lombard compared to Frank? I doubt it. The Normans, for example, had a well-established set of ethnic myths about their savage energy, their reckless and expansionist ambitions, myths which they themselves used positively and which some of their enemies such as Muslims and Byzantines accepted, only now as negative attributes (Bartlett 1993: ch. 4). The answer must be found outside the realm of ethno-symbolic discourse, above all in the centralisation and consolidation of the Norman polity of England.[53] It is 'regnum' and 'regnal identity' which account for the shift. However, I see little in the way of investing this regnum with the trappings of a sacred territory or ethno-scape – key terms in Smith's ethno-symbolism – although the cult of English saints may have something of this quality. Neither do I discern an important place for any myth of ethnic election; the myth of descent which includes Brutus and Constantine is hardly 'English'.[54] Finally, I see precious little readiness for elites to sacrifice themselves for their ethnic community. Political loyalties were defined in terms of rulership (subjects of the kings of England or of France) or, when there were factional disputes, in terms of regional origins (Normans, Flemings or Poitevins now labelled as foreigners who have acquired too much influence over the king).

This central point may be made for many examples. Why do themes of ethno-symbolism not figure in detailed historical accounts of early modern France or England? Why can Scotland be brought so bloodlessly into union with England, first as a personal union in 1603 and then as a union of states in 1707, and the only significant ideological-political movement mobilised against this take up the Stuart cause, not any ethnic one? Why is Irish pressure for autonomy in the eighteenth century couched in terms of historic institutions and liberties and not ethnicity or nationality?[55] The answer in all cases is simple and the same: because such ethnic myths or memories do not matter. People have plenty of other ways to provide collective identity, usually to do with how they represent their interests within political-territorial institutions.

The appeal to the nation as a distinct, complete, inclusive society which sets itself up as the source of political authority comes with the rise of secular, popular politics in the modern period. This was first expressed in the American and French revolutions where a strong and mobilising sense of identity was explicitly modern, repudiating links to a discredited and despised past. It is only with the complex of reactions to this democratic nationalism that we find appeals to myths of descent, golden ages, pure languages and sacred homelands figuring centrally in the rhetoric of political movements. However, before outlining a modernist account of the connection between such discourse and modern nationalism, it is important to confront some other ethno-symbolic arguments.

Smith is well aware that the modern mass nation is precisely that: modern. To establish links with earlier ethnies or even pre-modern nation formation one needs to recognise the differences between the two. One way of achieving this is to argue that in some cases there was an elite sense of national identity which then spread downwards (e.g. through a process of political reform such as took place in France and England). In other cases there was a democratic sense of national identity, usually associated with smaller scale societies in which perhaps peasant farmers or urban dwellers in city-states were more significant. These could expand horizontally (e.g. the federal arrangements of the Swiss) to produce a more modern nation.[56]

The argument bears a certain resemblance to nineteenth-century concepts of 'large' and 'small' or, more disagreeably expressed, 'historic' and 'non-historic' nations, and to the twentieth-century distinctions between political and cultural, civic and ethnic, Eastern and Western nations. Historic nations built on the elite ethnic identities formed within well-established institutions and a public culture; subordinate ethnies excluded from such institutions and culture constructed national identity from non-elite features such as language and popular customs.[57]

However, it does not appear to me that modern nationalism developed from either of these kinds of ethnies and their myth-symbol complexes. First, all nationalist conflict focused on elites. The so-called subordinate nations were movements mobilised by counter-elites such as the Uniate and Greek Orthodox churchmen of Rumania, or the emergent Czech-speaking bourgeois elites of nineteenth-century Bohemia. Certainly ethnic arguments were used, often sincerely, to legitimate their interests but these had to be painstakingly constructed. Their principal 'truth' resource was not a fund of continuous ethnic memories but the fact that Rumanian and Czech were distinct languages despised by the established elites of the regions who spoke Magyar and German respectively. These elite figures nevertheless had to assemble grammars and dictionaries of the national language, write plays and novels and histories about the nation, collect folklore and song, often after themselves learning as adults to speak their 'own' language. One may wish to present this, as they did, in terms of discovery or recovery, of memory and identity, but of so buried a legacy that it required the kind of effort and artifice that others, including myself, would rather call construction or even invention.

Even in the case of so-called aristocratic nations, modern national ideologies were for the most part constructed *against* the pre-modern elites. One thinks of the passionate patriotism of the parliamentarians and radicals in the English revolution, and of Jacobins in the early 1790s. Insofar as an ethnic past was invoked, it was based on such myths as the Norman or Frankish yoke, precisely to *reject* existing elite ideology. Yet these never became very significant as nationalist ideas. Later, in the nineteenth century, some of these ideas were taken up, but now as race ideology, which for long remained in marginal and ambivalent relationship to dominant nationalist discourse.

Ethnic arguments are entangled with non-ethnic ones, elite claims with demotic ones. For example, one can sometimes account for the relative significance given to 'civic' or 'ethnic' arguments in terms of the territorial logic of the nationalist objective. Movements bent on reforming the existing territorial state tend to stress institutional identities; those aiming at bringing together a number of states into one focus on historic and high cultural ties, those seeking the separation of a peripheral region will stress as far as possible a distinct ethnic and linguistic identity. However, there is always a mixture of themes, due partly to the varied intellectual heritage of the elites involved, and different situations tend to select one rather than another. The balance can shift rapidly over time and be held in different ways by competing groups.[58]

None of this can be explained in terms of the pressure exerted by an existing stock of ethnic myths. Rather, in a negative way one can say that the clear non-existence of any ethnic characteristics such as a distinct dialect or religion will make it that much more difficult to construct a nationalist ideology appealing to such distinctions. Otherwise, providing there is some credible material with which to work, political and cultural elites will construct a diverse set of identities in attempts to mobilise popular support to take control of the modern state.

Where modernists have frequently gone wrong is in failing to recognise that there were important ways in which the national idea was used in pre-modern societies. Above all this was in the form of the regnal idea but also to buttress an ethnography of the civilised and the barbaric, occasionally to make appeals for support beyond elites, sometimes to invoke the idea of a chosen people.[59] Only in the first, regnal form does the national idea have a continuing and central political significance but one securely tied to the monarchy. There has to be disruption and transformation before this idea can be appropriated in the modern form of nationalism, turned against any creed of sovereignty from above, whether that be justified in dynastic or religious terms. It is not continuity but discontinuity, the discontinuity introduced by modernity, which needs emphasis.

Notes

1 Smith (1998) provides a judicious summary of the various positions.
2 See chapter 10, this volume.
3 For the notion of regnal identity see below, and Reynolds (1997).
4 This is a radically simplified scheme. In the 'real' history of nations names are

invented, discarded, modified and appropriated by different groups; Also the game never ends, so 'victory' is always provisional.

5 At the level of biological explanation neo-Darwinianism avoids the dangers of tele-ology (even if biologists use intentionalist language) but does not provide any specific causal explanation. Rather it specifies a set of formal conditions: descent with modifi-cations which are selected on the basis of their fitness under competitive conditions. Social scientists have not yet been able to agree on an equivalently precise set of conditions for processes of cultural selection. Whether they ever will is a matter of debate.

6 Krishan Kumar in his essay in this book has focused attention on the late modern period. However, in his book (Kumar 2003) he devotes a great deal of time to a critical appraisal of claims about national identity made for the medieval and early modern periods. I largely agree with his arguments. Rather than repeat them here, I refer readers to his book. Furthermore, I have already considered the English example at some length in another publication (Breuilly 2005). Again, to avoid repetition I refer the reader to that book. Here I will focus on fresh arguments which were not developed in those other publications.

7 This is the title used in the translation and edition of Bertram Colgrave and R.A.B. Mynors (1969). I will refer to this work by the commonly used abbreviation *The Ecclesi-astical History*. For purposes of quotation and citation I use the Penguin translation of 1955 published under the rather different title of *A History of the English Church and People* (Bede 1955).

8 This is a view shared by many medievalists who go on to argue that the fiction created by Bede became influential in the age of Alfred as something resembling an Anglo-Saxon polity took shape.

9 There is no consensus on just how Bede used his key term 'Angli'. See Brooks (1999). On the linguistic history see Crystal (2004: chs 1–3).

10 Bede pioneered the measurement of time, both in his use of a single chronological system in his history and in other work on the calendar and, in particular, the dating of Easter.

11 The rulers sometimes have the title of king but they are more like tribal chiefs. Else-where (Breuilly 2005) I have suggested we know little about how deep or lasting was conversion; modern missionary evidence suggests not much at first.

12 Nevertheless, I think the claims made by Reynolds for a widespread sense of English identity at this time go beyond what the evidence will reasonably bear.

13 The translation of Latin texts such as Bede's *Ecclesiastical History* was a matter of necessity. Danish incursions in the north of England had destroyed the Latinate civil-isation of which Bede himself was an eloquent expression. At best, Alfred could only hope for a small elite literate in Old English.

14 Bede did transfer the notion of a chosen people from the Israelites to the English. However, the projects of *conversion* or *expansion* make it impossible to equate Bede and Alfred with the self-centred Old Testament focus on one people seeking to survive and to sustain their faith against alien and hostile pagans. It is also difficult to equate with the rhetoric and education of Roman Christianity, a supra-ethnic faith and institution. In 1066, although differences between Anglo-Saxons and Normans are alluded to, for example, in the Bayeux Tapestry, they are fairly minor matters such as hairstyles. There were, of course, many elite interconnections between the two polities.

15 The most extensive claims that there was a strongly rooted system of government that can reasonably be called a 'nation-state' are made in Campbell (2000). For a succinct summary of the continuity in institutions see Elton (1992: ch. 2). For criticisms of such arguments in relation to 'nation' see Kumar (2003: 47–48); in relation to 'state' see Foot (2005).

16 The case for continuity was made powerfully by Victorian historians such as E.A. Freeman and Bishop Stubbs, and are given popular expression in J.R. Green (1893) *A*

Short History of the English People. A fine account of these views is provided in Burrow (1983). Kumar (2003: 202ff.) argues persuasively that this construction was part of the real 'moment of Englishness' which took place in the late Victorian and Edwardian period. How and why medieval historians have continued to affirm, amend or challenge is considered in Foot (2005).

17 There is a tendency to conflate 'England' with the south of the country. That is, of course, not a vice confined to medieval historians.

18 This type of criticism may be applied, for example, to Elton's book *The English* (1992). It is extraordinary that this appears in a series called 'The Peoples of Europe'. Elton's book would be more accurately entitled 'The Government of England'. He provides lucid and powerful accounts of the origins and developments of central political institutions. He then asserts at periodic intervals without any evidence that such institutions can be correlated with a widespread sense of national identity. I agree with Elton that the construction of a coherent, centralised and powerful system of monarchical government in England has deeply marked what terms such as England and English mean, but one cannot sustain claims about popular culture and identity without other kinds of evidence. A book in which Thomas Cromwell is given more space than the subject of English literacy and literature is never likely to do that.

19 By the seventeenth century there are many more recent developments which could account for such a sense of national identity.

20 For these figures – extremely approximate given the paucity of evidence – see the opening two chapters in Carpenter (2004).

21 It is debatable how far the great majority of the population, those who laboured manually, benefited from this but it is quite clear that higher social groups did.

22 The following paragraphs are heavily indebted to Thomas (2003).

23 Also important was the lack of any system of fortified castles in Anglo-Saxon England and a favourable topography, especially in southern and central England.

24 I develop these points in more detail in Breuilly (2005). See Clanchy (1983) and Gillingham (2000) for many supporting examples for the period *c.*1170 to 1270.

25 It is difficult to see how Hastings (1997) can argue the case for 'national identity' for the period *c.*1066 to the mid-fourteenth century given that for him so much hinges on a written vernacular. English ceased to be such for this period. The concepts of national identity formulated in this period are of a completely different order from any based on language. Arguments about continuity in a sense of national identity which has affinities to modern nationality (before 1066, from 1066 to the period in which Middle English came to prevail as a written vernacular, after this period) are based on the arbitrary yoking together of completely different uses of names such as England and English. That is, of course, precisely how nationalist myth-making works.

26 This is the principal criticism made by R.R. Davies in an otherwise sympathetic review of Thomas (2003: 1308–1310) in *English Historical Review*.

27 I draw especially upon Gillingham (2000) and Davies (2000).

28 Indeed, Carpenter (2004: 16–19) argues that as parts of Wales and Scotland displayed developments which made them appear more like England, so the negative stereotyping declined.

29 See especially Gillingham (2000: 3–18). Davies (2000) similarly argues that the political use of such an ethnographic category is strongest when English kings were pursuing a project of bringing the British Isles as a whole under their control, and faded along with that project.

30 For a succinct summary see Kumar (2003: ch. 4). Carpenter (2004) argues that 'Scottish' identity developed as a product of another Norman-shaped monarchical consolidation. Being Scottish was as much a regnal identity as being English.

31 Two centuries later Shakespeare would depict Henry V on the eve of Agincourt moving in disguise among common men, with ethnic stereotypes of Scot, Irish and Welsh now presented as equally patriotic in support of their king. Such imagery was not deployed

in the early fifteenth century. Shakespeare's characters can only be understood in late sixteenth-/early seventeenth-century terms. In *Henry V* ethnic stereotyping negates the link between ethnicity and political loyalty. In the early fifteenth century ethnicity was something the enemy possessed, not an attribute of one's own subjects. See Kumar (chapter 14, this volume) for the problems of using Shakespeare to argue the case for early modern English national identity.

32   The wine trade probably provides the most important explanation for the 'loyalty' of the hinterland of Bordeaux. Settlers also moved from England to these territories.

33   In Breuilly (2005) I included a section on medieval political thought which stressed the importance of arguments about the common good as legitimating rule. However, the argument that a ruler must promote the interests of his subjects does not entail characterising those subjects as a special group (a nation in an ethnic sense) and certainly does not support arguments about 'sovereignty from below' (a central tenet of nationalism).

34   See now Kumar (2003: ch. 4) for a cogent critique of arguments about sixteenth-century English nationalism.

35   Elton (1992) in ch. 4, 'From Cromwell to Cromwell', is typically lucid and persuasive at this level. Equally typically he devotes far more space to Thomas Cromwell than to Oliver Cromwell, precisely in order to delineate the 'state-building' work initiated by the former and which survived the Civil War. A fine recent account of this state-building as an impersonal process rather than an intentional project is Braddick (2000).

36   For the 'invention' of this argument, which breaks with Bede's linkage between the English and Roman Christianity, see Jones (2000).

37   In part it is this feature which enables Braddick to argue that local officials are agents of the central state. See also Corrigan and Sayer (1985).

38   In Breuilly (2005) I criticise the claims that have been made for John Foxe's *Book of Martyrs* as an expression of English nationalism which left a deep imprint on the minds of many English people in the late sixteenth and early seventeenth centuries.

39   Many readers admire the figure of Sir John Falstaff but more because he is larger than life than heroic.

40   By 'popular' I do not mean necessarily large scale but rather extending down the social scale.

41   In Breuilly (2005) I deal in some detail with the case of the Dutch Revolt against Spanish rule in order to counter arguments by Gorski (2000) that this represented an authentically modern form of nationalism.

42   To adopt the phase used by Colonel Rainborough in the Putney debates.

43   A recent work arguing that the confessional conflicts of the Reformation bore marks of nationalism is Marx (2003).

44   I first developed these arguments in Breuilly (1993: 76–81).

45   One interesting absence is that of the cities of northern Italy which did, after all, give rise to the secular, modern political ideas of Machiavelli. That is bound up with the larger question of why reformed religion of the Protestant kind largely failed in Southern Europe. See now MacCulloch (2003: chs 5, 7 and 9).

46   See Chapter 14 (this volume) and Kumar (2003: ch. 6).

47   That did not prevent such nationalism, either in the form of opposition as with Pan-Germanism in the Habsburg Empire and Turkish nationalism in the Ottoman Empire, or as state-inspired as with the Russianisation drive in the Romanov Empire. Note, however, that these only developed in the late nineteenth and early twentieth centuries in response to other forms of nationalism.

48   In a way this is the weak, non-political equivalent of the turns of other imperial groups – Russians, Habsburgs, Ottomans – towards the national idea.

49   I develop the point about public culture further in Breuilly (2005) where I also enquire into why the 'national' idea is notable by its *absence* in medieval political thought.

50   I am much indebted to the work of Patrick Geary for this question. See Geary (2002), a

writer who in my view Smith dismisses too easily due to his views of the ethnie as a contingent construct.

51 A derivation of 'Frank' was used in the Far East in the seventeenth century to designate Portuguese invaders, and the Chinese used it later indiscriminately to label Westerners. See Bartlett (1993).

52 Such as Argentineans, Nigerians and Australians.

53 Bartlett (1993) makes the point in ch. 2, 'The Aristocratic Diaspora', that this thin elite stratum cannot in itself introduce ethnic or language change into the majority population, as we have observed with the Normans in England. But this does not mean that the *name* cannot be transferred to the majority group, as it was with the Franks in France.

54 Indeed, although English kingship was nominally hereditary, the actual transmission of title was in constant dispute, and many of the sacred incumbents met violent deaths at the hands of domestic enemies.

55 See the essay on eighteenth-century Ireland by Ian McBride in Zimmer and Scales (2005).

56 He elaborates these arguments in Smith (1986).

57 The argument is also a repudiation of Gellner who contended that national identity was actually 'high culture' making a pretence of being popular.

58 For a good example of the complex mixture of themes which cannot be divided into ethnic or civic, aristocratic or demotic, see Vick (2002).

59 Although such peoples were often singled out for punishment or even destruction rather than triumph and longevity.

References

Allmand, C. (1988) *The Hundred Years War*. Cambridge: Cambridge University Press.

Bartlett, R. (1993) *The Making of Europe: Conquest, Colonization and Cultural Change, 950–1350*. Princeton, NJ: Princeton University Press.

Bede (1955) *A History of the English Church and People*. Harmondsworth: Penguin.

Braddick, M.J. (2000) *State Formation in Early Modern England c.1550–1700*. Cambridge: Cambridge University Press.

Breuilly, J. (1993) *Nationalism and the State*. Manchester: Manchester University Press.

Breuilly, J. (2005) Changes in the political uses of the nation: continuity or discontinuity? In O. Zimmer and L. Scales (eds) *Power and Nation in European History*. Cambridge: Cambridge University Press.

Brooks, N. (1999) *Bede and the English*. Jarrow.

Brooks, N. (2004) 'English identity from Bede to the Millennium'. *Haskins Society Journal* 14: 33–51.

Burrow, J.W. (1983) *A Liberal Descent: Victorian Historians and the English Past*. Cambridge: Cambridge University Press.

Campbell, J. (2000) *The Anglo-Saxon State*. London: Hambledon.

Carpenter, D. (2004) *The Struggle for Mastery. The Penguin History of Britain 1066–1284*. London: Penguin.

Clanchy, M.T. (1983) *England and its Rulers 1066–1272: Foreign Lordship and National Identity*. Oxford: Blackwell in association with Fontana.

Corrigan, P. and Sayer, D. (1985) *The Great Arch: English State Formation and Cultural Revolution*. Oxford: Blackwell.

Crystal, D. (2004) *The Stories of English*. London: Allen Lane.

Davies, R.R. (2000) *The First English Empire: Power and Identities in the British Isles, 1093–1343*. Oxford: Oxford University Press.

Elton, G.R. (1979) 'Parliament in the sixteenth century: functions and fortunes'. *The Historical Journal* 22(2).

Elton, G.R. (1992) *The English*. Oxford: Blackwell.

Foot, S. (1996) 'The making of Angelcynn: English identity before the Norman Conquest'. *Transactions of the Royal Historical Society* 6: 25–49.

Foot, S. (2005) The historiography of the Anglo-Saxon 'nation state'. In O. Zimmer and L. Scales (eds) *Power and Nation in European History*. Cambridge: Cambridge University Press.

Geary, P.J. (2002) *The Myth of Nations: The Medieval Origins of Europe*. Princeton, NJ: Princeton University Press.

Gillingham, J. (2000) *The English in the Twelfth Century*. Woodbridge: Boydell Press.

Gorski, P. (2000) 'The Mosaic Moment: an early modernist critique of modernist theories of nationalism'. *American Journal of Sociology* 105(5): 1428–1468.

Greenaway, D. (2002) *Henry of Huntingdon: The History of the English People 1000–1154*. Oxford: Oxford University Press.

Greenfeld, L. (1992) *Nationalism: Five Roads to Modernity*. Cambridge, MA.: Harvard University Press.

Hastings, A. (1997) *The Construction of Nationhood: Ethnicity, Religion and Nationalism*. Cambridge: Cambridge University Press.

Jones, E. (2000) *The English Nation: The Great Myth*. Stroud: Sutton Publishing.

Jones, W.R. (1979) 'The English Church and royal propaganda during the Hundred Years War'. *Journal of British Studies* 19(1): 18–30.

Kumar, K. (2003) *The Making of English National Identity*. Cambridge: Cambridge University Press.

MacCulloch, D. (2003) *Reformation: Europe's House Divided 1490–1700*. London: Allen Lane.

Marx, A. (2003) *Faith in the Nation: Exclusionary Origins of Nationalism*. Oxford: Oxford University Press.

Reynolds, S. (1997) *Kingdoms and Communities in Western Europe, 900–1300*. Oxford: Clarendon Press.

Rollason, D. (2002) 'Bede's *Ecclesiastical History of the English People*'. *The Historian* 73: 6–10.

Smith, A.D. (1986) *The Ethnic Origins of Nations*. Oxford: Blackwell.

Smith, A.D. (1998) *Nationalism and Modernism*. London: Routledge.

Smith, A.D. (2003) *Chosen Peoples: Sacred Sources of National Identity*. Oxford: Oxford University Press.

Thomas, H.M. (2003) *The English and the Normans: Ethnic Hostility, Assimilation and Identity 1066-c.1220*. Oxford: Oxford University Press.

Vick, B. (2002) *Defining Germany: The 1848 Frankfurt Parliamentarians and National Identity*. Cambridge, MA., and London: Harvard University Press.

Wormald, P. (1994. '*Engla Land*: the making of an allegiance'. *Journal of Historical Sociology* 7(1): 1–24.

Zimmer, O. and Scales, L. (eds) (2005) *Power and the Nation in European History*. Cambridge: Cambridge University Press.

2   The dawning of nations

Walker Connor

I find it very uncomfortable trying to engage with either John Breuilly or Anthony D. Smith in a discussion on any aspect of nations – including their dating – because what they and I mean by nations are not congruous. Consider Breuilly's working definition of the nation which, as he notes, is drawn from Smith: 'Nation: a named human population occupying an historic territory and sharing common myths and memories, a public culture, and common laws and customs for all members.' As I noted in the recent special issue of *Nations and Nationalism* (Connor 2004: 37–38), this is not a definition that succeeds in differentiating the nation from other human groupings. It would not, for example, differentiate the notion of British from that of Welsh, or Belgian from Flemish, or Spanish from Basque. By contrast, my definition describes the nation as the largest group that shares a belief in common ancestry and it is the largest group that can be influenced or incited by appeals to common kinship. Is there a Welsh or Flemish, or Basque nation? Yes. Is there a British, Belgian, or Spanish nation? No. Nor is there an American, Argentinean, Filipino, Indian or Indonesian nation.

A nation, then, is neither a state, nor the population of a state without regard to its ethnic composition. Nationalism is identity with and loyalty to the nation, not to and with the state. The latter has traditionally been called patriotism. A current vogue is to differentiate the two loyalties (i.e. to nation and to state) as ethnic nationalism and civic nationalism respectively. But using the same noun – nationalism – is misleading because it nourishes the misconception that we are dealing with two variations of the same phenomenon. We are not.

And this is where I must part sharply with Smith's and, by extension, Breuilly's view of the nation. The history of political instability since the Napoleonic Wars has been largely a tale of tension between the two identities – ethnic and civic – each with its own exclusive standard for political legitimacy. Smith is determined that the two identities remain under a single rubric. Earlier this year, he wrote:

> Now while there is a crucial analytic distinction between the concepts of state and nation . . . in practice there is often a good deal of overlap in many cases; and given the connotations of 'patriotism' with kinship (*e.g.*, 'fatherland'), I doubt that we can draw any hard-and-fast line between it and nationalism. For example, I find it impossible to distinguish the 'patriotism' from the

nationalism of the Swiss, but they are quite different from, say, Rhaetian or Ticinese ethnic sentiment; yet such a distinction cannot easily be made in Connor's terms. As he asserts, what counts is sentient history, not actual history: the Swiss as a whole feel they have been a nation for many generations and possess a common foundation myth, even though the original 'Alemannic' forest cantons were later joined by others from different ethnic groups – as, after all, were the English, the French, the Greeks, or the Italians, only rather earlier.

(Smith 2004: 200)

The Swiss example is a telling demonstration of how grouping two essentially different and often competing identities under a single rubric can vitiate analysis. There is most certainly a Swiss civic identity (again, call it patriotism, civic consciousness, statism or etatism), although it is certainly stronger among the German than among the French Swiss. But the assertion that 'the Swiss as a whole feel they have been a nation for many generations' is simply not the case. In each war during the nineteenth and twentieth centuries when Germany and France were opponents, the French and German communities within Switzerland were sharply divided in their sympathies; political leaders have acknowledged that fear of such a divide has been an important factor in the state's policy of neutrality; an attitudinal poll has shown that a substantial majority of young French Swiss identify more closely with the French of France than with their co-citizens; another poll shows that a strong majority of the French Swiss feel that their linguistic or cantonal identity is more important than their identity as Swiss; voting patterns show an increasing polarisation along ethnic lines; the Swiss-German scholar, Jürg Steiner (Steiner 2001), who for decades ascribed little significance to the ethnic division, now perceives it as important and growing, and a not inconceivable, if unlikely, threat to the survival of the Swiss state.

To drive home the dangers to the study of nationalism occasioned by placing two quite distinct and potentially conflicting identities under a single rubric, consider Benedict Anderson's *Imagined Communities* (Anderson 1983). The subtitle of this well-received and highly cited work – *Reflections on the Origin and Spread of Nationalism* – would suggest that it is of key importance to the question, 'When is a nation?' In it Anderson refers to 'the nation-states of Spanish America or those of the Anglo-Saxon family' (p 49), to 'the nation-states of Europe' (p. 122), to 'Filipino nationalism' (p. 32), to 'Indian nationalism' (p. 64), to 'Ghanian nationalism' (p. 122), to 'Swiss nationalism' (p. 126), and to 'Burmese or Indonesian nationalism' (p. 126). With the possible exception of Costa Rica, none of the Spanish-American states could qualify as a nation-state; there are no 'Anglo-Saxon' nation-states; very few of Europe's states are nation-states; and India, Ghana, Switzerland, Burma and Indonesia are all ethnically heterogeneous. Despite borrowing all of the key phraseology, including nation, nation-state, national consciousness and nationalism, Anderson has written a book that deals far more with patriotism than with nationalism. Even if the terminology, albeit improper, was consistently applied, the harm to analysis would be real, but by interspersing valid examples of nations and their nationalism (such as that of the German and Hungarian (Magyar) peoples) with counterfeit ones (such as the Filipinos and Indians) the confusion is extended from terminology to essence. Treating as comparable entities Germans and Filipinos or Indian 'nationalism' and Magyar nationalism fatally compromises the analysis of either nationalism or patriotism.

Smith is correct that there can be 'a good deal of overlap in many cases'. For those with their own nation-state or for *staatvolk*, such as the English, or Castilians, the two obviously overlap and reinforce one another, but for the overwhelming number of nations the two loyalties are quite separate and often at loggerheads. If students of nationalism do not like the term 'patriotism', they should call it statism or etatism or civic consciousness or civic loyalty, but not nationalism. Analysis of a phenomenon requires that it be distinguished and isolated; it cannot be confused with a different phenomenon, the more so when the two represent two quite incompatible principles.

Despite, then, some serious qualms as to whether Smith, Breuilly and I are always discussing the same phenomenon, I was delighted to find myself in agreement with much that Breuilly has said today. I agree totally with his position that one cannot safely ascribe national consciousness to a people without evidence that it was not restricted to an elite, that it is necessary to establish that it was shared by other segments of the putative nation. In this, Breuilly's position is harmonious with most contemporary historians but not with earlier ones. Prominent historians of the last generation, such as Marc Bloc, Johan Huizinga, George Coulton, Sydney Herbert, Barnaby Keeney and Dorothy Kirkland, routinely dated the appearance of full-blown nationalism among many of the peoples of Western Europe to the Middle Ages. By contrast, my now fifteen-year and continuing review of contemporary historians specialising in a region, a state or a people indicates a broad consensus that national consciousness was absent among the people of their purview prior to the late nineteenth or early twentieth centuries. The principal exception to this consensus involves, as Breuilly has indicated, the English; here the debate concerning a medieval national consciousness burns brightly. To my knowledge, the most recent work on the subject is *The Making of English National Identity* by Krishan Kumar (Kumar 2003), who comes down in favour of a late nineteenth-century appearance.

More than a decade ago, I wrote a piece noting the general absence prior to the nineteenth century of evidence of a broad-based national consciousness among the many peoples who today are regarded as nations (Connor 1990). I noted four problems involved in dating the nation, the first of which read 'national consciousness is a mass, not an elite phenomenon, and the masses, until quite recently, semi- or totally illiterate, were quite mute with regard to their sense of identity(ies)'.

Smith's most recent criticism of my position may be found in the special issue of *Nations and Nationalism* (Smith 2004: 206 and 207). In general, he wants to reverse the burden of proof as advanced by Breuilly and most other professors of history. By contrast, Smith feels that in the absence of proof that national consciousness does not exist among the people writ large, we should assume that it does. To do otherwise is to accept 'an argument from silence'. This concept of burden-of-proof would clearly not be acceptable in modern legal systems, in effect requiring the defendant to prove his or her innocence, and is a piece with US Secretary of Defence Donald Rumsfeld's comment upon failing to find any 'weapons of mass destruction' in Iraq: 'Lack of evidence is not evidence of lack.' In any case, Smith is creating a straw man. No one to my knowledge has contended that the absence of evidence of popular national consciousness is in itself proof that it did not exist.

Nor need students of nationalism passively accept the historic illiteracy of the masses as precluding knowledge of their identity. On the contrary, I have beseeched students of nationalism to develop imaginative research techniques and to become sensitive to shreds of evidence of the perception(s) of group-self held by the people writ large. I have tried to probe into the view of group-self held by a number of peoples in various historical periods. I reported, for example, that the ostensible Belorussians, Carpatho-Rusyns, Croats, Dutchmen, Italians, Lithuanians, Luxemburger, Macedonians, Norwegians, Poles, Slovaks, Slovenes and Ukrainians who migrated to the USA in the nineteenth and early twentieth centuries were not cognisant of belonging to such nations (Connor 1991).

I have further suggested that some institutions such as slavery and serfdom or rigid caste and outcaste systems are apparently incompatible with a single encompassing national identity, and that when and where they are encountered we may presume a popular national consciousness is absent. A sense of common nationhood cannot bridge a cleavage as deep and unremitting as that between slave and landowner or caste and outcaste. How can the Japanese justify their treatment of the outcaste Burakumin? Quite simply by denying that the Burakumin are Japanese, all evidence to the contrary notwithstanding. Is it pure coincidence that an ethno-national consciousness has not prospered within the so-called Hindu belt of northern India? The Sikhs, the Muslim Kashmiri, the Christian and animist peoples of Assam have all experienced a growth in national consciousness, as have Hindu peoples of southern India, such as the Tamils, where the cleavages dividing the jatis are less rigid and weakening. But in the Hindu belt, where marriage across jati lines is anathema, how could a sense of a single jati-transcending nation nurture?

In this context, it does seem to me that the institution of nobility and its relationship to the appearance of nations deserves more attention. If blue blood and red blood do not mix, if heirs apparent seek their mates among foreign aristocratic houses, can they depict themselves convincingly as part of the people writ large, tied to that people through common ancestry? As recently as the First World War the House of Hanover changed its name to Windsor in order to deflect attention from the German roots it shared with the enemy. And the desire to emphasise common ethnic roots with the people writ large may now be seen in, *inter alia*, Denmark, Japan, Norway and Spain, where commoners are now spouses of today's or tomorrow's rulers. The studs and breeding mares of Saxe-Coburg have lost much of their allure in the age of popular nationalism.

Beyond noting the presence of many pre-modern (albeit surviving) institutions that inhibited the rise of popular national consciousness and in addition to the evidence gleaned from US immigrant attitudes, there are numerous pieces of evidence scattered throughout history of the lack of an embracing national iden-tity until quite recently. Consider the mass of ostensibly *Polish* serfs who sided against the Polish landlords in 1846, although the latter were fighting for Polish (read: ethnic) liberation. Or the case of Spain, where in the 1520s at a time when Spain was ruled by the Netherlands, a middle-class revolt against Dutch rule was put down by the Castilian nobility whose fears for their own social and political status outweighed any sense of patriotism or nationalism. Or the many citations by members of the upper classes in which they refer to the peasants as animals, a far cry from describing them as fellow members of the nation. Particularly poign-ant is a nationalistic-sounding tract written by Allessandro Tassoni in the seven-teenth century, urging an uprising against Spanish rule of Italy, rulers not 'of our blood nor used to Italian customs' (Gilbert 1975: 32). Nationalistic sounding indeed, but not truly nationalist, since Tassoni makes it clear that he is addressing only the nobility and not the commoners who he describes as devoid of courage and honour.

The relative ease or difficulty regimes had in inducing people to fight in their armies is also a possible index into the existence or non-existence of a national consciousness. Here is how Samuel Finer described the Prussian army of the eighteenth century:

> Only the scum, or most helpless of Europe's population would voluntarily join an army in those days. The King of Prussia had a thousand recruiting officers scouring not only his own lands, but also those of his neighbors to persuade, to con, or even to kidnap volunteers. It did not suffice.
>
> (Finer 1975: 142)

The need to rely on mercenaries and involuntary conscripts prior to the French Revolution is, I believe, a symptom of a very weak or absent nationalism. The British need to resort to impressments in order to staff their ships during wars in the eighteenth and early nineteenth centuries should certainly be a factor in any assessment of the health of English nationalism during this period.

In sum, I think that if, while reading histories, we remain constantly on the lookout for hints concerning the presence or absence of a broad-based national consciousness, we will learn a great deal more than Anthony D. Smith pes-simistically indicated in his recent piece 'History and National Destiny' (Smith 2004). Mining this information will be time consuming, and for most students of nationalism it will require a reordering of primary interest in ascertaining the view of group-self held by elites to that held by the people writ large. As suggested by many of the cases cited above, elite attitudes and policies can be important in discerning elite views of the nation. For example, if the rights of Englishmen include the right to vote, what can we say concerning an English nation for whom the franchise was restricted to less than 2 per cent of adult male members prior to 1832 and to some 3 per cent prior to 1867? Or how do we factor in the nineteenth-century British policy of foot-dragging on the creation and expansion of a public school system due to a fear on the part of the upper classes that a popular national consciousness would be the by-product and threaten their special prerogatives. So again, if students focus on what public policies can tell us concerning the existence or health of the nation, we may uncover quite a lot.

Have I encountered any evidence of nations prior to the eighteenth century? My research has concentrated on peoples today considered as nations and, again, is supported by a consensus of most historians who feel that claims to a lengthy history of national consciousness should be viewed with scepticism. However, if the standard of continuity were to be discarded, there are certainly some interesting cases. Breuilly mentions the Hussites whom I have never studied, but I have encountered historians who maintain that the Hussites represented early stirrings of a Czech/Bohemian consciousness. There were a number of tracts written by English Levellers in the early seventeenth century which manifest a popular national consciousness, but their ethos was not broadly shared beyond their membership. My early favourite would be the Altai Turks. An account of their sixth- and seventh-century history was etched during the eighth century on stones located on the Mongolian steppes. Unlike early European histories that focused on the elites, this history focuses on the attitudes of the people writ large which it terms 'the little people'. It states how the little people were once happy with their leaders before the latter sold out to the Chinese: becoming subservient to the Han, marrying Chinese women, and adopting the Chinese language, attire and way of life; and, seeing this eclipse of their golden age, it is related that 'the little people thus came to hate the Chinese'.

It is also possible that the study of the evolution of nations has been too Eurasian centred. In particular, it strikes me that many of the indigenous peoples of North America (e.g. the Hurons, Mohawks, Apaches) may well have possessed all of the prerequisites of nationhood prior to the coming of the Europeans. But overall, my point is that Smith perhaps need not be so pessimistic concerning our ability to lift the veil a little on popular identities prior to the modern era.

That is all I am able to contribute to the discussion on dating nations. I conclude by noting that I do not find the issue of the dating of nations very important. This is how I recently ended an article:

> I do not feel that the issue of 'When is a nation' is of key significance. Although today's nations may be modern phenomena, in a more important sense they defy dating. Stathis Gourgouris, Professor of Comparative Literature and Hellenic Studies at Princeton, has stated this seeming paradox with remarkable brevity and clarity (Letter to the Editor, *New York Times*, 9 May 1994):
>
>> My long term research into the nature of national formation and the development of nationalism in both Europe and Greece has taught me two insurmountable historical facts: (1) national symbols are always people's inventions, and (2) people often die for them with the satisfaction of serving eternal truth.
>
> (Connor 2004: 45)

Identity does not draw its sustenance from facts but from perceptions; not from chronological/factual history but from sentient/felt history. Failure to appreciate that national identity is predicated upon sentient history underpins a current vogue in the literature on national identity to bifurcate contributors in terms of (1) 'primordialists' and (2) 'social constructivists'/'instrumentalists'/'modernists'. What is missed in all this academic labelling is that, while from the viewpoint of objective history, today's nations are modern creatures, in popular perceptions they are, to borrow a word from Gourgouris, 'eternal', that is to say 'beyond time', 'timeless'. And it is not facts but perceptions of facts that underpin attitudes and behaviour.

References

Anderson, B. (1983) *Imagined Communities: Reflections on the Origin and Spread of Nationalism.* London: Verso.

Connor, W. (1990) 'When Is a Nation?', *Ethnic and Racial Studies* 3: 92–103.

Connor, W. (1991) 'From Tribe to Nation?', *History of European Ideas* 13: 5–18.

Connor, W. (2004) 'The Timelessness of Nations', *Nations and Nationalism* 10: 35–47.

Finer, S. (1975) 'State- and Nation-building in Europe: The Role of the Military' in C. Tilly (ed.) *The Formation of National States in Western Europe*. Princeton, NJ: Princeton University Press, pp. 84–63.

Gilbert, F. (1975) 'Italy' in O. Ranum (ed.) *National Consciousness, History, and Political Culture in Early Modern Europe*. Baltimore, MD: Johns Hopkins University Press, pp. 21–42.

Krishan, K. (2003) *The Making of English National Identity*. Cambridge: Cambridge University Press.

Smith, A. D. (2004) 'History and National Destiny: Responses and Clarifications', *Nations and Nationalism* 10 (1/2): 95–209.

Steiner, J. (2001) 'Switzerland and the European Union: A Puzzle' in Michael Keating and John McGarry (eds) *Minority Nationalism and the Changing International Order*. Oxford: Oxford University Press, pp. 137–154.

Question and answer I

Question 1

How is it possible for modernists to engage in effective debate with specialist medieval historians?

John Breuilly

I take the point about the difficulty of debating with medieval specialists, and there is always a danger that they will overwhelm any modernist critic with expertise. And no one ever really moves from the modern to the medieval period. The occasional medievalist like Ian Kershaw moves from the medieval to the modern period, but medievalists tend to be in a closed if distinguished guild, and it's quite difficult to penetrate. There are two possible ways forward. First, try to figure out precisely what medievalists are actually saying. Gillingham, for example, makes it clear that he doesn't believe there is any ethnic concept to the notion of English until the twelfth century. Of course he concerns himself not so much with political arguments as with ethnographic arguments in relation to people with different ways of life; people who don't have settled agriculture, don't live in towns, don't use money. In fact the ethnographic discourse he describes sounds like Tasitus describing Germans. Second – find your own medievalist. Fortunately they don't all agree with one another, so Sarah Foot, for example, is writing some wonderful stuff on how the concept of a state is inappropriate for medieval historians. Patrick Geary, who Anthony D. Smith dismisses quite unfairly in my view, is a constructionist in terms of so-called early medieval, late Roman nations. Do you know why Visigoths and Lombards are different from English and Germans? It's just that their names disappear earlier, that's all. So, I would say read between the lines and find your own pet medievalists.

Question 2

When was the first nation?

John Breuilly

When was the first nation? No idea. I don't think it's a very meaningful question. What I do think is important is how the term 'nation' is used. Some would argue that territory is important in such usage. The term is taking on a modern meaning when the nation is used to denote the political bearer of sovereignty and when that political bearer is not divided conceptually into a minority but is conceptually available to all. It may be practically closed down, women may be excluded from citizenship, certain kinds of foreigners may also be excluded but the meaning is extensive. French Jacobins argued that Bretons spoke a barbaric language that made it impossible for them to really appreciate the virtues of revolution, so they would need to be made French before they could be revolutionary. So there were all kinds of exclusions but the point is that conceptually membership of the nation is available to all, and for me that's pretty modern.

Question 3

When did the English become an *ethnie*? Second, how should we treat the Declaration of Arbroath? Is it a reflection of a real development of something like a nationalist consciousness in the fourteenth century?

John Breuilly

When the English became an *ethnie*, again I have no idea. I agree with Daniel Defoe: we are a bastard, mongrel people. As for the Scottish, I think of it as a spark in the night. Given that we've got these different usages of nation (ethnographic, monarchical), given that we've got ethnic notions which can sometimes be linked to aristocracy, and so aristocracies can express their interests in very ethnic terms. It's just that I don't think their ways of thinking translate into the modern period. I don't think that Professor Smith's so-called 'Aristocratic *ethnies*' works, this aristocratic ethnic sense is not extended to broader groups but challenged and displaced by modern, inclusive views of nationality.

Given that aristocratic elites can think like that, in particular moments, I can see how they can use a language that looks so modern to us. What's interesting is that the language then disappears. They don't use it next year. The propaganda used in the first ten years of the Hundred Years War was not continued later. We have no idea whether any substantial audience heard that propaganda and we don't know, even if they heard it, whether they believed it.

These observations lead me to say the following: The first thing is there is no overall approach that works. I am more and more aware of that. There are splitters and lumpers and I am a splitter. I think some of these questions are about nationalism as sentiments, feelings; some of them are about nationalism as politics and action; some are about nationalism as ideas or doctrines. I think there are different histories and they connect in different ways in different cases, but there is no general formula to how they connect, that's the first thing I want to say. The second thing is that I do disagree fundamentally with certain aspects of Walker Conner's views. For example, I find it impractical to define a nation in terms of what people really feel, because I don't even know what I really feel. All we can establish are certain uses of language connected to certain patterns of action.

Question 4

Women could not vote in France until 1945. Was there a French nation after 1789 then?

John Breuilly

I don't believe that we have to say that there's got to be a majority of people voting to say that the nation means something. I think that the nation means something from 1789 onwards. Eugene Weber's book is a significant book but I wouldn't conclude from it that the concept of nation is not important before the late nineteenth century. It seems to me that at the elite level across the whole country and right down to small-town elites, the concept of the nation already matters a lot. I don't think we can explain, for example, Napoleon's success in conscripting the number of troops that he does without understanding that national action and consciousness have become significant, although we need to look at which areas there was strong resistance and which areas there was not.

Question 5

Could the panel address the issue of language, particularly the significance of written language when discussing nationhood?

John Breuilly

The continuity of language is something which Adrian Hastings stresses, and I think it's one of the most important things in Hastings's work and also in Liah Greenfeld's work on nationalism. The significance of a written vernacular and the way in which words like 'nation' and 'people' are used in that vernacular is important. A written vernacular fixes the language, but nevertheless languages can change very quickly and there can be a gulf between written and spoken forms. There's a question of which particular form is accepted as the written form of the language. Justus Möser, an eighteenth-century German writer, argued that there was only one language in the world where the written form of the language as used by educated people bore any close resemblance to the spoken form of the language, and that was English. Even where we can talk about a written form of vernacular as being 'French' or 'Italian', it bore very little resemblance to the spoken language even of the people from the area where the dialect form was adopted as the basis of the written vernacular. So, I think the role played by written vernacular is vital but one needs to do much more than just establish the existence of such a vernacular. I'm also aware that there are people like Joshua Fishman who know far, far more about these things than I do.

Primordialism

Introduction

What we today refer to as primordialism is the oldest paradigm that has been employed to explain nations and nationalism. It was first adopted by nationalists themselves (though they did not call it primordialism) and then by some social scientists. It holds that nations are 'natural' and that is why they exert so much influence in human experience. A nation, according to primordialists, is a naturally occurring social grouping, often marked by cultural features such as a shared language, a single religion, shared customs and traditions, and shared history. In the writings of Johann Gottfried Herder, perhaps one of the earliest theorists of nations, for example, a nation is held to be natural and organic as opposed to the state which is seen to be an artificial creation (Evrigenis and Pellerin 2004: xxxv–xxxix). Because it is intrinsic for human beings to form this group, primordialists would maintain that we can find nations in any epoch of human history. They would not hesitate, therefore, to claim that the ancient Israelites, to take one example, constituted a nation, although they would not deny that there are nations which have emerged more recently. Because nations are part of human nature, they can be found anytime, everywhere. The emergence of a new nation is, then, often explained as an 'awakening' of a dormant entity.

Although the primordialist paradigm of nations and nationalism emphasises the timelessness of nations and often focuses on the antiquity or the Middle Ages, it has its roots in a wider study of modern society carried out by generations of sociologists and anthropologists, in particular that of social relations. The nature of modern society has always been at the centre of sociological studies, and one of the fundamental prepositions that has emerged so far is that rationality and calculability have become dominant at the expense of the power of kinship and blood tie – the 'givens' – in modern society. This notion underpins a variety of sociological ideas, from Tönnies' distinction between *Gemeinschaft* (community) and *Gesellschaft* (association) to Weber's 'disenchantment of the world'. Yet more and more sociologists and anthropologists have noticed that the power of the 'givens' or ascribed qualities is not weakening so fast. Cliford Geertz, who studied new states in Asia and Africa that achieved independence after the Second World War, for instance, has noted that 'the new states are abnormally susceptible to serious disaffection based on primordial attachments' (Geertz 1973/2000: 259). He then concluded that:

> The general strength of such primordial bonds, and the types of them that are important, differ from person to person, from society to society, and from time to time. But for virtually every person, in every society, at almost all times, some attachments seem to flow more from a sense of natural – some would say spiritual – affinity than from social interaction.
>
> (ibid.: 259–260)

Likewise, Edward Shils, widely regarded as one of the most vocal proponents of primordialism in sociology, has concluded that 'a certain ineffable significance' of 'the tie of blood' was alive and kicking in postwar East London (Shils 1957: 142). Both have pointed out that, contrary to what has been expected according to various modernisation theories, there remains something non-rational, ineffable and coercive in modern society that cannot be explained by referring to interests or rationality. Those that exercise such power include family, ethnicity and nations.

The primordialist perspective to nations and nationalism owes much to the discussion of primordialism in the field of ethnicity. There, the issue is whether ethnicity is part of human nature that cannot be changed (primordialism) or one of a wide range of resources that individuals mobilise in order to maximise their chances to achieve their goals (instrumentalism). In other words, is ethnicity something 'authentic' or 'constructed and manipulated'? Richard Jenkins has, however, pointed out that this is in fact a false dichotomy: as Geertz has agued, the primordial is powerful because it is *seen* as 'given', and there is no reason to dismiss a possibility of something 'fabricated' and 'manipulated' to be felt as 'natural' and 'primary' (Jenkins 1997: 46–47).

The discussion in the study of nations and nationalism mirrors, to a certain extent, that in the study of ethnicity. The primordial approach to nations and nationalism therefore focuses on what is regarded as the non-rational, ineffable yet coercive power of nations; Why does a nation command such intense loyalty as to sacrifice oneself in the name of the nation? Of course one answer to the question is that nations do not always command such loyalty; not everyone is willing to die for his or her nation. Many people have, in fact, gone out of their way to avoid being conscripted, for instance. However, there is no denying that there have been some cases where nations appear to have succeeded in commanding such intense loyalty although it was not conducive to the individual's apparent self-interests, and that is what the primordial approach to nations and nationalism tries to explain.

Primordialists have therefore put forward a preposition that nations command ultimate loyalty from individuals because nations are primordial, part of human nature. There are some variations in explaining why that is the case. Some base their arguments on human nature, especially various requirements for the human minds to survive. Others would look to biology and explain the primordial power of nations from the socio-biological point of view.

One of the examples of the former is given by Shils. Shils defines a nation as being 'constituted by its collective self-consciousness, the referents of which are birth in a specifically bounded territory, residence in that bounded territory or descent from person resident in that bounded territory' (Shils 1995: 94), and argues that the phenomenon of nations is 'a necessity of human existence in society' because of 'the necessity of the human mind to find sacrality not only in the spiritual transcendental sphere but in the primordial transcendental sphere as well' (ibid.: 109). In short, nations cater for the fundamental needs of human beings to locate themselves in time and place and to belong to something sacred, and are thus part and parcel of human existence. He therefore does not hesitate to assert that nation 'has repeatedly happened in world history' (ibid.: 109). The conclusion is that nations are not necessarily modern phenomena and that nations did exist in the antiquity or the Middle Ages; in other words, nations can be old.

The most well known proponent of the socio-biological explanation is given by Pierre L. van den Berghe, whose contribution may be found in the next section. According to van den Berghe, a nation is 'a politically conscious ethny, that is, an ethny that claims the right to statehood by virtue of being an ethny' (van den Berghe 1981: 61). Ethnies, van den Berghe argues, are simply extended kinships. Despite a variety of modernisation theories, kinship ties remain powerful even in modern society because of a general behavioural principle of all animals including human beings 'to favour kin over nonkin' (ibid.: 18). 'Favouring kin over nonkin' is the essence of nepotism, and it is an essential feature of human beings as well as other species because this is the most efficient way of maximising the chance of survival of one's genes. This principle of kin selection is combined with those of reciprocity – which accords a 'mental kinship' to unrelated humans – and of coercion to enable humans to form large-scale ethnies whose numbers sometimes run into millions. Moreover, human beings are different from other animals in that human behaviour is conditioned not only by genetics but also by ecology, and more importantly, culture (ibid.: 5). Culture facilitates the maintenance of the myth of common decent, by which any ethny is bound together. But the myth, according to van den Berghe, cannot be invented and 'has to be rooted in historical reality to be accepted' (ibid.: 27). Human nature therefore comes first and culture – manipulation – comes later.

In this variant of primordialism, the oldness of nation is not an issue. However, because its explanatory framework is timeless in that it is not conditioned by any temporary requirements, it is not illogical to conclude that this version of primordialism also allows for a possibility of pre-modern nations.

The primordialist approach to nations and nationalism has been subjected to a wide range of criticism like any other perspective in social science. When nationalists put forward a primordialist explanation in arguing the case for independence, or more generally for the right to self-determination of what they deem to constitute a particular nation, their argument is often dismissed as irrational and unscientific, and moreover destabilising the existing international order.

In academic discussions, primordialism comes under attack because it is often seen as a declaration of failure on the part of scholars to understand the world around us. One of the best-known critiques of primordialism, if somewhat misplaced, is voiced by Jack David Eller and Reed M. Coughlan (1993). They see a mortal danger in employing the concept of the primordial in explaining ethnicity and nations because this 'leads to a mystification of emotion, a desocializing of the phenomenon, and in extreme cases can lead to the positing of a biological imperative of bond-formation' (ibid.: 192). They continue:

> The source of this fallacy, and the cause of most of the confusion regarding the primordial concept, is the failure of sociology and anthropology to deal intelligibly with emotion. Primordial ties are likened to kinship, but here again the assumption is that kin simply are bonded.
>
> (ibid.)

In short, relying on the concept of the primordial for Eller and Coughlan means to admit that social sciences cannot explain emotion and therefore primordialism is a position that any serious scholar should not assume. There have been many comments made on the validity of their criticism of primordialism (see e.g. Smith 1998: 155–159). What is worth pointing out here is that their criticism is permeated by the 'fear' of being non-scientific and irrational, and as a result, perhaps, their critiques towards primordialism are sometimes unfair and harsh.

What primordialism brings to the study of nations and nationalism is the issue of loyalty and emotion that modernist approaches are often unable to address directly. For this reason, the two positions rarely meet in discussions about nations and nationalism. This is not to deny that primordialism has some strength in explaining certain aspects of nations and nationalism while it is not very effective in others. The way forward for students of nations and nationalism, then, is not to choose between the two, but to try to complement one approach with the other to achieve a deeper understanding of the issue.

References

On general discussion of primordialism in the study of ethnicity and nationalism

Jenkins, R. (1997) *Rethinking Ethnicities: Arguments and Explorations*, London: Sage.
Smith, A.D. (1998) *Nationalism and Modernism: A Critical Survey of Recent Theories of Nations and Nationalism*, London: Routledge (also for a critique of primordialism).

On primordial approaches to nations and nationalism

Evrigenis, I.D. and Pellerin, D. (trans. and ed.) (2004) *Johann Gottfried Herder: Another Philosophy of History and Selected Political Writings*, Indianapolis, IN: Hackett.
Geertz, C. (1973, 2000) *The Interpretation of Cultures: Selected Essays*, New York: Basic Books; esp. 'The integrative revolution: primordial sentiments and civil politics in the new states', first published in C. Geertz (ed.) (1963) *Old Societies and New States: The Quest for Modernity in Asia and Africa*, New York: Free Press of Glencoe, pp. 105–157.
Rex, J. (2002) 'The fundamentals of the theory of ethnicity', in S. Maleševič and M. Haugaard (eds) *Making Sense of Collectivity: Ethnicity, Nationalism and Globalisation*, London: Pluto, pp. 88–121.

Shils, E. (1957) 'Primordial, personal, sacred and civil ties: some particular observations on the relationships of sociological research and theory', *British Journal of Sociology*, 8 (2), pp. 130–145.

Shils, E. (1995) 'Nation, nationality, nationalism', 1 (1), pp. 93–118.

van den Berghe, P. (1981) *The Ethnic Phenomenon*, New York: Elsevier.

Critique of primordialism

Eller, J.D. and Coughlan, R.M. (1993) 'The poverty of primordialism: the demystification of ethnic attachment', *Ethnic and Racial Studies*, 16 (2), pp. 183–202.

Özkirimli, U. (2000) *Theories of Nationalism: A Critical Introduction*, Basingstoke: Macmillan.

3 The primordial, kinship and nationality

Steven Grosby

In examining the category of the primordial and its relation to nationality, it will be useful to begin by taking a step back from that examination and consider briefly religion. To do so will situate the subsequent discussion of the primordial and its relation to nationality in such a way as to clarify both its character as one of a number of heterogeneous orientations of human conduct and its heuristic utility for an investigation into the tensions present in the constitution of any nation.[1]

Persistence and variability

The observation that no human society has existed without religion is a commonplace. However, far from obvious are the conclusions to be drawn from the evidence that supports this observation. To acknowledge the ubiquity and persistence of religion does not represent a refusal to recognise that there have always been individuals who have either been so passive in their acceptance of a religious tradition as to appear indifferent to it, or who have professed a rejection of religion altogether, including in antiquity, as is clear from the mere mention of the names Democritus, Epicurus, Lucretius, Carneades and probably the Chinese Wang Ch'ung (27–100 CE). Indeed, the existence of non-believers and the challenge they represent to a religious tradition are attested to in the Hebrew Bible (Psalm 14:1; 53:1–3; Job 21:14–16).

These individuals from antiquity indicate that our understanding of the rejection of religious belief should not be exploited in the service of maintaining the fashionable historicism that insists upon an unequivocal contrast between, on the one hand, the religiously infused and putatively culturally homogeneous *Gemeinschaften* of the distant past (which should have precluded the disbelief of such individuals) and, on the other, the putatively secularised and supposedly culturally homogeneous *Gesellschaft* of what the historicists refer to as 'modernity' (which none the less displays considerable attachments to religious beliefs). The perspective of such a historical disjunction of human understanding, conduct and relation is a relic of an antiquated theoretical schema that should be abandoned. To be sure, *Gemeinschaft* and *Gesellschaft* are useful categorial abstractions to describe a contrast between two directions of human conduct, respectively, binding relations that are temporally enduring and territorially specific, and temporally episodic relations that are expediently self-serving. However, this categorial contrast must not be understood to represent a hard-and-fast historical distinction between the relations of the past and those of the present. In antiquity, individuals and their families were often motivated by expedient self-interest and the accumulation of private property, for example, the Athenian Themistocles' greed for money as recounted by Herodotus in *The History* (8.112). In antiquity, there were certainly temporally episodic relations of the marketplace, for example, policies during the 'Old Assyrian period' (2000–1800 BCE) to maximise profit in the geographically extensive trade of copper and tin (Veenhof 1972; Muhly 1973), or extensive commerce and use of contracts in Han China (210 BCE–220 CE). As Max Weber once remarked, those who fail to recognise that capitalism (where goods are produced for the market, and property – including land – is an object of trade) existed in antiquity should be sent back to the kindergarten of history (which is not to gainsay important differences between ancient and modern forms of capitalism). Today, individuals are often motivated by ideals that indicate their acknowledgement of enduring and binding relations, as manifested in, for example, acts of charity or patriotism.

Tönnies' categories of *Gemeinschaft* and *Gesellschaft* are better understood as representing patterns of conduct commingling in varying degrees in all periods of time. Only by recognising that both self-interest, narrowly understood as the maximisation of individual pleasure, and the transcendence of the self, broadly understood as the abnegation of the self, are co-existing patterns of human conduct can one take into account the historical persistence of religion as well as an accompanying scepticism. Only by doing so can one appreciate the paradox of nationality and the heterogeneity of human conduct recognised by Adam Smith (1982 [1759]: 192): 'There is many an honest Englishman, who, in his private station, would be more seriously disturbed by the loss of guinea, than by the national loss of Minorca, who yet, had it been in his power to defend that fortress, would have sacrificed his life a thousand times rather than, through his fault, have let it fall into the hands of the enemy.' The problem is to account for such paradoxical combinations of attachments, rather than avoid them through the adoption of obfuscating and overly facile periodisations implied by such rubrics as 'the age of secularisation' or 'modernity'.

Certainly, there are periods where one pattern of relation predominates over another; and, in this regard, some have argued that the current age is one lacking in religious belief. To what extent is this so? It is incumbent on the analyst who questions the polemical intention and thereby analytical merit of the category of 'modernity', because it misrepresents the evidence of what it has meant to be human, to address the best case for this weak argument. I thus put aside the continuing adherence of much of the world's population to Christianity, Islam, Hinduism and Buddhism that is itself sufficient to undermine the argument, and turn to the 'progressive' Western intellectual. Here, it is a question of a more nuanced, hence more accurate, understanding of the categorial distinctiveness of religion (Grosby 2001b), namely the evidently inexpungable, metaphysical orientation in human affairs that asserts a meaning to life derived from reference to an other-worldly being (god) or power(s), or an other-worldly ideal condition (for example, universal harmony, such that 'the wolf will dwell with the lamb and the leopard will lie down with the goat' (Isaiah 11: 6), Eden or Nirvana). From this perspective, that is, the human thirst for hope, expressed by what Talcott Parsons (1965[1938]) characterised as existential, non-empirical ideas that, as such, are not capable of verification, the religious orientation of today's progressive Western intellectual exhibits much similarity with the ideal of a universal harmony of the Roman Stoics, including that of Cicero who combined fidelity to that ideal with an overt scepticism about the existence of the gods (Momigliano 1987). This by no means unique similarity indicates that it is an error not to recognise continuities between the culture of the modern Occident and that of antiquity.

To recognise the persistence over time and ubiquity across civilisations of religious beliefs does not mean that those beliefs have not undergone changes, even transformations. It is possible that, in antiquity, scepticism about the existence of the gods might be correlated with what Karl Jaspers (1953) and S.N. Eisenstadt (1986) characterised as the 'axial age breakthrough', since the latter represented the subjection of previously existing religious traditions to critical evaluation that, in turn, led to degrees of rationalisation – the elimination of magic and the search for conceptual coherence – of the doctrines of what Max Weber described as the 'religions of the book'. This rationalisation, as exemplified by the ancient Israelite prophets, Platonic philosophy, Buddhism and to a lesser extent Confucianism, carried with it the potential for the ostensible rejection of religion.

Even granting the possibility of such a correlation, it is none the less difficult, if not impossible, to point to any particular set of sociological or economic factors which may have served as a necessary precondition for that conceptual break-through, its concomitant rationalisation of religious doctrine, and further specula-tion on humanity's place in the universe that could lead to the rejection of a religious tradition. It was indeed the case that in ancient Greece, Israel, India and China the period of the 'axial breakthrough', from approximately the seventh century BCE to the third century BCE, saw large-scale wars and the consolidation of states with codified legal codes. The result of such developments – requiring the emergence of ascendant political and religious centres, the marshalling of large resources, and a degree of predictability in legal and economic relations: a 'public culture' – was a relative systemisation in various spheres of human conduct. Nevertheless, massive military conflict, state formation that included large-scale irrigation (Egypt, Mesopotamia) and extensive, written legal codes had certainly existed previously, at least in the ancient Near East, but without resulting in the transformation of religious conception characteristic of the 'axial breakthrough'. Despite these developments within the pre-axial civilisations, one observes only vague anticipations of this rationalisation of the understanding of humanity's relation to the universe (for example, the proto-monotheistic descrip-tion of Marduk in the Babylonian *Enūma Eliš*). Moreover and of the utmost importance, where the axial breakthrough subsequently occurred, the system-isation of conduct of the various spheres of human activity was noticeably uneven. For example, ancient Greece never developed a political centre; ancient and medieval Judaism remain resistant to philosophical speculation, despite impressive legal codification (Mishnah, Talmud) and the prestige of Maimonides; and commercial activity and law throughout much of the history of Islamic civilisation did not achieve sufficient independence from the principle of *taqlîd*, obedience to (requiring an imitative extension of) the *Shari'a*, despite the occasional expression of *ijtihâd* (individual judgement or innovation, for example, the *hiyal*) for further legal and economic rationalisation to occur.[2]

However disconcerting to social historians, the pursuit of definitive preconditions that would account for the rationalisation of religious belief should be met with scepticism. Of course, this scepticism in no way denies that the development of conceptual coherence of a religion may be influenced by various factors, for example, whether or not a religion achieves institutional independence, or, as in the case of the ancient Israelite worship of Yahweh, evidently war and military defeat that required a new understanding of what it meant to be 'chosen'. It in no way denies that such a development may be in the service of other 'interests', such as the consolidation of power, for example, the Roman emperor Constantine's role at the Council of Nicea. Furthermore it in no way denies that a particular religious orientation may be combined with other orientations of understanding and conduct, each influencing the other (either to facilitate or to limit further rationalisation) in a tension-filled but relatively stable centre of a society or civilisation, the existence of which remains the valuable insight, since Herder, of the *Geisteswissenschaften* and the central assumption of the 'ethno-symbolic' approach to the study of nationalism. However, such a conclusion means that religion has its own set of categorially specific problems revolving around the positing of an other-worldly (in the sense that it asserts conditions which transcend human experience) meaning to the existence of the individual, the relation of the individual to his or her society, and the place of both the individual and that society in the universe in the face of worldly events, above all death, that otherwise call into question that meaning (Nilsson 1960). The proper conclusion is that the assertion of meaning to human existence follows a logic of its own that is relatively independent from other activities of life.

Notwithstanding the widely variable manifestations of religion throughout history; the dramatic transformations that religion has undergone such that one may speak warily of its uneven evolution – warily because of the antinomies inherent to the category between, on the one hand, the significance attributed to the propagation and continuation of life itself and, on the other, a meaning that transcends, hence conditions, that propagation and continuation; and even the rejection of religion: the historical evidence justifies the observation that religious belief is a persistent, albeit variable orientation of human understanding. The variability of the historical expressions of religion should not obscure from the analyst the fact of this persistence. The conundrum is how to account for this civilisational ubiquity and historical persistence.

One solution to this puzzle is the explanation that religion functions as one factor of solidarity necessary for any society to exist over time. In the attempt to rid the social sciences of metaphysical assumptions, this functionalist accounting of religion was put forward by Durkheim, Radcliffe-Brown and Gellner, all of whom in varying degrees also historicised the account, for example, Durkheim's and Gellner's religiously infused categories of respectively 'mechanical solidarity' and 'agro-literate society' in contrast to, respectively, 'organic solidarity' and the diffuse 'high culture' of industrial society. Such a functionalist analysis of religion is not without merit, since it elucidates the relations of the orientations within what is only the relatively stable centre of any society. However, in its factually inaccurate subordination of those relations to a historical disjunction, this functionalism suffers from numerous weaknesses. It suffers from an inaccurate understanding of ancient societies, the structures of which have too often been understood in terms of the anthropological studies of Australian and African tribes.[3] Thus, for example, it is too simplistic to characterise Han China as merely an agrarian society whose literacy was confined to the ruling stratum, when, according to the first-century CE *Han shu*, the officials of both the central and provincial governments numbered 120,285 – officials who may have originally been from rural areas where they first studied the 'five classics' and who, after 132 CE, were required to pass written examinations (Twitchett and Loewe 1986: 463–466).[4] The society of Second Temple Judah was clearly literate, as was perhaps the late monarchy of the period of the First Temple.[5] Moreover, the centrality of a written text for the continued existence of a social relation is clear from the Copts with the translation of the Bible into Sahidic at the end of the third century CE (Frend 1982). This historicism has also led to a misappreciation of early medieval Europe, as Adrian Hastings (1997) has argued.

This historicist functionalism suffers, above all, from an inability to recognise tensions, religious and other, within what has wrongly been viewed as the homogeneous centre of ancient societies. Sharp tensions were clearly possible in those ancient societies where the axial breakthrough occurred, as the examples of the religio-political movements of the Taoist influenced 'Yellow Turbans' and 'Five Pecks of Grain' in late second-century CE China and the messianic divisions within late Second Temple Judaism (Maccabees, Pharisees, Essenes, Zealots, Sicarii, Bar-Kokhba) indicate. In these examples from antiquity, religion did not function to 'reaffirm and strengthen the sentiments on which the social order depends' (Radcliffe-Brown 1952: 169). These are examples of threats to civil order, involving mass mobilisations of populations organised around fidelity to sharply conflicting conceptions of the way the world ought to be. It would be to go too far to characterise such movements in antiquity as examples of the more recent 'ideological style of politics' that represents a repudiation of politics properly understood. However, the millenarian and often Manichaean elements of this 'ideological style' owe their origin to the ancient religions of the 'axial breakthrough' – yet another fact that challenges the periodic disjunction implied by the category 'modernity'.

At stake here is not merely a proper appreciation of ancient societies. The historicist periodisation implied by the category 'modernity' also suffers from a refusal to recognise both the persistence of religion in today's societies and the tensions within those societies' relatively stable yet heterogeneous centres. The societies of today are not culturally homogeneous, as human conduct has always been and continues to be heterogeneous. Religious beliefs persist, and their enthusiastic expressions often pose a threat to civil order, as is clear today in Islamic and Hindu civilisations; for example, the assertion by the Rashtriya Swayamsevak Sangh and the Bharatiya Janata Party of *Hindutva*, 'Hinduness', that has posed grave dangers to the continued existence of Muslim and Christian minorities in India. To anticipate the subsequent discussion of the category of the primordial and its relation to territorial attachments, one weakness in Gellner's analysis of nationalism was to posit the existence of a culturally homogeneous modern society, thereby being unable to account for such heterogeneity, an example of which is the 'regionalism' found in a number of Western industrialised societies, for example, Scotland, Wales, Northern Ireland, Catalonia, Euzkadi, Flanders, Quebec, Corsica, Breton.

Max Weber's important contributions to the social sciences and historical analysis were twofold. First, in his unparalleled studies of religion he recognised existential, non-empirical ideas as factors influencing human conduct. Second, he further recognised a heterogeneity of human conduct through the formulation of: (1) its distinct spheres (economic, political, aesthetic, erotic and intellectual), each with is own categorially specific axioms (Weber 1946 [1915]); (2) types of social action (instrumentally rational, value-rational, affectual and traditional); and (3) types of authority (rational, traditional and charismatic) (Weber 1978 [1921]). The rejection of Weber's insights into the heterogeneity of human conduct has had a baneful influence on the understanding of religion, nationality and human conduct in general.

This evident heterogeneity of human orientation is not to gainsay that, as Walter Burkert (1996) argued, 'religion keeps to the tracks of biology'. Indeed, since human beings are part of the animal kingdom, how could it be otherwise? In this regard, the theorists of evolutionary biology are correct to pursue human traits, *qua* human, as probable morphological adaptations to the environments of the Plio-Pleistocene era that made those traits possible, such as: upright posture; the opposable thumb that facilitates the fashioning of tools; an enlarged complex brain, much of whose development is extra-uterine; and, in contrast to most of the rest of the animal kingdom, the underdetermination of an instinctual apparatus. Evidently concomitant with these latter two evolutionary developments is, in the phrase of philosophical anthropology, an 'openness of the mind' (or, as reformulated in the less edifying naturalistic idiom of evolutionary psychology and cognitive science, the 'brain's processing module is not dominated by a specific instinct') to different environments, including those created by humans that, once objectivated out of the ebb and flow of life, provide various foci of attention – structures of tradition – to which human conduct is oriented.

The biological givens of human existence (for example, the evolutionary mechanism of 'inclusive fitness', which situate humanity within the animal kingdom) provide the parameter of needs (for example, procreation, avoidance of pain, preservation) that account for the persistence of various patterns of human action. However, the evolutionarily emergent 'openness of the mind' not only to different and new environments but also to the internal life of the individual, that is, self-consciousness, carries along with it the awareness that life itself is a problem. The imperfect solutions to this problem are varied and heterogeneous. The biological necessities of human existence become subject to evaluation along the lines of meanings conveyed by qualitatively different, emergent and developing traditions. For example, even the biologically compelling drive to procreate and to establish relations for procreation are subject to different evaluations, and are thus susceptible to variability of different forms of mating (monogamy, polygamy, promiscuity) – a wide variability within a species that is unique to humans. Indeed, humans have the capacity to reject altogether what may otherwise be this behaviourally compelling drive to procreate, as one finds expressed in the quintessentially ascetic Matthew 19:12: 'and there are eunuchs who have made themselves eunuchs for the sake of the kingdom of heaven.' Thus there is a degree of indeterminacy in human conduct – what is usually referred to as the human capacity of 'choice' or 'freedom' – arising both from the tensions *between* different orientations of conduct and tensions *within* any particular tradition of conduct. Thus, while the mechanisms of the necessities of biological existence provide a framework for various patterns of human action, there is no direct relation between those mechanisms and their cultural expressions.[6]

In positing the very existence of humanity itself as a problem requiring a response, this 'openness of the mind' makes possible the recognition of the distinction, as formulated by Aristotle's in *The Politics*, between 'living' and 'living well', or, as formulated by Adam Smith in *The Theory of Moral Sentiments* between 'what is useful' and 'what is proper'. The problem of determining what it is to live well or what is proper represents the evidently inexpungable importation of a meaning of life into what thus can never be merely a biologically deterministic strategy of the struggle of life. This unavoidable metaphysical element in human affairs represents the foundation for the conceptual world of religion, where, in recognition of and in response to the facts of suffering and death, a meaning or purpose to life is asserted that transcends what may otherwise be the meaninglessness of the biological mechanism. For the axial age, world religions of the book, the positing of such a meaning (including the belief in a universal life-force in Stoicism or in the work of Henri Bergson) establishes, both in antiquity and today, an acute tension between such an ideal other-world and the brute reality of this world, as those religions have elevated that meaning to existence over existence itself through the formulation of criteria (for example, universal brotherhood) by which to judge, as Hobbes put it in *The Leviathan*, that 'nasty, brutish, and short' reality.

However, indicative of the heterogeneity of human experience, there is another category of meaning with attendant social relations that attributes significance to human existence, the 'primordial'. It is also persistent throughout time, ubiquitous across civilisations, and yet the historical expressions of its attendant social relations are widely variable. As with religion, the wide variability in primordial relations – a variability that has been awkwardly characterised as the 'family resemblances' of 'polythetic classification' (Needham 1975) – should not obscure from the analyst the fact of the persistence of this orientation.

The primordial

The meaning in human affairs that justifies the heuristic utility of the category of the primordial refers not to a universal standard that qualifies the existence of life, as in Matthew 19:12, or to the Platonic conception of 'the good', but to the generation and transmission of life itself. Specifically, the meaning characteristic of the primordial centres on the significance attributed to the facts of birth; that is, nativity. Thus, the beliefs conveying this significance are about life-giving and life-determining connections formed through birth to particular persons and birth in a delimited area of land of varying dimensions. Primordial beliefs are therefore about the relational modes of attachment constitutive of lines of descent, both familial and territorial – what is referred to as 'kinship'. Primordial beliefs about the creation, transmission and, hence, one order of life are the cognitive references to the objects – the actual or perceived biological connection – around which varying structures of kinship from the family to the nation are formed (Grosby 1994, 2001c).

It is often assumed that there is a categorially pure, original form of kinship which is narrowly gentilic; that is, a relation of descent based on the perceived 'tie of blood'. It is this form of kinship that one means when one uses the term 'family'. This assumption should be put aside, because the evidence indicates that kinship may be constituted not only along the axis of familial descent but also along a second axis constituted through the shared image of a territory, specifically descent in – being 'native to' – that territory. There are thus two axes of descent; and neither one precludes the other (Lowie 1927: 51–73).[7]

From everything we know anthropologically and historically about human beings, they have always been members of both families and larger territorially constituted collectivities to which kinship has been attributed. This attribution of kinship to the relation between members of a territorial collectivity has often been obscured, as in the formulation of a historical 'movement from status to contract' (Maine 1970[1861]: 165), by viewing that territorial relation as being merely juridical (usually expressed as 'citizenship'). This is a mistake, as further indicated by the necessity to draw a distinction between the self-consciousness of two admittedly historically intertwined forms of relation, 'nation' and 'state'. Our understanding of kinship must be broadened to include the 'we' that arises from the understanding of the self and the self's relation to those who are perceived as sharing in the territorial referent of that self-understanding. Throughout history, in both ancient and modern societies, one observes, to resort to a metaphor and idiom, a 'territorial contamination' of the otherwise putatively 'pure blood'. Thus one element in the uneven process of the transformation of an area of land into a 'territory' is that the inhabitants of that territory recognise it to be a relational referent of kinship – the status of being a 'native of the land': a source of life. This territorial referent of kinship is the 'pagan' recognition of telluric power; and it persists today within the monotheistic civilisations, in our understanding, however latent and partial, of our term 'homeland' and the attachments to that homeland known as patriotism. The combination of the narrowly gentilic terms of kinship – mother and father – with the territorial reference to land in the terms 'mother-land' and 'fatherland' conveys the significance of this second axis of descent which ought not to be dismissed as either a vestige of 'primitive mentality' or a capricious metaphor (Grosby 1995).

Insofar as one is justified in recognising, as heuristically useful, the category of 'pagan', referring to the perception of powers of vitality that are manifested in, for example, ancestor worship or deities of the land, for the *Religionswissenschaften* and comparative historical analysis, there is an overlap of references between the categories 'pagan' and 'primordial'. Indeed, understood this way, the term 'pagan' refers to primordial relations within the world of religion. Such an under-standing of pagan, insofar as one is justified in isolating this category from early Christian polemic which insisted on a generalised contrast between the recogni-tion of these sources of vitality and an ethical monotheism, is thus to be dis-tinguished from the systematic doctrine implied by the term 'paganism' (Grosby 1996). Similarly, primordial relations are to be distinguished from a doctrinally systematic view of human attachment implied by the term 'primordialism'. Finally, 'nation' – *a relatively extensive territorial relation of nativity* (the word 'nation' being one of those instances where the etymology of the term indicates that the original meaning to which the term refers has not been so 'emptied' as to obscure its original significance (see Freyer 1998[1928]: 116–127), thus, 'nation' from the Latin *natio* that, in turn, is derived from *nativus-nasci*: 'native', 'to be born from'[8]) – is to be distinguished from the ideological doctrine of nationalism, that, as an ideology, represents the subordination of all forms of experience to a vision of a unitary orientation to the world. The formulation of the category of the prim-ordial situates the anthropological category of kinship and the religious category of pagan within the broader context of a philosophical anthropology having to do with the classification of heterogeneous social relations.

It was the systematic assertion of the putatively ultimate uniformity of human experience (e.g. Platonism, Thomism, behaviourism) that was challenged in the initial formulation of the category 'primordial' by Edward Shils (1975[1957]).[9] Thus, central to the philosophical anthropology of the so-called 'primordialists' (Smith 1998: 151–159; Horowitz 2002) is the recognition of the heterogeneity of human experience, what William James (1987[1909]) had earlier referred to as 'pluralism' (Grosby 2002b). Implicit in this recognition was the acknowledgement of an evolutionarily emergent indeterminacy of human understanding and con-duct, predicated upon an 'openness' of the mind to the world. Explicit in this recognition was an acknowledgement that for any social relation there was neces-sarily always meaning around which a particular social relation is formed. This meaning, once lifted (or 'objectivated') out of the ebb and flow of life (either as an idea or material symbol), contributes to the existence of a particular, developing tradition, the continued existence of which is none the less dependent upon it being continually, if often latently, reaffirmed (Grosby 2001a). Furthermore, traditions and their respective meanings coalesce in qualitatively different directions, corresponding to different problems that confront life, such as not only the generation and transmission of life, but also the compulsion to conceptual coherence, and, of course, death. To reformulate this process in a more fashionable and often frivolous idiom, in order for an 'invented' tradition to persist over time, there must be an 'interest' in that tradition.

To be sure, as David Hume (1888 [1739]: 484) observed, since humanity is an inventive species, its traditions (and the institutions and social relations that bear them) are not given 'in nature'; they are in this sense 'artificial', having been made possible through 'the intervention of thought and reflection' often in response to new demands. Yet, as Hume also observed, though traditions are 'artificial', their existence should not be viewed as 'arbitrary'. The merit of this latter observation opens up the question of what it means to be human; that is, the formulation of a philosophical anthropology, as ascertained through consideration of the historical evidence. The problem thus arises to ascertain the likely patterns of characteristics of often conflicting 'interests' such that always changing and respectively heterogeneous traditions (e.g. religious, primordial, civil) exist and persist. The emphasis on the 'invention' of traditions is useful as a necessary refutation of the timeless organicism of ideological nationalism and obscene racialism (Hobsbawm and Ranger 1983); but beyond this important contribution, it offers little to our understanding of the classification of human experience and social relations, specifically the seriousness of nationality in human affairs.

The analysis of nationality ought not to avoid situating its investigation within the context of what the existence of nations reveals about humanity. In this regard, it is to the credit of the ethno-symbolic approach to nationality that it has recognised humanity's perennial, albeit variable, 'interest' in kinship; that is, in primordial relations. The primordial component in this approach is conveyed by Anthony D. Smith's (1986, 2004) focus on what he calls 'ethnic' attachments; that is, the presumption of descent. The component of tradition is conveyed in his focus on 'the centrality of symbolic elements' which places this approach within the *Geisteswissenschaften*, and which thus sharply distinguishes his analysis of a number of historically fluid processes from the deterministic 'sociologism' of Gellner.

There are indeed perennial human traits (e.g. the avoidance of pain, the tie of the umbilical cord of the mother to her infant, self-disclosure (and deception), death). These traits are not merely brute facts; the consciousness of each results in anxiety-provoking problems to which there is no definitive solution. For example, the male lacks the assurance of biological descent that the unambiguously traceable connection of the umbilical cord to the infant provides the mother, thereby raising one perennial problem of kinship – the determination of who is the father. The solution to this problem has resulted in various strategies of relation between male and female of which monogamy is one. The problem of self-disclosure and deception manifests itself in the perennial difficulty of calibrating what the relation should be between the individual and the other (Plessner 1924: 58). The consciousness of the extinction of the self poses the problem of a meaning to human existence, the solutions to which have varied widely, ranging from the desire to overcome the anxiety arising from the awareness of death through the perpetuation of the self through one's recognised kin (whether through one's family or nation or both) to the positing of a universal purpose to human existence as in the world religions. Given the biological fact of the anxiety of cognitive indeterminacy evidently arising from the instinctual underdetermination of the human species as compared to the rest of the animal kingdom, there is a human need for conceptual coherence to minimise such anxiety. The solution to this need – functioning perhaps as the human equivalent to a more developed and, hence, limiting instinctual apparatus found in the rest of the animal kingdom – is the development of traditions that structure, but do not eliminate, that cognitive indeterminacy we refer to as choice.

It is ironic that the so-called primordialists such as Edward Shils, Clifford Geertz, Steven Grosby and S.N. Eisenstadt, who have always recognised the inexorable presence of meaning-bearing traditions – the despotism of significance – in human affairs, should be the ones who have brought implications of perennial human traits into the *Geisteswissenschaften*, specifically into the investigation of nationality through discussion of kinship and territory. The postulate fundamental to sociology that human actions are limited to or determined by the environment, or the behavioural assumptions fundamental to sociobiology (for example, 'genetic favouritism' (van den Berghe 1981, 2001)), economic theory and the theory of rational choice (the maximisation of one's own advantages – conceived as wealth, power, or some pleasure as determined by one's passions and interests under the pressures of circumstances, including cultural, that delimit the range of choice) are not to be rejected. However, the heterogeneity of experience, including the ability to evaluate one's actions and thus reject what might otherwise be behaviourally compelling, poses complications to this postulate and these powerful theories that, in turn, require their qualification. These complications and qualifications suggest that the provenance of historical analysis should be a comparison of one societal configuration of traditions (and the tensions within that configuration) with that of another society, rather than the pursuit of causal mechanisms that would account definitively for a historical periodisation of human affairs.

The formulation of the category of the primordial to indicate the perennial, if variable, significance that humans attribute to recognised sources of vitality (what Weber referred to as *Sippen* or *Erbscharisma*) and their attendant relations was never intended, at least by Shils, Geertz and Grosby, to be a predictive model for human behaviour; and that it should be judged by such a criterion only reveals the temptation of reductionism that rejects the complications arising from the heterogeneity of the orientations of experience. The difficulty here consists in taking into account, on the one hand, the biological reality of existence and, on the other, the indeterminacy of action, the historical variability of any social relation, and this heterogeneity of orientations. None the less, there is nothing in the formulation of the category of the primordial that precludes the postulation of various speculative models for the emergence and persistence of primordial relations (Horowitz 2002). Thus it may be likely that the emergence of forms of primordial relations (e.g. family, clan, nation) represents an evolved strategy to minimise the cost of facilitating 'inclusive fitness' and adaptation (van den Berghe 1981, 2001; Gil-White 1999, 2001) through the promotion of trust and cooperation.

While acknowledging this likelihood, there is nevertheless a well founded prejudice against these speculations beyond the often made objection to their logical circularity. The conceit of these behaviourist speculations is revealed in their avoidance of facts that do not eliminate but compromise their explanatory power; for example, the ascetic self-abnegation of life as in the renunciation of sexual activity of the Buddhist Sangha, or, for Christianity, as expressed by Paul in 1 Corinthians 7:1,7: 'Yes, it is a good thing for a man not to touch a woman . . . I should like everyone to be like me [celibate].' One observes in these examples the importation of the tradition of another meaning of life to which conduct should accord. The neo-Darwinian 'response' to such self-abnegation is that it involves individuals and not a species. Yet the admittedly interesting behaviourist attempts to provide an account for persistence and ubiquity of the primordial relations of kinship are further compromised on an aggregate level, when there are declines of fertility, even declining populations, of nations that have achieved a higher standard of living.

It seems to me that there is no getting around the fact of the heterogeneity of orientations of human conduct, the tensions such a heterogeneity implies, and the capacity to choose among them. There is no getting around the cognitive element – meaning – present in human, *qua* human, affairs. This meaningful element is recognised in the formulation of the category of the primordial, since the empirical existence of primordial objects of vitality – the physical fact of bio-logical connectedness – do not themselves compel the formation of collectivities of kinship. It is only when such objects are perceived as being significant that they become objects of attachment; it is only when they become objects of shared belief (and, as such, always subject to modification) that primordial relations of kinship are formed. Thus the objects of primordial relations (for example, 'blood' as in the belief in a putatively common blood line) do not necessarily exist in the manner in which those who refer to them believe (Grosby 2001c).

This much is clear: humans make classifications of the self and the other in accordance with their beliefs. One set of beliefs is about the primordial objects of biological connection, including territorial co-residence. On the basis of such classifications, humans form groups, membership in which influences their con-duct. However, complications that have always been recognised in the philo-sophical anthropology of the so-called 'primordialists' involve precisely this element of belief, however biologically compelling as in the case of the primordial, in the formation of any social relation: (1) a belief may always be repudiated; and (2) beliefs are necessarily malleable, especially as they are brought into accord with other beliefs. This is merely to state a consequence of the heterogeneity of experi-ence. As to (1), individual humans and groups of humans may decide not to procreate. They may reject kinship altogether, as in Jesus' statements in Matthew 10: 35–8 and Mark 3: 33–5, or as Max Weber (1951: 237) formulated it, 'the great achievement of ethical religions was to shatter the fetters of the sib [by] establishing the superior community of faith in opposition to the community of blood, even to a large extent in opposition to the family'. Humans may not form nations. Indeed, throughout history, the perspective of universal empire has existed and continues to exist as an alternative to nationality. As to (2), social relations formed around a meaning can never be thoroughly stable, since other orientations with their attendant beliefs (and interests) intrude. There are always a multitude of criss-crossing and fluctuating beliefs, the saliency of any particular one in comparison to another varying according to the social relation in question and the demands of the day. The more extensive the social relation, for example, the national state (itself an uneasy combination of a rationalising tendency through the rule of law and the primordial, parochial tendency of kinship (Schnapper 1998)) in contrast to the family, the less homogeneous and less relatively stable it is. There is empirically no thoroughly stable, 'fully formed nation'; to posit such represents a misunderstanding of the character of nationality, often in the service of maintaining simplistic historical periodisations.

The primordial, history and nationality

There is nothing in the formulation of the category of the primordial that precludes recognition of a periodisation of the appearance and greater likelihood for the continued existence of a particular form of kinship such as nationality. Eisenstadt (2003a: 75–134; 2003b: 723–757), for example, has made frequent recourse to the category, as one of 'three major codes in the construction of collective identity', both in his analysis of a historical periodisation of what he calls 'multiple modernities' and in his masterful comparisons of civilisations (Eisenstadt 1986, 1996). Indeed, Shils (1975[1961]) thought that the existence of a nation, *qua* community, assumed a diminution of the distinction between centre and periphery, the most obvious but by no means only historical manifestation of which is the process of reaching political decisions known as democracy – a political process that, along with the belief in equality, is, as Tocqueville argued in *Democracy in America*, more prevalent today.

None the less, as Anthony D. Smith (1998: 158–161) noted, the recognition of the nation as a form of kinship has been accompanied by a tendency to be less concerned with delineating sociological preconditions and cultural mechanisms that might account for the emergence of nations and a periodisation of nationality (the work of S.N. Eisenstadt representing an exception to this tendency). As I have suggested, there are several reasons for this tendency. One has been the result of the focus on formulating patterns of attachment (or ideal types) in the attempt not only to refine the earlier formulations of Tönnies and Weber but, above all, also to understand better the particular features of any society in a way that raises analytically significant problems. Second, this formulation was part of a broader philosophical anthropology, the aim of which was to attain 'a coherent view of man's nature, of the meaning of the society which is given by man's nature and by the exigencies of coexistence, and of the transformations that societies can undergo within the scope of the limited potentialities so far known in the course of evolution and history' (Shils 1980: 33). Thus, historical transformations have been situated within the context of perennial, heterogeneous orientations with their respectively different problems. The justification for this approach was the intention of the opening section of this chapter. This approach has situated nationality within the continuum of forms of kinship, thereby accounting for a lack of emphasis in distinguishing nation from 'ethnie', although let it be noted that empirically the distinction is blurred. This approach further accounts for the scepticism towards disjunctive historical periodisations implied by categories such as 'modernity' or the 'age of nationalism' to describe a period that contained the Austro-Hungarian empire, the Ottoman empire, the empire of the Soviet Union, and continents such as Africa and much of Asia where the category of nation is applied with difficulty.

That there is a variability, even transformation, in human affairs is acknowledged; and, indeed, the recognition of numerous changes in how humans have perceived and thereby organised themselves was the point of departure for Shils' (1997) writings on civility, and Geertz's (1963) writings on the 'new states'. Regarding nationality, the relative stability of a territorially extensive and temporally deep community of a nation, constituted as a community out of a shared collective self-consciousness of what are viewed to be enduring attachments attendant to birth in a territory, would be facilitated by technological advancements in transportation and communication. This is obvious. Thus there is merit in Ernest Gellner's (1983, 1996) formulation of the 'high culture' of the industrialised societies of 'modernity' and Benedict Anderson's (1983) analysis of 'print capitalism'; indeed, they represent little more than workmanlike adaptations of Shils' formulation of the historical shift that has taken place in the relation between centre and periphery. Where they depart from Shils' analysis is in their impressionistic historicism, by failing to recognise that distinctions between centre and periphery, however ameliorated by access to the centre through merit (whether achieved through education or democratic election or accumulation of wealth) rather than birth, nevertheless remain. Moreover, overly facile periodisations (of which 'globalisation' is the most recent) often obscure continuing distinctions and new tensions by ignoring that technological advancements in communication make more likely wider dissemination and adherence to conflicting attachments.

Once one frees oneself from the tyranny of impressionistic disjunctive periodisations, one can then address those facts that are obscured by such rubrics. For example, historically significant expressions of diffuse 'high culture' such as the territorial expansion of the world religions, the dispersion of texts such as the Chinese 'five classics', and the codification and promulgation of Roman Law, took place in the absence of the technological advancements of industrialised society. Rather than leading to an avoidance of history, the formulation of the primordial opens up consideration of the evidence from antiquity and the Middle Ages which complicates our understanding of nationality in history, because explicit in that formulation is the rejection that any particular society, culture or epoch is so unique that no general categories can elucidate the nature of that society, culture or epoch. In what follows, I refer briefly to only some of this evidence beyond that already presented by John Armstrong (1982), Adrian Hastings (1997) and Anthony D. Smith (2004b).

As I have written at length on the applicability of the category 'nation' to a number of societies of the ancient Near East, in particular ancient Israel (Grosby 2002a), I emphasise here only two additional points. The first is to draw attention to the classification employed several times in Genesis 10, where the *gôyim*, the widely accepted translation of which is 'nations' (Speiser 1960; Cody 1964), are distinguished from one another by presumptive ancestry, language *and* bounded territory. The second is to observe that the Israelite opposition to the Seleucids beginning in 168 BCE, and to the Romans from 67 CE to 72 CE and from 132 CE to 135 CE is inconceivable without the existence of a national collective self-consciousness.

The central place of Buddhism in the constitution of the Sinhalese territorial relation of a nation goes back to the Sinhalese histories of the fourth and fifth centuries CE, the *Dīpavamsa* and the *Mahāvamsa*. There one finds the myth of the visit of the Buddha to Sri Lanka, during which he freed the island of its original, supernatural and evil inhabitants, the Yakkahs. As a result, the Buddha had sanctified the entire island, transforming it into a Buddhist territory. These histories thus asserted a territorial relation between being Sinhalese and Buddhism, the stability of which was derived from a perceived order of the universe, that is, the actions of the Buddha. The reaffirmation of that relation may be observed today in the shrines throughout the island: at Mahiyangana, where the supposed collarbone of the Buddha is kept; at Mt Samantakuta, where the Buddha's supposed fossilised footprint may be seen; and the most important one at Kandy, supposedly containing the relic of the Buddha's tooth.

The central place of the emperor that provides the foundation and continuity of the belief in the distinctiveness of Japan is put forth in the early eighth-century CE *Kojiki* and *Nihon Shoki*, where it is asserted that the emperor was descended from the sun goddess Amaterasu, and that Japan itself was created by the parents of the sun goddess. In the Sinhalese and Japanese histories and the Israelite account of being a chosen people, one finds, through a process of making myths more historical and making actual events more mythical (Brown 1993: 506), an assertion of the territorial distinctiveness of the society that is justified by reference to a perceived order of the universe which, as such, provides a conceptual stability to what might otherwise be understood to be capricious. Such mythical appeals – earlier referred to as existential, non-empirical ideas – to legitimate the distinctiveness of the collective self-consciousness of territorial kinship are also found in modern societies; for example, in the Declaration of Independence of the United States. It may be possible that a society will be constituted without such an appeal on a purely contractual basis; but it has not happened yet, which, of course, is not to gainsay the important developments in European constitutional law (see e.g. van Caenegem 1995).

Should ancient Israel, Sri Lanka and Japan be considered nations? Our use of the term 'nation' implies a stability (and consequently greater cultural uniformity) of a self-referential territorial relation that would distinguish it from those apparently more amorphous and transitory social relations which Anthony D. Smith classifies as 'ethnie' or 'ethnic groups', such as the Aramaeans of the ancient Near East and the Vandals and Avars of the early Middle Ages. The attempt to express this stability categorially as a distinguishing criterion is reasonable. However, the societies of the Sumerians and Hellenes existed for centuries. Evidently, on the one hand, the primacy of the attachments to the various city-states within those cultural configurations of ancient Sumeria and Greece justifies our excluding them as nations; yet, on the other, the stability and duration of their pantheons suggest a significant degree of cultural uniformity that was recognised to be distinctive, especially by the Hellenes during their war with Persia. Here we face a categorial quandary that is not so easily dispatched by the distinction between 'ethnie' and nation. Perhaps Friedrich Meinecke's (1970 [1907]) distinction between *Kulturnation* and *Staatsnation* still holds merit.

In any event, modifying slightly Anthony D. Smith's (2004a) reasonable enumeration of the processes necessary for the formation of a nation, then ancient Israel, Sri Lanka and Japan display the following characteristics: collective self-designation; written history; degree of cultural uniformity; legal codes; ascendant centre; and the conception of a bounded territory. This does not mean that differences between ancient nations and modern nations do not exist. For these earlier nations, religion played a greater role in the formation of a distinctive cultural uniformity than for today. One also observes a far more intrusive law of the land today than in these ancient societies. None the less, legal standardisation is to be observed in the history of ancient Israel and most certainly in the Japanese 'Ritsuryō State' of the seventh through ninth centuries CE, where laws divided the country into provinces, established a differentiated ministerial apparatus responsible for household registration, taxes, allocation of rice fields, military conscription and a religion that included a 'Council of Kami Affairs' which supervised the worship of Shinto kami at both court and local levels.

On the question of legal standardisation, one should not overlook those developments in England beginning with Henry II (1133–1189 CE) which led Pollock and Maitland (1895) to refer to the emergence of a national body of law during this period, such as: a permanent court of professional judges; local disputes adjudicated increasingly in accordance with the law of the land through frequent visits of itinerant judges, thereby checking capricious decisions previously made by local sheriffs; and the institution of the jury. The result of these and other legal developments was that the king, as representative of the nation and its laws, and his agents were seen as protectors of the property and rights of the individual and public order (i.e. the 'king's peace') throughout the land. Then, in 1215, there was the Magna Carta, with its fourteenth clause that by 1295 culminated in the institution of a legislating Parliament. It is difficult not to conclude that the result of these legal developments was the emergence of the territorial relation of the national community of England. It should also be noted that Henry II's *Assize of Arms* (1181), requiring that a man need only have bow and arrows, represented a mass mobilisation of an army that, as such, undermined further the primacy of the relation between local lord and tenant (Keeney 1947: 538–539).

In all of these cases, there is an intimate relation between the formation and continued existence of a nation and the consolidation of the political power and sovereignty of a state. It may be that a state often generates over time beliefs in the kinship of the members of the state, although when it does so it draws upon, and usually transforms, already existing traditions. Sometimes new beliefs about the putative continuity of the present with the past that seeks to provide legitimacy and stability to the present are asserted, for example, that the Germans of the nineteenth century were related to the ancient Cherusci, as represented by the *Hermannsdenkmal* (Mosse 1975). Such often factually spurious assertions indicate the hold of the primordial on the human imagination. It may also be that a nation seeks a state, as did Israel during the period of the Second Temple or Poland during the nineteenth and twentieth centuries, so that the nation, through its representatives, may act in the world to safeguard the processes of the generation and transmission of life. In any event, the social relation of the nation should not be collapsed into that of the state.

While a historical analysis must be based on facts, one historian may emphasise certain facts different from those emphasised by another historian. Clearly a historian may reach conclusions different from those drawn here about ancient Israel, Sri Lanka, Japan and medieval England. To be sure, complications exist. Just the existence of the Samaritans makes clear the difficulties in understanding ancient Israel as a nation. Clearly, the mythological account of the Yakkahs, subdued by Buddha, was intended to legitimate King Dutthagāmani's subsequent historical defeat of the Tamils, thereby justifying the sovereignty of the Buddhist king throughout what the early Sinhalese histories portray as a territorially uniform island. Needless to say, this ideal of a territorially uniform island stood in contrast to long periods of instability and regional conflicts during much of the early Anurādhapura period of Sinhalese history (137 BCE to 718 CE) between the southern part of the island, Rohana, and the central kingdom of Anurādhapura. Furthermore, Tamils and Tamil territory have always existed throughout the history of the island in ways which indicate an intermingling of Tamils, Sinhalese and their respective religious traditions. In Japan, regional differences between territorial (note well!) clans that led to the civil war of 672 CE persisted, until being undermined if not by the centralised Tokugawa Shogunate (1603 CE) then by the Meiji Restoration (1868 CE). These kinds of unavoidable historical complications have led to disputes among historians about the existence of nations. How should these disputes be understood?

Such disputes may be beside the point if they lose sight of the fact that no social relation evinces a stability as if it were thoroughly objective. It must always be kept in mind that with all social relations, and especially with the territorially extensive and temporally deep nation, we are dealing with uneven processes of attributed significance of recognition involved in the always complicated formation of a variegated collective self-consciousness. This is true for numerous territorial relations of kinship from antiquity and the Middle Ages of which the above cases are only a few examples. One could just as well ask what is the significance of the resilience of the term *īrāniyyat*, 'being a Persian', in contrast to being an Arab from the time of the Persian Buyids (945 CE to 1060 CE); or the significance of the Moroccan cult of the eighth-century CE Islamic Idris championed by the Marinids from the fourteenth through fifteenth centuries CE and later by the 'Alawites from the seventeenth through eighteenth centuries in the formation of an Islamic nation of Morocco as a counterpoint to divisive tribal loyalties; or whether or not Korea was a nation beginning with the Koryŏ era (tenth to four-teenth century CE) – examples that are also replete with complications. Thus for the historian it is often a matter of weighing the saliency of the development of one particular process as compared to another.

Anthony D. Smith's (2004a) reasonable enumeration of the processes necessary for the existence of nations – self-definition, myth and memory-making, terri-torialisation, public culture and legal standardisation – is, as I have observed above, an attempt to clarify the perquisites for the existence of stable, geographic-ally extensive territorial relations of kinship. However, there are ambiguities involved with all of these processes. I have already alluded to the theoretical and empirical difficulties here in distinguishing nations so understood from societies such as the Sumerians and Hellenes, both of which certainly had self-definition, myth and memory-making and degrees of a public culture, and legal standardisa-tion. Furthermore, these processes are also often evident in the continued exist-ence of empires, where the primordial attribution of kinship, while present (for example, the Chinese description of the foreign *Di* and *Rohn* as being less than human (Loewe and Shaughnessy 1999); or the territorial designation for the land of Assyria with a term for its respective population – a designation that self-referentially represents order in contrast to the chaos of the foreign barbarian (Machinist 1993)) is subordinated to a universalising vision of a civilised life (for example, the Chinese conception of *li* emanating from the *Zhongguo*, the centre) that presumably thus distinguishes these empires from nations. Moreover, legal standardisation cuts two ways. The law of the land is necessary for establishing a sociologically uniform territory; but the process also carries with it the potential for undermining a bounded territory through freedom of contract and a market for real property – consequences of the rationalisation of economic activity. Necessary for nationality is the saliency or ascendancy of an attributed territorial kinship as compared to these other heterogeneous processes. Focusing on this criterion may blur the lines seemingly distinguishing 'ethnic groups' from nations. However, empirically the situation is always complicated; and thus the criticism of 'neo-perennialism' is water off a duck's back.

One must never lose sight of the fact that as processes of collective self-consciousness, the features as enumerated by Anthony D. Smith are necessarily replete with tensions and uneven development. This is certainly so for the societies of antiquity and the Middle Ages, where as Friedrich Meinecke (1970 [1907]: 16) noted, the territorial relation (in particular its public culture) rests heavily on its collective representation: *pars pro toto*. Of course, the centre, even though viewed as representative of the nation, and thus worthy of deference, is also viewed warily, even at times openly resented. The centre may be viewed as the guarantor of peace or even health (Bloch 1973 [1923]), but it also taxes. This uneven processual character, with its unavoidable tensions and ambiguities, of each of what Smith has designated as the necessary features of nations is also characteristic of modern nations. Regarding 'territorialisation' today, there is 'regionalism'. One must remember, as Walker Connor (1972) observed, that less than 10 per cent of all of the contemporary states are homogeneous from an ethnic viewpoint. There is also the temptation to empire (the European Union). Both are but a few of the many factors that contribute to the tensions, the fragmented quality, of the national state's public culture today, of which resentment of the centre is yet another. There are also competing claims to represent the centre – claims that involve disputes over what is the proper understanding (the process of 'memory-making') of the asserted temporal continuum of the nation between present and past. Disputes over self-definition remain, including over the determination of membership (expressed in differences over laws of immigration and citizenship). This and more should be obvious; but the fluidity and heterogeneity of attachments have been obscured by conceptual clumsy, disjunctive periodisations of human affairs.

That there is variability in human affairs is obvious. However, it is our task to interpret that variability in significant ways which illuminate what it means to be human, including the heterogeneity of human experience. The aim of the formulation of the category of the primordial and its bearing on the study of nationality through situating the nation within the continuum of forms of kinship is to do just that.

Notes

1 I gratefully acknowledge support of a research fellowship from the Earhart Foundation in the writing of this chapter.
2 For the *hiyal*, see Schact (1964) and Udovitch (1970). For the possibility of the Islamic law of inheritance as an obstacle to economic development in the Islamic Middle East, see Kuran (2003).
3 For Gellner's inaccurate understanding of the 'vertical cultural cleavages' of 'agroliterate' societies of the ancient Near East, in particular ancient Egypt, see Routledge (2003).
4 Gellner (1983:16) acknowledged the literacy of the Confucian bureaucracy, but his acknowledgement is an example of the tyranny of a theoretical schema riding roughshod over such a fact.
5 For literacy in the late monarchy of the First Temple, see Mazar (1992: 515). Challenging Mazar's conclusion is Niditch (1996: 39–59). See also Schneidewind (2004).
6 The behaviourist or philosophical naturalist may object to this conclusion by insisting that 'choice' or 'freedom' is merely the consequence of either the lag of evolutionary adaptation or the excessive cost of information to maximise efficiently one's pleasure or preference. Such objections have the appearance of 'just so' stories in the service of maintaining the exclusivity of the explanatory mechanism of the posited initial condition. The neo-Darwinian temptation to explain all aspects of culture by recourse to the biological mechanism of evolutionary adaptation should be rejected because we are never in a position to determine what current cultural manifestation is or is not a consequence of the mechanism of adaptation. Such a determination requires the

perspective of many thousands of years. This is one objection to the otherwise suggestive article by Horowitz (2002).

7 The recognition of this second axis of descent in Asia and the ancient Near East is the anthropological significance of Rowton (1973, 1974, 1977).

8 The territorial implication of kinship of the terms 'natio-nativus' is found in other languages. In addition to Herodotus' description of a territorial kinship of Hellenes in Book 8 of *The History*, Plato's use of *génos* in Book 5 of *The Republic* implies a familiarity binding those born as Hellenes, as if they were members of the same familial household. In the Semitic languages, there is the biblical Hebrew *'ezrach ha 'arets*, 'native of the land' where *'ezrach*, 'native', is likely derived from the verb *zarach*, 'to rise' or 'to come forth', and thus not from the Arabic *sarih* as argued by W. Robertson Smith (1889). Furthermore, the ancient Hebrew *gôy* and the Akkadian *gāyum* refer to collectivities of territorial kinship. Note also, despite Bernard Lewis' (1992) argument restricting the earlier use of the Arabic *watan* to a place of residence (although there are occasional usages indicating a conflation of familial relation with geographical collectivities), Ibn Khaldûn's repeated use in *The Muqaddimah* of *'asabiyya*, signifying a 'group feeling' of a collective self-consciousness of kinship beyond the family.

9 For an overview of the term 'primordial' in the literature of the social sciences and its relation to the categories of Tönnies and Schmalenbach, see Grosby (2001c).

References

Anderson, B. (1983) *Imagined Communities*, London: Verso.

Armstrong, J. (1982) *Nations before Nationalism*, Chapel Hill: North Carolina University Press.

Bloch, M. (1973 [1923]) *The Royal Touch*, London: Routledge & Kegan Paul.

Brown, D. (ed.) (1993) *The Cambridge History of Japan, Vol. I*, Cambridge: Cambridge University Press.

Burkert, W. (1996) *Creation of the Sacred: Tracks of Biology in Early Religion*, Cambridge, MA: Harvard University Press.

Cody, A. (1964) 'When is the chosen people called a goy', *Vetus Testamentum* 14: 1–6.

Connor, W. (1972) 'Nation-building or nation-destroying?', *World Politics* 24: 319–355, reprinted in *Ethnonationalism: The Quest for Understanding*, Princeton, NJ: Princeton University Press 1994.

Eisenstadt, S.N. (1986) *The Origins and Diversity of Axial Age Civilizations*, Albany, NY: State University Press.

—— (1996) *Japanese Civilization: A Comparative View*, Chicago, IL: University of Chicago Press.

—— (2003a) 'The construction of collective identities and the continual reconstruction of primordiality and sacrality', in *Comparative Civilizations & Multiple Modernities*, Leiden: Brill, pp. 75–134.

—— (2003b) 'Mirror-image modernities: contrasting religious premises of Japanese and U.S. modernity', in *Comparative Civilizations & Multiple Modernities*, Leiden: Brill, pp. 723–757.

Frend, W.H.C. (1982) 'Nationalism as a factor in anti-Chalcedonian feeling in Egypt', in S. Mews (ed.) *Religion and National Identity* Oxford: Blackwell, pp. 21–38.

Freyer, H. (1998 [1928]) *Theory of Objective Mind: An Introduction to the Philosophy of Culture*, Athens, OH: Ohio University Press.

Geertz, C. (1963) 'The integrative revolution: primordial sentiments and civil politics in the new states', in C. Geertz (ed.) *Old Societies and New States*, New York: Free Press, pp. 105–157.

Gellner, E. (1983) *Nations and Nationalism*, Ithaca, NY: Cornell University Press.
—— (1996) 'Do nations have navels?', *Nations and Nationalism* 2(3): 366–370.
Gil-White, F.J. (1999) 'How thick is blood?', *Ethnic and Racial Studies* 22(5): 789–820.
—— (2001) 'Are ethnic groups biological species to the human brain?', *Current Anthropology* 42/4: 515–554.
Grosby, S. (1994) 'The verdict of history: the inexpungeable ties of primordiality', *Ethnic and Racial Studies* 17: 164–171.
—— (1995) 'Territoriality: the transcendental, primordial feature of modern societies', *Nations and Nationalism* 1(2): 143–162.
—— (1996) 'The category of the primordial in the study of early Christianity and second-century Judaism', *History of Religions* 36(2): 140–163.
—— (2001a) 'Mind and collective consciousness', in T. Luigi (ed.) *New Horizons in Sociological Research*, Aldershot: Ashgate, 257–276.
—— (2001b) 'Nationality and religion', in M. Guibernau and J. Hutchinson (eds) *Understanding Nationalism*, Oxford: Polity, Press, pp. 97–119.
—— (2001c) 'Primordiality', in L. Athena (ed.) *Encyclopaedia of Nationalism*, New Brunswick, NJ: Transaction, pp. 252–255.
—— (2002a) *Biblical Ideas of Nationality: Ancient and Modern*, Winona Lake, IN: Eisenbrauns.
—— (2002b) 'Pluralism in the thought of Oakeshott, Shils and Weber', *Journal of Classical Sociology* 2(1): 43–58.
Hastings, A. (1997) *The Construction of Nationhood*, Cambridge: Cambridge University Press.
Hobsbawm, E. and Ranger, T. (eds) (1983) *The Invention of Tradition*, Cambridge: Cambridge University Press.
Horowitz, D.L. (2002) 'The primordialists', in D. Conversi (ed.) *Ethnonationalism in the Contemporary World*, London: Routledge, pp. 72–82.
Hume, D. (1888 [1739]) *A Treatise of Human Nature*, Oxford: Clarendon Press.
James, W. (1987 [1909]) 'A pluralistic universe', in B. Kuklick (ed.) *William James: Writings 1902–1910*, New York: Library of America, pp. 625–819.
Jaspers, K. (1953) *The Origins and Goal of History*, New Haven, CT: Yale University Press.
Keeney, B.C. (1947) 'Military service and the development of nationalism in England, 1272–1327', *Speculum* 22(4): 534–549.
Kuran, T. (2003) 'The Islamic commercial crisis: institutional roots of economic underdevelopment in the Middle East', *Journal of Economic History* 63(2): 414–446.
Lewis, B. (1992) 'Watan', in J. Reinharz and G.L. Mosse (eds) *The Impact of Western Nationalism*, London: Sage, pp. 169–179
Loewe, M. and Shaughnessy, E.L. (eds) (1999) *The Cambridge History of Ancient China: From the Origins of Civilization to 221 B.C.*, Cambridge: Cambridge University Press.
Lowie, R.H. (1927) *The Origin of the State*, New York: Harcourt, Brace & Co.
Machinist, P. (1993) 'Assyrians on Assyria in the first millennium B.C.', in K. Raaflaub, (ed.) *Anfänge politischen Denkens in der Antike*, Munich: R. Oldenbourg, pp. 77–104.
Maine, H.S. (1970 [1861]) *Ancient Law*, Gloucester, MA: Peter Smith.
Mazar, A. (1992) *Archaeology of the Land of Israel*, New York: Doubleday.
Meinecke, F. (1970 [1907]) *Cosmopolitanism and the National State*, Princeton, NJ: Princeton University Press.
Momigliano, A. (1987) 'The theological efforts of the Roman upper classes in the first century B.C.', in *On Pagans, Jews, and Christians*, Middletown: Wesleyan Press, pp. 58–73.
Mosse, G. (1975) *The Nationalization of the Masses*, Ithaca, NY: Cornell University Press.
Muhly, J.D. (1973) *Copper and Tin*, New Haven, CT: Yale University Press.

Needham, R. (1975) 'Polythetic classification: convergence and consequences', *Man* (NS) 10: 349–369.

Niditch, S. (1996) *Oral World and Written Word: Ancient Israelite Literature*, Louisville: Westminster John Knox.

Nilsson, M. (1960) 'Religion as man's protest against the meaninglessness of events', in *Opuscula Selecta*, Lund: C.W.K. Gleerup.

Parsons, T. (1965 [1938]) 'The role of ideas in social action', in *Essays in Sociological Theory*, Glencoe, IL: Free Press, pp. 19–33.

Plessner, H. (1924) *Grenzen der Gemeinschaft: Eine Kritik des sozialen Radikalismus*, Bonn: Friedrich Cohen.

Pollock, F. and Maitland, F.W. (1895) *The History of English Law Before the Time of Edward I* Cambridge: Cambridge University Press.

Radcliffe-Brown, A.R. (1952) 'Religion and society', in *Structure and Function in Primitive Society*, New York: Free Press, pp. 153–177.

Routledge, B. (2003) 'The antiquity of the nation? Critical reflections from the ancient Near East', *Nations and Nationalism* 9(2): 213–234.

Rowton, M.B. (1973) 'Autonomy and nomadism in Western Asia', *Orientalia* NS 42: 247–258.

—— (1974) 'Enclosed nomadism', *Journal of the Economic and Social History of the Orient* 17: 1–30.

—— (1977) 'Dimorphic structure and the parasocial element', *Journal of Near Eastern Studies* 36: 181–198.

Schacht, J. (1964) *An Introduction to Islamic Law*, Oxford: Oxford University Press.

Schnapper, D. (1998) *Community of Citizens*, New Brunswick: Transaction.

Schneidewind, W. (2004) *How the Bible Became a Book: The Textualization of Ancient Israel*, Cambridge: Cambridge University Press.

Shils, E. (1975 [1957]) 'Primordial, personal, sacred, and civil ties', in *Center and Periphery: Essays in Macrosociology*, Chicago, IL: University of Chicago Press, pp. 111–126.

—— (1975 [1961]) 'Center and periphery', in *Center and Periphery: Essays in Macrosociology*, Chicago, IL: University of Chicago Press, pp. 3–16.

—— (1980) 'The calling of sociology', in *The Calling of Sociology and Other Essays on the Pursuit of Learning*, Chicago, IL: University of Chicago Press, pp. 3–92.

—— (1997) *The Virtue of Civility*, Indianapolis, IN: Liberty Press.

Smith, A. (1982 [1759]) *Theory of Moral Sentiments*, Indianapolis, IN: Liberty Fund.

Smith, A.D. (1986) *The Ethnic Origins of Nations*, Oxford: Blackwell.

—— (1998) *Nationalism and Modernism*, London: Routledge.

—— (2004a) 'The genealogy of nations: an ethnosymbolic approach', conference paper presented at the Association for the Study of Ethnicity and Nationalism 14th Annual Conference, 23–24 April, London: LSE.

—— (2004b) *The Antiquity of Nations*, Cambridge: Polity Press.

Smith, W.R. (1889) *Lectures on the Religion of the Semites*, London: Adam and Charles Black.

Speiser, E.A. (1960) 'People and nation of Israel', *Journal of Biblical Literature* 79: 157–163.

Twitchett, D. and Loewe, M. (eds) (1986) *The Cambridge History of China, Volume I, The Ch'in and Han Empires 221 B.C.–A.D. 220*, Cambridge: Cambridge University Press.

Udovitch, A.L. (1970) *Partnership and Profit in Medieval Islam*, Princeton, NJ: Princeton University Press.

van Caenegem, R.C. (1995) *An Historical Introduction to Western Constitutional Law*, Cambridge: Cambridge University Press.

van den Berghe, P. (1981) *The Ethnic Phenomenon*, New York: Elsevier.

—— (2001) 'Sociobiological theory of nationalism', in A. Leoussi (ed.) *Encyclopaedia of Nationalism*, New Brunswick: Transaction, pp. 273–279.

Veenhof, K.R. (1972) *Aspects of Old Assyrian Trade and its Terminology*, Leiden: Brill.

Weber, M. (1946 [1915]) 'Religious rejections of the world and their directions', in H.H. Gerth and C. Wright Mills (eds) *From Max Weber*, New York: Oxford University Press.

—— (1951) *The Religion of China*, New York: Free Press.

—— (1978 [1921]) *Economy and Society*, Berkeley, CA: University of California Press.

4 Comment on Steven Grosby

The primordial, kinship and nationality

Eric Hobsbawm

I

All debates about human nature and its characteristics and malleability, however far they delve into the past, are about the present, both because they are formulated in terms of current ideas and because every answer has social or political implications. If this were not so, the arguments about the relative importance of nature and nurture, inheritance and environment, would be considerably less passionate, not to mention they would be less likely to have the murderous consequences they often did in the twentieth century. The arguments about a supposed genetic predisposition of human males to the virtues of hunter and warrior are not about what happened in prehistory but about the social implications *today* of the behaviour of business executives and others who like to describe their virtues in the metaphors of aggression and war. Whatever similarities to war and conquest may be read into the activities of some tycoon of take-overs or share-price levitation, they are not the activities conducted on real battlefields, past or present, nor indeed do they call for similar qualities or develop similar sets of values.

When we talk about nations and nationalism it is essential to keep in mind that we are talking about today and tomorrow and not about the past, for this, above all, is a text which, by definition, can only be read backwards. If we did not know what nations are or ought to be today, we would not even discuss their past and its significance in their formation. If Granada had successfully resisted the Spanish reconquest, its schools would today teach Granadine national history while its scholars would rebut claims from Rabat that it was merely a northern extension of Morocco. 'Padania' is a 'nation' which did not even exist notionally until invented in the late 1980s by a regional demagogue to justify the secession of the north from Italy (Avanza 2003). Unlike its component regions such as Piedmont, Venetia, Lombardy and Friuli this conglomerate concept lacks all the characteristics of a 'nation' usually claimed by nationalist movements. It has therefore attempted to create the common past so indispensable to the nationalists' 'nation', and to justify the claim never to have been properly 'Italian', or even Roman, by a process of highly unpersuasive historical acrobatics. But if northern Italy were to secede, the invented 'nation' would exist and its invented history would be taught in the schools, though one hopes not in the universities of Padania.

Since the borders of educational systems are overwhelmingly congruent with those of politically independent or autonomous territories, this applies not only to imagined nations but to real ones as well. The great geographer Vidal de la Blache voiced the problem with Gallic lucidity: 'How did it come about that a fragment of the terrestrial surface, neither peninsula nor island, something that as a whole has no unity in terms of physical geography, rose to the status of a country in the political sense, and in the end became a fatherland?' (Guiomar 1986: 569, my translation). It is only in retrospect, when we know the answer – the nation-state France in something like its nineteenth-century borders – that this question makes sense. Conversely, before the era of incipient disintegration, or at least decentralisation, of the traditional European 'nation-states', such questions as those exercising historians today about the nature, the history or even the age of 'Great Britain' or the relationship between the English and the other peoples of these islands would not have been asked.

II

Two things divide modernists from primordialists in the debate about nations and nationalism. Both agree that social groups (the 'we's) have always asserted a collective identity, distinguishing themselves from other groups (the 'thems'), often in similar ways by ensembles of shared symbols and historical narratives. Whether this reflects primordial structures of social life or, at a greater remove, Darwinian patterns for species survival, need not concern us here. Unlike 'primordialists', 'modernists' believe that, however long the real or ascribed historical continuity between groups claiming the same name, earlier collectives cannot be confused with the modern, essentially class- or rather literacy-linked concept of the linguistic nation and the essentially state-linked concept of 'nationalism'. Most of them also agree with Frederik Barth's view (Barth 1989) that a group's boundaries' (who or what 'we' are not) determine its nature rather than its pre-existent ethnic or cultural content and that these boundaries are historically impermanent and open to change.

None of this means that nation-states, or the movements aspiring to this status, do not make use of sentiments derived from primordial structures of social life, such as kinship or the distinction between ingroups and outgroups, or from supposed memories of a real or imagined past. The more modern nationalism is, the more essential it is to demonstrate its eternity or at least its ancient roots. No historian denies this. Hence the importance of 'proto-nationalism' and acceptable 'invented traditions' as assets that modern national states can mobilise to create popular loyalty and patriotism, though the USA and Australia prove that a proto-national past is not indispensable. Indeed, there are cases where discontinuity is an essential element in defining national origins – the Swiss myth of foundation and liberation being a notable early example (Marchal and Mattioli 1992: 17–18; Zimmer 2003: ch. 1).

In the paper prior to this conference[1] Professor Grosby argues that social group identity is primary, deriving from 'modes of attachment constitutive of lines of descent, both familial and territorial', which have only to be prolonged, as it were, to constitute modern nations. He seems to me to underestimate three aspects of our problem: history, the state and the problem of scale as well as (in common with all previous students of nationalism, including the present discussant) that of gender.

Let me take the last two aspects first. His view that the various 'patterns of human conduct . . . are found commingling in varying degrees in all periods of time' is either trivial or, if it assumes that the mixture is unaffected by historical development, it is wrong, particularly so in the era of accelerating fundamental transformations since 1750 and especially since 1950. Religion may be a permanent feature of the human landscape, but it is absurd to deny the unprecedented secularisation of the eighteenth to twentieth centuries, not least (as Zionism demonstrates) in Jewish public life. To this extent what Grosby calls 'disjunctive periodisations' are essential for any study of 'nations', all the more so since he (rightly) notes the 'intimate relation between the formation and continued existence of a nation and the consolidation of the political power and sovereignty of a state' (Grosby 2005: 72). Indeed, I have argued that 'the most decisive criterion of protonationalism [was] the consciousness of belonging or having belonged to a lasting political entity' (Hobsbawm 1991: 73–76). Only political rule from above and a suitable supra-local religion could create a common consciousness of belonging together for the inhabitants of large territories, as later only public educational systems, could ensure their mass identification with the proposition state = nation.

However, nothing has been subject to more profound historical transformations than 'the institutions of political rule, especially in the past half-millennium, e.g. the change from the Old Regime in France which envision[ed] its sovereignty in terms of its jurisdiction over subjects not over a delimited territory' (Sahlins 1989: 6).[2] A clear distinction between the various eras of the state and popular politics is all the more crucial, since so much of the presumed traditions and symbols surviving from the 'nation's' alleged antiquity come, not from a supposed 'popular memory', but are the product, generally of rulers and ideologists, at specific historical moments. They are innovations, even when they 'indicate the hold of the primordial on the human imagination' (Grosby 2005: 72).

In short, the problem is not 'how to account for . . . civilisational ubiquity and historical persistence' (ibid.: 59) but for the different ways in which the ubiquitous and perennial actually expresses itself over time, especially given the speed with which most profound cultural changes have actually taken place in the past half-century. To put it brutally, what needs explaining is not why different ethnic communities have functionally co-existed throughout history amid friction and occasional massacre, but why the systematic elimination of peoples from a territory by 'ethnic cleansing' or 'genocide' only became a general characteristic of large zones of the globe in the twentieth century.

III

Primordialism is dangerous for both historians and sociologists. It confuses socio-cultural analysis by failing to distinguish between the essentially state-aspiring nineteenth- to twentieth-century 'nation' from ensembles of communities politically dispersed by their structure, such as the ancient Hellenes, the Kurds, Pathans, the Atlas Berbers, the Balkan highland communities and other clan societies, which, though distributed over what may be a large geographical zone, possess(ed) something like a common consciousness of being part of a wider 'people' recognisably distinct from other 'peoples', but were often acephalic and segmentary societies specifically opposed to any wider lay territorial power, native or foreign. It confuses socio-political analysis by failing to distinguish, as the nineteenth-century politicians did so clearly, notably in the Habsburg empire, between achieved national reality (with or without a recognised group history) and indeterminate national potential (e.g. between Czechs and Ruthenes (see Magocsí 1992)).

Primordialism risks unduly extending historically limited propositions like 'most human beings revere their own language' (Grosby 1995: 148) or 'heterogeneity is one of the essential characteristics which distinguish an empire from a national state' (ibid.: 145). The Ottoman system of rule via *millets* was 'relatively irrational' (ibid.: 146) only by post-1789 criteria of statehood. Even national states are familiar with special treatment for sub-territories (as in Britain) or indirect government by the central power through intermediate levels of rule and autonomous corporations (as in pre-partition Poland (Mączak 1997: 79–90)). State homogeneity by a single written language was only relevant to minorities before mass literacy, homogeneity of the spoken language was impracticable. For that matter, precise linear frontiers of an ideally coherent and continuous state territory are (as the North American use of the word 'frontier' still testifies) historically novel.

This brings me to the problem of scale. This is particularly relevant to the question of territory, central to Grosby's argument, because operational communities with a consciousness of common descent, possible territorial attachment,[3] and popular traditions and memories are almost invariably sub-national by any of the criteria in the literature. It is wrong to confuse the arbitrary and shifting political boundaries of the modern territorial state with the boundaries so essential to the daily reproduction of ancient settled agrarian societies, and therefore necessarily more precise long before state frontiers. It is illegitimate to see 'the attachments to that homeland or motherland or fatherland known as patriotism' (Grosby 2005) as a sort of prolongation of the emotional attachment to land, kin, local cult and locally rooted memories at the local level. Even when such attachments have become embedded in the loyalty to a state, as in nineteenth-century Serbia, the difference from modern patriotisms is striking.[4]

Small groups with potentially intercommunicating membership find it easier to develop collective consciousness than do vast masses. Italy, which existed for the educated from Dante's day, did not become a reality for most Italians until well into the twentieth century. Conversely, in human relations as in numbers, there is a threshold of everyday experience beyond which the collectivity cannot be actually envisaged by most people, but only in the form of recognition symbols (e.g. flags, anthems, images), or a process of shrinkage that substitutes persons, singular or plural (e.g. football teams), for the abstractions of 'people' or 'country'. Here the language of kinship and community is necessarily metaphorical. The relation between the members of a rule-defined descent group such as the traditional Balkan kindred (see Kaser 2002) is entirely different from that between the inhabitants of a supposedly ethnic nation-state, whose effective links cannot be with real ancestors or kin, i.e. not in time but in social space: laterally with other inhabitants or more usually upward with group-inclusive institutions such as state or religion. Beyond a certain threshold all communities are 'imagined communities', and changing communities. In addition, apart from the historic state that defines the extension the 'nation' to which they are deemed to belong, the heritage from a past they claim to have in common is also likely to be an ex-post facto construction, however much historical continuity research can establish.

In short, interesting as the study of the primordial characteristics of human societies is, it is not a useful guide to the phenomenon of nations and nationalism in the contemporary era.

Notes

1 *The Primordial, Kinship and Nationality*. This is quoted from the print-out copy submitted to the conference, but (Crosby 2005) refers to Chapter 5 of this book.
2 See also Guenée (1986) and Nordman (1986).
3 In lands of colonisation and thinly populated regions of shifting agriculture and livestock raising, as in many parts of Eastern Europe and the Middle East, the roots between territory and emotional attachment in such communities may be slow to develop. See Adanir 1989.
4 For the relation between a Serb peasant, the king and other Serbs outside his region in the period 1914 to 1941, see Popovic 1989. I am indebted to Professor Dejan Dimitrievitch for drawing my attention to this illuminating first-person novel.

References

Adanir, F. (1989) 'Tradition and rural change in Southeastern Europe during Ottoman rule', in D. Chirot (ed.) *The Origins of Backwardness in Eastern Europe: Economics and Politics from the Middle Ages until the Early Twentieth Century*, Berkeley: University of California Press, pp. 131–176.

Avanza, M. (2003) 'Une histoire pour la Padanie: La Ligue du Nord et l'usage politique du passé', *Annales, Histoire, Sciences Sociales* 58(1), pp. 85–108.

Barth, F. (ed.) (1989) *Ethnic Groups and Boundaries*, London: Allen & Unwin.

Grosby, S. (1995) 'Territoriality: the transcendental, primordial feature of modern societies', *Nations and Nationalism* 1(2), pp. 143–162.

Guenée, B. (1986) 'Des limites féodales aux frontiers politiques', in P. Nora (ed.) *Les lieux de memoire II La Nation*, Paris: Gallimard, pp. 11–63.

Guiomar, J. (1986) 'Le Tableau de la géographie de la France de Vidal de la Blache', in P. Nora (ed.) *Les lieux de memoir II La nation*, Paris: Gallimard, p. 569.

Hobsbawm, E.J. (1991) *Nations and Nationalism since 1780*, Cambridge: Cambridge University Press.

Kaser, K. (2002) 'Historisch-anthropologische Fragestellungen', *Historicum*, 76(3), pp. 28–29.

Mączak, A. (1997) 'Broken salad bowl or nations – professions in early modern Poland', in M. Řezník and I. Slezáková (eds) *Nations – Identities Historical Consciousness: Volume dedicated to Prof. Miroslav Hroc*, Prague: Charles University, Faculty of Philosophy.

Magocsí, P.R. (1992) 'The birth of a new nation, or the return of an old problem? The Rusyns of East-Central Europe', *Canadian Slavonic Papers*, 24(3), pp. 199–223.

Marchal, G.P. and Mattioli, A. (eds) (1992) *Erfundene Schweiz: Konstruktionen nationaler Identität*, Zürich: Chronos Verlag.

Nordman, D. (1986) 'Des limites d'État auf frontiers nationales', in P. Nora (ed.) *Les lieux de memoire II La Nation*, Paris: Gallimard, pp. 11–63.

Popovic, D. (1989) *Le Livre de Milutin*, Paris: Stock.

Sahlins, P. (1989) *Boundaries: The Making of France and Spain in the Pyrenees*, Berkeley: University of California Press.

Zimmer, O. (2003) *A Contested Nation: History, Memory and Nationalism in Switzerland 1761–1891*, Cambridge: Cambridge University Press.

Question and answer II

Question 1

Do you accept that ethnic groups existed before 1780 and if so does this not place some sort of limit on the possible transformation of human social relations?

Eric Hobsbawn

The question is about the origin of nations, I don't believe in looking for a single date from when we can start talking about modern nations and nationalism. It seems to me ridiculous not to think of, shall we say, the England of the Shakespearean historical dramas as having the qualities of what we would today regard as a nation. However, I think there is a major difference between what we might call the original French Revolutionary concept of the nation which is: one state or one territory and everybody living in it belongs to that nation, and the opposite, the Mazzinian which sees the nation as a pre-existing body of people with common characteristics – typically ethnic and linguistic – each of which should form a state and only one state. The world should be divided into states, each of which represents one such nation. I believe the original sense is the one which makes more sense; the other one has turned out to be the most disastrous innovation in the twentieth century and remains so in the twenty-first century.

Steven Grosby

The formulation of this question put to Professor Hobsbawm contains implicitly its own answer that has merit; but it is a complicated matter. Much has been written about the 'invention of tradition', 'imagined communities' and 'construction of identities'. All of these fashionable phrases attempt rightly to capture the recognition that humanity creates its own forms of association, and that these forms vary across time and civilisation. This recognition rests on the solid anthropological foundation of the 'openness' of the human mind. This variability of social relations indicates, following Hume, that they are 'artificial' (or 'invented', 'constructed'). However, just because social relations are 'artificial' does not mean that they are necessarily 'arbitrary', suggesting the possibility of limits on the transformation of social relations. Humanity has always displayed a tendency to divisiveness, expressed perennially in distinctive groups of kinship of varying kinds constituted around beliefs in a common ancestry. It is this tendency that Anthony D. Smith has drawn attention to in his use of 'ethnic' and '*ethnie*'. When the emphasis on the 'invention of tradition' or 'construction of identity' diverts our attention from pondering the significance of this perennial tendency, as often appears to be its intention, then it serves the nefarious end of trivialising the signi- ficance of nationality in human affairs. Yet humanity has also displayed other, universal tendencies, for example, science, monotheism, and, politically, empire. Herein exists the analytical problem. How to account for the heterogeneity of orientations that surely are not arbitrary, but none the less are not narrowly determined by our biological constitution?

Question 2

Historically academic debates have produced numerous classifications of nations: imagined and real, historic and unhistoric, revolutionary and non-revolutionary, nation-states and non-nation-states. Is this a way to downgrade some nations, to consider them as less valuable and of less existence?

Eric Hobsbawn

In the nineteenth century the Austrians produced the distinction between historic and unhistoric nations or, if you like, between nations and nationalities. Their empire contained ethnic groups which had to be recognised as being potential but not necessarily definite nations, but which had to be treated as collectives with rights (e.g. of language). The essence of Austrian thinking was that 'nationalities' could not be exclusively identified territorially, although to some extent they could. Now clearly the Slovenes were recognised as a nationality. The Slovenes, so far as I am aware, did not become a full nation and the idea of Slovene independ- ence as such did not arise until after 1945. What the relationship between Slovene nationality or the Slovene nation and the various states of which the Slovenes were part of historically is a difficult and complicated question. The fact is the idea of an independent Slovene nation-state is the product of our own time and the first such state appears in the 1990s. However, there are cases like the Ruthenes discussed by Professor Magocsí in Canada, that is to say groups which have some sort of ethnic or if you like, historic coherence or even vague forms of consciousness but which are not and were not actually ever likely to become nations although, potentially, they might have become so. The world is full of them. Whether they will is another matter. In fact, I believe they are only likely to ask to become so insofar as the states of which they have hitherto formed part disintegrate, which is of course happening today, but if they don't disintegrate, they are not likely to succeed. In the course of the twentieth century the Ruthenians belonged successively to Austria-Hungary, Czechoslovakia, Romania, the USSR and Ukraine, and for about three weeks part of them had a statelet in the

Carpathians. At one stage it looked as though they might conceivably regard themselves not as Ukrainians but as something else, perhaps as Ruthenians. But history has settled the problem in a different way and it is not very likely that they will get much further than they are at present unless Ukraine in turn disintegrates.

Steven Grosby

Our classifications are obviously abstractions that cannot do justice to the unavoidable fluidity of processes involved in the constitution of any nation. There is no such thing as a 'fully formed' or 'classic' nation. The ambiguities of the temporal element (where a past is brought into the present) and territory (where none the less local attachments persist) in the always developing and variegated collective self-consciousness of a nation makes this so. That is why I have sought a 'minimalist' definition of the nation as a 'territorial community of nativity'. Of course, much is implied in the terms 'territorial', 'community' and 'nativity'. In any event, a great deal has been written recently about the inadequacy of the classifications to which this question refers, such as the contrast between 'ethnic' and 'civic' nations. There certainly is a proclivity for historians, political scientists and sociologists to understand the nation from the limited perspective of modern egalitarianism. This proclivity should be rejected. 'Public cultures' certainly existed in antiquity, although often borne by religion. Some ancient cultures (for example, ancient Israel) displayed a remarkable degree of literacy. Finally, as Meinecke observed long ago, all nations, modern and ancient, indeed all social relations beyond friendship, have a structure of *pars pro toto*, for example, in medieval England, the king as responsible for peace and as final protector of the property of the individual. It is a mistake for Walker Connor to insist that a nation requires the modern conception of citizenship to exist; although clearly the diminution (but not elimination) of the distinction between the centre and periphery is characteristic of our times.

Question 3

Are the Jews a nation, were they a nation or can they be a nation?

Eric Hobsbawm

It doesn't matter what the argument is, whether the Jews are or were a nation; some people thought they were, some people thought they weren't. The fact is Israel as a national and territorial state is an absolute *novum* in history. It has absolutely nothing to do even with the few years in which there was a unified Kingdom of Israel in the days of whatever it is, David and Solomon. A secular Jewish territorial state was not even thought of before the end of the nineteenth century. Whether it is a good thing or a bad thing is a matter which we don't need to discuss, it is a novel thing. It has no precedent.

Finally the question about modern politics.

I think we must distinguish between the declining importance of the concept of the nation as a state-building organisation and the continuing importance of identity groups of which ethnic groups are a fairly obvious example. Identity groups continue to exist and flourish. Their significance may even increase, but in my view identity politics of which ethnic politics such as is found in countries, particularly multi-ethnic countries where politicians appeal to the ethnic, communal or tribal vote, are not the same and should not be confused with a discussion of nations and nationalism.

Steven Grosby

I have spent twenty years arguing that ancient Israel should be considered a nation. I certainly agree with Professor Hobsbawn that Israel today is a nation. I wish to answer the question 'Are the Jews a nation?' bliquely. One of the points of the six pages of comments with which I began this session was that the proper understanding of the nation must tolerate ambiguity. The processes that constitute the nation are processes of a developing self-consciousness that is always varied, flexible and ambiguous. It varies by class and status; it varies over time; it varies by region. Of course, scholars are obligated to develop categories. Anthony D. Smith has carried out this obligation very well. None the less, these categories have trouble capturing the ambiguities of the processes of this development. I have come to the conclusion that a proper understanding of nationality must, however difficult, entertain ambiguities. The Jews, as distinct from Israelis, are an ambiguous category. Well, there are many ambiguities. There is of course a very strong monotheistic element to the Prophets and the first eleven chapters of Genesis. This goes without saying. There is also, in my view, a very strong primordial component to Judaism formed by a putative ancestry, Abraham, Isaac and Jacob: the chosen people. So, there is an ambiguity here about how to understand the Jews. My friend Professor Eisenstadt characterises the Jews as a civilisation. Others refer to the Jews as a nation. Many simply describe the Jews as a religion. I like to circumvent the problem by pointing to the ambiguity. The important point is that ambiguity is the norm for all social relations. As I said earlier, social relations are not made out of stone; there is a subjective development involved. There is our minds; there is thus a cognitive element and an evaluative element. The development of self-consciousness is always flexible and contradictory. Sometimes it is even subject to dramatic innovation – what my respondent calls the invention of tradition. I agree that sometimes, or maybe often, this is the case. It could not be otherwise.

Ethno-symbolism

Introduction

Is it possible to offer a coherent summary of the main premises of ethno-symbolism without comparing them with the so-called modernist approaches? Reading texts written by either ethno-symbolist theoreticians or their critics one really doubts that possibility. A critique of the modernist approaches is usually the starting point of ethno-symbolists' explanations of their views.[1] At this point we will try to break with this tradition.

The main advocate of ethno-symbolism and, indeed, the author who is mainly responsible for its name and meaning – Anthony D. Smith – insists that ethno-symbolism should be seen as an approach, not a theory. If we put aside the 'modesty' explanation, we may assume that the father of ethno-symbolism either does not see it as an integrated hypothetico-deductive system or doubts its predictive possibilities. Whatever the case, the explanatory virtues of this approach are beyond any doubt.

What makes this approach to the study of nations and nationalism distinctive is its historical, cultural and sociological character, all at once. In most simplistic terms, the ethno-symbolic approach argues that nations have their origins in ethnic groups. Its main concern is the nature and characteristics of specific social groups and collectivities: how they are formed and transformed, and why they persist or cease to exist. Ethno-symbolists find the answers to these questions predominantly in the domain of culture and its interrelations with the structure of a society through agency in time. In this respect ethno-symbolists see ethnic groups and nations not as an epiphenomenon of social development but as a *sui generis* entity.

What is the nation?

In the ethno-symbolic view the nation is necessarily a *historical* social group. It is a community of 'history and destiny' (Smith 2001: 23). Hence, 'what nation is' is not only defined by its present form. This current form cannot be grasped without an exploration of what the nation has been and what it may be in the future. Ethno-symbolists maintain that whatever dramatic historical changes may have occurred at some point in history and consequently given birth to modern nations, these nations cannot be understood without an exploration of the forms from which they have emerged. Rather than being an unilinear evolutionist approach, ethno-symbolism bases its method of analysis on a conception that a social group, a community, is not determined but necessarily *conditioned* by its past. Hence they 'adopt a method of analysis that treats collective cultural identities over *la longue durée*, and seek to locate modern nations within a continuum of historical forms of cultural community' (ibid.). The nation is not invented.

For this reason a study of ethnicity, or *ethnie*, is the first step towards under-standing modern nations. In his early work Smith (1986: 32) defines *ethnies* as 'named human populations with shared ancestry myths, histories and cultures, having an association with a specific territory, and a sense of solidarity'. Such a community, through various social and historical processes, becomes a nation. Smith's earlier definition of the nation is one of the most quoted definitions.[2] However, in this volume Smith reformulates this definition and ultimately shifts the emphasis in relation to the nature of the nation – from a community that possesses certain characteristics to a community that undergoes several processes of acquiring these characteristics. Now, the nation is 'a named and self-defined community whose members cultivate common myths, memories, symbols and values, possess and disseminate a distinctive public culture, reside in and identify with an historic homeland, and create and disseminate common laws and shared customs' (see page 98). The new definition of the nation emphasises even more strongly historicity of the nation. The nation does not simply appear at some specific period in history – a social group *becomes* a nation.

This clearly defines nations as *cultural*, symbolic communities. Smith emphasises that 'it is the sense of cultural affinities, rather than physical kinship ties, embodied in a *myth* of descent, shared historical memories and ethnic symbolism, that defines the structure of ethnic communities; and the same is true for any nations created on the bases of cultural affinity' (1998: 192, emphasis in original). In this sentence Smith emphasises a one-way relation between culture and structure: it is the cultural domain that formats a new social structure – the nation. Culture for ethno-symbolists means not just symbols, traditions or rituals, but rather the meanings and orientations to collective action that these evoke (Hutchinson 2001: 76). Hence, a nation is not defined simply by possession of a set of cultural traits. It can only be defined within a sphere of socio-cultural interaction, where the members of the community acquire their specific identity. This national identity is then defined as 'the maintenance and continual reinterpretation of the pattern of values, symbols, memories, myths and traditions that form the distinctive heritage of the nation, and the identification of individuals with the heritage and its pattern' (Smith 2003: 24–25).

When is the nation?

The ethno-symbolic approach examines this question increasingly from a *socio-logical* perspective. Smith argues that the modern Western nation and nationalism are of course modern phenomena, but that there are 'ethnic roots' which 'deter-mine, to a considerable degree, the nature and limits of modern nationalisms and nations' (Smith 1986: 18). The ethnic community, characterised by its isolation, passivity and cultural accommodation, has been forced to change into a more activist, mobilised and politically more dynamic community – the nation. In his earlier work Smith argued that this process of transformation has occurred over time through triple revolutions: the division of labour, a revolution in the control of administration, and a revolution in cultural coordination (ibid.: 131). These three revolutions have developed social surroundings which prefer centralised and culturally homogenised states.

In this volume Smith goes a step forward in explaining the processes of so-called nation formation. While these above-mentioned triple revolutions have redefined the social structure of a community in a particular historical period we call modernity, ethnic communities have been undergoing a set of social processes that, through time, have changed the 'nature' of the group: its own structure, dominant culture and patterns of social interaction. Since Smith elaborates these processes in some detail in Chapter 5, we will mention them only briefly here. Processes that are necessary for the formation of the nation are self-definition, myth and memory-making, territorialisation, public culture and legal standardisation.

Defining the nation as a community that undergoes a set of social processes in time makes the task of pinpointing a historical period when the nation emerges a more difficult one. The new approach that Smith introduces in this volume rejects historical determinism of both primordialist and modernist approaches to the study of the nation. He opens a space for examining different stages of emergence of the nation throughout history and calls for social historical analyses of specific nations. Hence, he would argue, such analyses would reveal that certain social processes and characteristics of modern nations could be found in antiquity and in the Middle Ages among specific communities. With the emphasis on social processes, the ethno-symbolic approach undermines further the importance of modernity in the emergence of the nation and opens a broader space for seeing their development and formation in pre-modern times.

How do nations persist?

While the ethno-symbolic approach claims the central importance of ethnic communities in determining the 'nature' of the nation and the processes of 'nation-building', it holds that the answer to the question of the persistence of the nation should be sought elsewhere. In his recent book *Chosen Peoples* (2003), Smith tries to examine the 'strength and scope of national identities, and the passions they evoke' (ibid.: 3). He maintains that the reason for the persistence of the nation lies in its sacred character. 'The reasons for the durability and strength of national identities can only be understood by exploring collective beliefs and sentiments about the "sacred foundations" of the nation and by considering their relationship to the older beliefs, symbols and rituals of traditional religions' (ibid.: 4). At this point Smith builds upon Durkheim's notion of the role of religion in the creation and maintenance of solidarity among the members of a community. According to Smith, the 'pre-existing cultural resources' such as memories, myths, symbols, values and traditions of the community that have been regarded as sacred and in the domain of religion in pre-modern times are becoming 'nationalised'. The selection of a set of myths as national is not seen as a process of social engineering or, as some modernists would claim, a case of invention of the nation. While Smith would agree that nations are imagined, they are also 'perceived as "real" and "substantial", and often "enduring" communities by their members' (ibid.: 22). Nations, Smith claims, 'combine elements of faith and ethnic communities to produce a new synthesis, which draws much of its strength and inspiration, as well as many of its forms, from older religious beliefs, moral sentiments and sacred rites' (ibid.: 23). In this perspective, the religious character of nationalist belief systems explains the persistence of nations.

This brief summary falls short of describing the whole richness and thoroughness of the ethno-symbolic approach. However, it demonstrates that the process of nation formation may be described in terms of 'active dynamism, the transformative power, which is characteristic of what we call "nation-building"' (Smith 1999: 175). Dynamism in Smith's theory of nation formation is reflected in the interrelations between structure (the five processes of institutionalisation of national culture), culture (myth-symbol complex), and social interactions of the members of a community (as active proponents of the five processes). In addition, the ethno-symbolic approach emphasises the importance of the 'origins' of the nation that provides a picture of the structural and cultural conditioning associated with the emergence of the nation.

In the past this approach has been labelled as an evolutionist, culturally deterministic, historicist, idealistic approach. The new stage of development of the ethno-symbolic approach offered in this volume would surely force its critics to re-examine these labels.

Notes

1 See e.g. Smith (1998, 2002, 2003) and Hutchinson (1987, 1994, 2000).
2 Smith used to define nation as 'a named human population occupying an historic territory and sharing common myths and memories, a public culture, and common laws and customs for all members' (Smith 2003: 24).

References and further reading

On ethno-symbolist approaches to nations and nationalism

Armstrong, J. (1982) *Nations before Nationalism*, Chapel Hill: University of North Carolina Press.

Hutchinson, J. (1987) *The Dynamics of Cultural Nationalism*, London: Allen & Ulwin.

Hutchinson, J. (1994) *Modern Nationalism*, London: Fontana Press.

Hutchinson, J. (2000) Ethnicity and modern nations, *Ethnic and Racial Studies*, 23(4), pp. 651–669.

Hutchinson, J. (2001) Nations and culture, in M. Guibernau and J. Hutchinson (eds) *Understanding Nationalism*, Cambridge: Polity Press.

Smith, A.D. (1986) *Ethnic Origins of Nations*, Oxford: Blackwell.
Smith, A.D. (1991) *National Identity*, London: Penguin.
Smith, A.D. (1998) *Nationalism and Modernism*, London: Routledge.
Smith, A.D. (1999) *Myths and Memories of the Nation*, Oxford: Oxford University Press.
Smith, A.D. (2001) Nations and history, in M. Guibernau and J. Hutchinson (eds) *Understanding Nationalism*. Oxford: Polity Press.
Smith, A.D. (2002) When is the nation?, *Geopolitics*, 7(2), pp. 5–32.
Smith, A.D. (2003) *Chosen Peoples*, Oxford: Oxford University Press.

Critique of ethno-symbolism

Breuilly, J. Dating the nation: how old is an old nation?, in Chapter 1 of this book.
Gellner, E. (1996) 'Do nations have navels?', *Nations and Nationalism*, 2(3), pp. 366–370.
Özkirimli, U. (2000) *Theories of Nationalism: A Critical Introduction*, Basingstoke: Macmillan.

5 The genealogy of nations

An ethno-symbolic approach

Anthony D. Smith

'When is the nation'? The conventional answer to this question is one that may be characterised as 'modernist'. By modernism I refer to the view which holds that:

- nationalism is recent and novel;
- nations are recent and novel;
- both nations and nationalism are products of 'modernisation' and the conditions of modernity.

Although it had its forerunners, this was a perspective that became prevalent in the 1950s and 1960s with the works of Karl Deutsch, Elie Kedourie and Ernest Gellner. In their view, both the ideals of nationalism, the ideology and movement, and the form and content of the nation, as a type of community and culture, were historically and sociologically modern. That is, they were both recent and novel. They emerged in the wake of the French and American revolutions, and they embodied a new kind of society and political order.[1]

This perspective challenged the earlier conventional wisdom, which was that nations were perennial and immemorial, as was national sentiment, if not the ideology of nationalism. The earlier 'perennialist' approach, which saw nations in every continent and epoch, echoed the claims of the nationalists themselves from the late eighteenth to the mid-twentieth centuries. According to the modernists, this was nothing more than a case of 'retrospective nationalism', an anachronistic view that signally failed to make elementary distinctions between historical contexts. On the contrary, asserted the modernists, nations emerged in the wake of nationalism. Indeed, they were, for the most part, creations of nationalism. From the late eighteenth century onwards, first in Europe and North America and then elsewhere, we can chart the rise of nations in terms of the designs and activities of its self-styled nationalists, as they seek to imitate and adapt the models of neighbours and colonial powers. It is really only since that time that the modern territorial 'nation-state' has become the universally accepted norm of political organisation and government. Before the onset of modernity, we find clans, tribes, city-states, empires and religious civilisations, but never nations. After that watershed, nations become the primary political unit, and these pre-modern identities recede and lose their hold.[2]

Two ideal types of the nation

What, in the eyes of the modernists, is so singular and special about the nation that it has become the dominant political form across the globe? The answer lies in the peculiar features of the nation. For modernists, the nation is a form of human community possessed of the following characteristics:

- a well-defined territory, with a definite centre and clear and recognised borders;
- a legal-political community, with a unified legal system and institutions in a given territory;
- mass participation in social life and politics by all the members or 'citizens';
- a distinctive mass public culture disseminated through a system of standard-ised, mass public education;
- collective autonomy institutionalised in a sovereign state for a given nation;
- membership in an 'inter-national' system or community of nations;
- legitimation, if not creation, by and through the ideology of nationalism.

This undoubtedly provides a clear and coherent definition, but the combination of these features produces a pure or ideal type, not of the nation per se, but of a particular kind of nation, namely the *modern nation*. This is a particular variant of the general type of the nation, and it possesses its own peculiar features. These derive from the fact that it is a product of a particular milieu: that of eighteenth-century Western Europe and North America and of its rationalist, Enlightenment culture. This was the kind of nation imagined and created by a specific kind of nationalism, the civic-territorial kind, and, as Hans Kohn documented, it flourished in a particular part of the world, namely Western Europe and North America. It is not the kind of nation imagined, let alone created, in many other parts of the world, where different kinds of nationalism flourished, even though attempts to create the Western kind of nation were made in parts of sub-Saharan Africa, to whose very different conditions the civic-territorial concept had to be adapted (Kohn 1967 [1944]).[3]

Now, if the concept and features of the modern nation reflect those of eighteenth- and nineteenth-century Western Europe and America (that is, the period of the onset of modernity), then to assert that the nation must be modern on the basis of this particular ideal type amounts to a tautology. Moreover, it is one that rules out any different definition of the concept of the nation, outside of the West and outside modernity.

However, even more important, the modernist definition of the concept of the nation is a partial one: it covers only one kind of nation and only one type of nationalism. A particular version of a general concept is made to stand for the whole range covered by that concept, and it is a version that is the product of a particular time and place, of whose culture it bears the hallmarks.

There are several reasons for attempting to find a new definition and a broader, alternative ideal type of the nation. There is, first, an empirical problem, since one of the key features of the modernist definition is mass participation; that is, the involvement of its members in the social and political life of the nation. Walker Connor has explained this stipulation as requiring a majority of its members to be aware of belonging to the nation, which, in a democracy, would mean that they must participate in politics and therefore be able to vote. Thus no nation could be said to exist prior to the early twentieth century, since in the vast majority of cases women were not enfranchised until after the First World War. But such a radical modernism, besides forcing us to rewrite the very terms of European and American histories, conflates a sense of belonging with political participation and enfranchisement, and militates against Connor's other observation that the nation emerges in stages (even if we cannot so term it until there is mass political participation) (Connor 1990; cf. Smith 1998, ch.7).

The second reason stems from the ethnocentrism inherent in the modernist ideal type of the nation. As we saw, its peculiar features arose out of the time and place of its conception by a Western territorial-civic version of nationalism. It was for this reason that Hans Kohn found it necessary to complement it with another concept of the nation based on a very different version of nationalism. In Eastern Europe and Asia, he claimed, we find such a different concept because it arises from an 'ethnic' version of nationalism. In this ethnic variant, the nation is seen as being possessed of:

- genealogical ties, or rather presumed ties of ethnic descent traceable down the generations;
- vernacular culture, a culture that is not only public and distinctive, but indigenous in terms of native language, customs and arts;
- nativist history, a belief in the values of indigenous history and its peculiar interpretation of the world;
- popular mobilisation, a belief in the need to rouse 'the people' as the source of national values.[4]

Of course, the nation of the ethnic nationalists also shares some of the features of its territorial-civic counterpart, including collective attachments to a well defined territory (the ancestral homeland), the ideal of citizenship for all 'the people', the goal of autonomy, usually in a sovereign state, and legitimation of the – pre-existing – nation by (ethnic) nationalism. However, the main difference is that, for ethnic nationalists, the 'nation' is already present at the onset of modernity and nationalism in the form of pre-existing ethnic communities such as those of the Poles, the Serbs, the Arabs and the Persians. Thus, for example, the Arab nation, in this 'perennialist' view, is descended from the Arabic tribes of the Saudi peninsula, and has continued to exist throughout history, at least from the time of the Prophet, bound by genealogical ties, vernacular culture (notably Qu'ranic Arabic), a nativist version of history, and the ideal of 'the Arabs' of Islam as the repository of virtues, who only need to be mobilised to gain political autonomy. Of course, the modernist failure to include this kind of nationalism and its ethnic conception of the nation stems from its theoretical rejection of any necessary linkage between ethnicity and nationhood (Suleiman 2002).

Third, the modernist ideal type precludes any consideration of the question of 'pre-modern nations'. For modernists, there was neither room nor need for nations in pre-modern epochs, if only because, as Gellner argued, the culture of the tiny elites was entirely different from the many cultures of the vast mass of the population, the peasantry, and they had no incentive to spread their culture downwards. (The clergy did have such an incentive, but they generally lacked the resources to impose their culture on society.) Thus if we should chance on a pre-modern nation somewhere, it is purely fortuitous. Generally, the nation is a modern phenomenon, because it is the product of modernity and of the nationalism that modernity fosters (see Gellner 1983: ch. 2).

Modernism, then, gives us an ideal type of the nation that is both arbitrary and restrictive, ruling out, as it does, any conception of the nation that does not conform to the canonical modern Western nation. But must we accept this definitional fiat with all its attendant problems? Can we not frame a more generic definition and a broader, more inclusive ideal type, that will nevertheless distinguish the category of the 'nation' from other kinds of collective cultural identity?

I think we can do so, and thereby arrive at a more satisfactory ideal type, provided we recognise that its 'features' or elements are also social and cultural processes. It is the working out of these processes and their combination over time that can produce communities and collective identities which approximate to this broader pure or ideal type of the nation. Many of these processes are already familiar in the literature of ethnicity and nationalism, and some indeed are accepted by modernists. However, others are omitted or downplayed in their definitions, notably, of course, those that stem from a sense of ethnic community and collective cultural identity; and I shall be examining more closely the differences, as well as the relationship, between ethnic communities and nations later in this chapter.[5]

The main processes that, I would argue, are necessary for the formation of nations include:

- Self-definition: a growing sense of identity in a population, including naming by self and others, which encourages the differentiation of 'us' from 'them', and reveals to the members a progressive understanding of 'who they are'.
- Myth and memory-making: the creation and cultivation of distinctive myths, memories, values, traditions and symbols, which over time form the cultural heritage of the community and mark it out from those outside its boundaries.
- Territorialisation: the generation of collective attachments in a community to particular historic territories or ancestral homelands, within recognised borders, and residence in the homeland of a substantial part of the community.
- Public culture: the creation and dissemination of a distinctive public culture of shared traditions, values, symbols and knowledge to increasing numbers of the members of the community.
- Legal standardisation: the creation and dissemination of common laws and

shared customs, and their growing observance by increasing numbers of the members of the community.

Of course, in particular cases, other processes may be at work contributing to nation formation, but the above appear to be fundamental for creating communities that approximate to the broader ideal type of the nation that I think is most useful for the purpose of tracing the genealogy of nations. When we can show that a community exhibits a sufficient development of these processes, and that they combine and reinforce one another, then there is a prima facie case for designating it a 'nation'. This allows us to propose a definition of the nation as a named and self-defined community whose members cultivate common myths, memories, symbols and values, possess and disseminate a distinctive public culture, reside in and identify with a historic homeland, and create and disseminate common laws and shared customs.[6]

Ethno-symbolic premises

What are the main assumptions behind the selection of these particular processes and the ensuing ideal type of the nation? There are three assumptions that are crucial. The first is the centrality of symbolic elements – myths, memories, traditions, values, rituals and symbols – in the formation and persistence of nations. These constitute the basic elements for the analysis of the distinctive character of nations. A second assumption is that many of these elements derive from prior ethnic and ethno-religious symbols, myths, memories and traditions among the same or related populations. Together, these two assumptions address the question of the distinctive character of the nation, the question of 'Who is a nation?' The third assumption is that such ethno-symbolic elements, though subject to change, can resonate among populations for long periods of time, even before the age of modern nationa*lism.* This means that the analysis of the formation and persistence of nations requires an investigation of processes across different epochs of history over the long term (*la longue durée*).[7]

The phrase 'the same or related populations' needs some explanation. It refers to ethnocultural attributes; that is, attributes of groups regarded as (presumptively) ancestrally related. (We are dealing here with *myths* of descent, imputed rather than biological ancestry.) Such groups are bound by ties that are more or less pervasive, intense and complex. Of these, the simplest are ethnic categories whose members share some elements of common culture and perhaps a common terrain, but possess no collective proper name, no myth of descent and no shared memories or solidarity. These are generally fluid ethnic groups with an oral culture. More complex groupings may have a collective name, a myth of common ancestry and some measure of elite solidarity as a result of shared activities; these we may term ethnic networks or associations. Most developed of all are those groups whose members, in addition to possessing a myth of common descent and a developed sense of named identity, have shared memories and traditions, often textual, and a considerable measure of solidarity. These we may call ethnic communities or *ethnies* (to use the French term). Thus an *ethnie* may be defined as a named human population with myths of common ancestry, shared historical memories, common elements of culture and a measure of solidarity (Smith 1986: ch. 2; Eriksen 1993).

In light of this, we may elucidate the second assumption given above to mean that many of the symbolic elements of nations derive from the myths, traditions, memories, symbols and values of earlier ethnic categories, ethnic networks or *ethnies* that are *presumed* to be identical with or related to the members of the nation in question. The focus of an ethno-symbolic investigation of the formation and persistence of the nation, then, is the nature and variety of its symbolic elements (myths, memories, symbols and the like) and their linkages, social and institutional, with prior *ethnies*, ethnic categories or ethnic networks.

Let me try to spell this out a little more clearly. For ethno-symbolists, the relationship between ethnicity and nationhood is central. In this, they differ from both perennialists and modernists, for whom this relationship is irrelevant or quite secondary. (Thus the perennialists conflate *ethnies* and nations, while the modernists regard *ethnies* as secondary or irrelevant to a theory of nationalism.) Nations and *ethnies* for ethno-symbolists are both forms of cultural community, sharing a high degree of self-definition, and a fund of myths, memories and symbols. But nations differ from *ethnies* in terms of:

- the residence of many members of the community in a particular historic territory or homeland;
- the dissemination of a distinctive public culture to the members (as opposed to elements of common culture);
- the spread of standard laws and customs among the members.

This suggests that, at a general level, one may regard nationhood as a specialised development of ethnicity, although specific nations cannot always be traced back to one or more particular *ethnies*. What is required for a nation to emerge is the combination of the main processes enumerated above; and that means the development of the key elements of 'ethnicity' (self-definition, myths of ancestry, shared memories) as an intrinsic part of the processes of nation formation. However, equally important for the formation of nations are institutional processes: hence the central role accorded to the creation and spread of a distinctive public culture and to the dissemination of public laws and shared customs, and to the vehicles of transmission of law and culture.[8]

Finally, there is the ethno-symbolist insistence on analysis of cultural elements over *la longue durée*. Not only does this imply that nations must be analysed quite separately from the modern ideological movement of national*ism*; it opens the way to long-term analysis across different epochs. By bringing together the (ethnic) past or pasts and the present, ethno-symbolists encourage investigation of the different ways in which they can be linked and reinterpreted.

The most obvious form of linkage is that of *continuity* from the ancient or medieval epoch to the modern. Thus we may want to claim that particular nations can be traced back into the (early or late) medieval epoch or even to antiquity, as Adrian Hastings has argued in a number of cases in medieval Western Europe; or, what is more likely, that members of these often modern nations draw on the symbolic elements of earlier *ethnies* to which they claim kinship and an ancestral relationship, as later Tsarist Russia did with medieval Muscovy and Meiji Japan with the Japan of the Heian and Nara empires. Here our understanding of the ethnic past frames our conception of the present, as much as the latter highlights aspects of that past (Hastings 1997: chs.2–4).[9]

A second type of linkage is through the *recurrence* of ethnicity and nationhood, both among particular groups and at a general level. In this view, both *ethnies* and nations are recurrent phenomena, forms of social organisation and cultural community that may be found in every period and in every continent, that are constantly emerging, flourishing and being absorbed or submerged. This is the picture of ethnicity and nationhood to be found in John Armstrong's great cultural panorama of medieval civilisations in Christian Europe and the Islamic Middle East, with its insistence on the persistence, but also the changing nature, of ethnic and national identities (Armstrong 1982).

Finally, the connection of past and present may be made through the *discovery* and *appropriation* of ethnic history. Typically, a new national community and polity is elaborated by priests, scribes and intellectuals who select for this purpose symbolic elements from earlier 'related' ethnic or national cultures. In the modern epoch, authenticity becomes their guiding light, the need to discover and use all that is genuine and indigenous, to construct national communities that will be pure, original and unique. But, even in antiquity, we find movements and regimes that seek to create communities modelled on visions of earlier ethnic cultures and religious traditions – for example, in ancient neo-Sumerian Ur, in Assyria under Ashur-bani-pal, and Sasanid Persia under Chosroes I, not to mention later Republican Romans yearning for the certainties of an earlier age, or the later Judaic commonwealth harking back to the faith and simplicity of the Mosaic era (See Roux 1964: chs 10, 22; Frye 1966: ch. 6, esp. pp. 258–262).

Social and cultural sources of national identity

On the basis of these ethno-symbolic assumptions, we can consider the question of the origins and persistence of nations under two related headings. The first enquiry is sociological, and here we may ask: When is *a* nation? In other words, what, at a general level, makes or constitutes any nation? The second enquiry is historical, and here we have to address the question: When is *the* nation? That is to say, when in the historical record do we first encounter the category of nation and when does it become widespread? When do nations in general emerge, and when do they become the historical norm?

Let me start with the sociological enquiry. Here I am concerned with the symbolic elements of nationhood, and with the general processes of national formation – self-definition, myth and memory cultivation, territorialisation and so on. It is on and through these elements and processes that what we may term the 'cultural resources' of national identity are created and crystallised. Some of these cultural resources come to be treated as both 'sacred' and 'usable' resources; they are revered, canonical, set apart, but may also be used for political ends, as Tilak used the cult of the dread goddess Kali for patriotic purposes. This process of sanctification of symbolic elements derives from, and is often modelled on, the processes of sanctification in earlier religious traditions. In a nationalist epoch, its epitome is, once again, the cult of authenticity. In earlier epochs, ethnicity is rarely separated from religious tradition; and as a result the cultural resources which can be sanctified and used by pre-modern ethnic or national leaders and by modern nationalists come with a definite religious aura which imbues even secu-larising nationalisms with a 'sacred' quality, such as we witness in the *fêtes* of the French Revolution or the commemorative rituals of communist revolutions.[10]

Now, while all the general processes of nation formation listed above are rele-vant, it is these sacred sources of national identity that are of particular signifi-cance for the formation and persistence of nations. In certain of the myths, memories, symbols and traditions of national community, territory, history and destiny, we can discern the key elements which help to differentiate nations over many generations, and serve as 'sacred foundations' of the persistence of national identities. In general, we could say that the more of these sources, and the more intense and potent they are, the more likely are we to observe the formation and persistence of *a* given nation, and the stronger and more durable the members' sense of national identity. Conversely, the less of these 'foundations' and the more attenuated they are, the more fragile and less enduring the sense of national identity among a nation's members.

Myths of ethnic election

The first of these sacred sources is a specific type of collective myth: myths of ethnic election, the idea that a given people or community was 'chosen' by the deity for a special purpose. Such myths take two forms (though in practice they often overlap). In the first, there is an enduring collective belief in a covenant with God, by which He chooses and sets apart a people provided that its members fulfil certain moral and ritual obligations. Its prototypical expression may be found in the Pentateuch or *Torah* given to the children of Israel on Mount Sinai, but we can also discern elements of it in early medieval Monophysite Armenia and Ethiopia, and among the early modern Americans, the Afrikaners, Ulster-Scots and early Zionists, all of whom sought to cultivate holiness, moral virtue and spirituality in their own communities apart from the wider world.[11]

In the second type of election myth, the community is entrusted by the deity with a sacred task or mission. This can take several forms: defence of a sacred realm, conquest of barbarous tribes, conversion of the heathen and provision of an example – bringing 'a light to the Gentiles'. In earlier epochs, the king and his nobles assumed the burden of the mission, notably in *antemurale ethnies* and nations. This was particularly the case in the Judaeo-Christian tradition – in Poland, Hungary and Catalonia, in the 'shatter zone' between religious civilisations. But we also find it in more secure kingdoms such as those of England, Scotland, France and Muscovy-Russia, and in secular form, in their modern counterparts. Something of this sense of chosenness for a collective mission also emerged in cultural communities and states outside the Judaeo-Christian tradition – in Safavid Persia, modern Egypt and twentieth-century Japan.[12]

Territorialisation of memories

The second of these key sacred sources stems from collective attachments to historic lands deemed to be 'sacred'. In this special development of the 'territorial-isation of memories', given *ethnies* become bound up with particular landscapes in a two-way process: on the one hand, through the naturalisation of ethnic history, and on the other hand, by historicising nature and making it part of the develop-ment of the ethnic community. The result is the birth of an 'ethnoscape' in which certain ethnic communities appear to be 'rooted' in 'their' historic homelands; in Steven Grosby's words, 'a people has its land and a land has its people' (Grosby 1991: 240).

But the mutual possession of landscape and people is only the first step towards nationhood. The homeland requires not only 'history' but bounded space and specifically recognised borders. This is often achieved in and through warfare, but it can also be a reward of ethnic election and fulfilment – a 'promised land'. A further development sees the homeland as not only promised but blessed and sanctified. This can come about in a number of ways. Most obviously, the land on which the prophet or saint walked and preached becomes holy and set apart from everyday life. This reverence and separation may be extended to the exploits and example of heroes and geniuses, notably their tombs and memorials. One may go further, and derive the sanctity of the land from the holiness of the people, or at any rate, their aspirations to holiness. Above all, the idea of standing on 'holy ground' emerges in the context of reported miracles and especially of the final resting places of one's ancestors. Although most powerfully evocative in the graveyards of fallen patriots, these holy sites extend to temples, cities, battlefields, excavations and museums, where we are bidden to reflect on the sacred nature of 'our past' in 'our homeland'.[13]

Golden ages

The general process of the cultivation of myths, memories and traditions can result in the creation of an 'ethno-history' for the community. Instead of strands of myth, memory and so on, a single panorama of the ethnic past fills the collective horizon, albeit one that may change, even within a generation. (In fact, there is usually more than one such 'panorama', containing alternative tableaux, at any one moment in time.) This becomes a potent resource, because, unlike the kind of 'objective' causal historical enquiry fostered by professional historians, an ethno-history presents a developmental series of historical tableaux, which highlight in easily memorised terms the 'key events' and turning points of the ethnic past or pasts.[14]

Among the most memorable of these illuminated episodes are those periods of ethno-history that are felt to be great and glorious, the 'golden ages' of the nation. Here, the message of the nationalists draws from a particularly deep well: it is the community itself that was great and glorious, just as it will be once again, when it is restored to its historic status. Thus the later visions of an idealised ethnic past not only help to shape the popular understanding of that past, but also important aspects of the present – something that was evident, in the most vivid manner, among Hellenisers and Byzantinists in nineteenth-century Greece, or among Pharaonicists and Arab Islamists in early twentieth-century Egypt (see Campbell and Sherrard 1968: ch. 1; Gershoni and Jankowski 1987: chs 6–8).

However, even before the advent of nationalist ideologies, the quest for recovery of golden ages was plainly visible. We met it in ancient Sumer, Assyria and Persia, and to these we may add the striking example of medieval Ethiopia where the so-called 'Solomonic' dynasty from the fourteenth century ousted the previous Zagwe dynasty and set about remodelling the religious culture and society of Ethiopia in the light of the 'Semitic' Christian culture of the ancient kingdom of Axum a thousand years earlier. As with the more modern quests, the desire to rejuvenate the community by returning to the values of a golden age demonstrates the growing need for antiquity, continuity, authenticity, dignity and national destiny (see Levine 1974: ch. 7; Henze 2000: ch. 3).

Sacrifice and destiny

Finally, the need to achieve the true destiny of the nation is revealed in the more recent development of a cult of national struggle and sacrifice. There are intimations of such sacrifice in earlier epochs; one thinks of the ideal of fame and glory in ancient Greece and Rome, and of ideas of sacrifice in the Bible, not to mention the heroic deaths of warriors for the cause of a religious civilisation during the Crusades or the long struggle by and against the Ottoman *ghazis*. But such forerunners are only sometimes related to *ethnies* or nations. We had to wait until the advent of national*ism* for the ideal of national destiny through sacrifice to take hold and become an essential sacred foundation and cultural resource of national identity.

At first, this ideal centred on the noble sacrifice of great men and women of heroism and genius, commemorated in elegies of verse, paint and stone from the seventeenth to the nineteenth centuries. However, with the advent of democracy, this was soon supplemented and overtaken by the choreographed ceremonies of remembrance of mass sacrifice of the fallen soldier-patriots which became so potent and decisive an instrument in the preservation and renewal of nations. The culmination of this trend in the cult of 'The Glorious Dead' of the two World Wars highlighted the dissemination of a distinctive public culture of modern democratic mass nations, demonstrated in the 'civic religion' of the people with its mass liturgies and solemn rituals.[15]

While there may be other sacred sources of national identity, as well as conducive external (geopolitical, social and cultural) conditions, the above seem to be the most significant and potent, and the stronger and deeper they run in the received traditions of a community, the more likely are we to witness the presence and persistence of a nation.

The genealogy of national identity

If beliefs in ethnic election, attachments to sacred homelands, memories of golden ages and the cult of destiny through sacrifice constitute some of the main social, cultural and religious sources of the sociological community of the nation, how are we to locate these sources and the more general, underlying processes of which they are specialised developments, in the sequence of historical epochs? In which periods, and under which historical conditions, do we find nations emerging?

Nations in the ancient world

Contrary to the modernist doctrine, we can already find evidence of the general processes of nation formation, and some of the cultural resources and sacred foundations of nationhood, in pre-modern epochs, starting with the ancient world. Several of these resources may already be discerned, for example, in ancient Egypt, in Second Temple Judaea and in early Christian Armenia, as Steven Grosby has demonstrated. Thus the peculiar geopolitical circumstances of ancient Egypt, for example, encouraged the rise of a fairly compact society from the early Dynastic period onwards. During the Old, Middle and New Kingdoms, we witness a well-developed self-definition of Egyptians in relation to neighbouring peoples, a rich corpus of myths, symbols, memories and traditions, clear attachments to the fertile land of the Nile valley, and by the time of the New Kingdom a distinctive public religious culture. Law and custom were also fairly uniform and standard-ised among the populations along the Nile valley, whose labour and production were controlled and regulated by a powerful centralised bureaucracy headed by the Pharaoh. Of course, there were important countervailing tendencies: the division between Upper Egypt and the Delta; the centrifugal pressures of the nomarchs and the regions they controlled, especially during intermediate periods of weak dynasties; the division between nobles, priests and scribes, on the one hand, and the mass of the working population, on the other; and the competition of rival priestly centres and cults, and their cosmogonies. Besides, there is little evidence of beliefs in collective ethnic chosenness or in a national destiny achieved through struggle and sacrifice. On balance, then, ancient Egypt may be described as only partly approximating to the ideal type of nationhood at particular moments in her long dynastic history.[16]

In early Christian Armenia and Second Temple Judaea, on the other hand, there is a closer fit with the ideal type of the nation that I outlined earlier. In both cases we find a strong and potent belief in divine election: in the Judaean case this belief privileged the community as a whole, in accordance with the Mosaic ideal of all Israel as a 'kingdom of priests' set apart for divine service, in Christian

Armenia, the object of election was the Gregorian Apostolic Church and by extension all its adherents, who in practice over time were confined to Armenians. In both cases, the myth of election was covenantal: God has made a covenant with a people or a church that, as a result, was sanctified and separated from all others, even when it sought to make converts further afield (see Novak 1995: ch. 4; Garsoian 1999: ch. 12).

In both cases, too, we find an ethnoscape with vivid territorial attachments, together with a recognition of a bounded ancestral homeland and of mutual belonging of land and people. History, that is to say ethno-history, was cultivated among both peoples from an early period, but it was an ethno-theological history that justified the ways of God to the children of Israel and to the Armenians, and explained the glory and the vicissitudes of these chosen peoples. Later Armenians in the period of the Bagratids in the eighth and ninth centuries looked back to a golden age of the early bishops, missionaries and martyrs from Gregory to Nerses, recorded in the early providential histories of Agat'angelos, Paustos Buzand, Elishe and Lazar P'arcepi. In the Armenian case, too, we find a well-developed ideal of collective martyrdom for faith and people, developed in the interminable wars with Zoroastrian Sasanid Iran and modelled on the example of courage and self-sacrifice of Jewish heroes from Joshua to the Maccabees. At the same time, the sharp class divisions between the Armenian landed nobles (or *naxharars*), the lesser nobles and the common people militated against the dissemination of common laws and customs and the development of a uniform public culture, despite the efforts of ecclesiastical leaders such as Mesrop Mashtots who invented a new script for the Armenian language (Redgate 2000: ch. 7; Nersessian 2001: chs 1–2).

Such divisions could also be found in Judaea, but the increasing prominence of the Pharisees resulted, especially after the destruction of the Temple and its Sadducean hierarchy, in a more egalitarian society based on the local synagogue. In the Mishnaic period, a wider observance of common laws and customs attuned to the common people, together with the dissemination of a single public religious culture, was initiated by the rabbis of Yavneh and later of Galilee. Thus, despite the loss of political independence, the Jews of Palestine achieved a relatively high degree of cohesion and autonomy under the Byzantine emperors, and preserved a more spiritual but none the less vivid image of the Holy Land (Neusner 1981; Davies 1982).

Despite these signal partial exceptions, ethno-symbolists, in contrast to perennialists, speak of ethnicity rather than nationhood as the hallmark of collective cultural identity in the ancient world. What we encounter among Sumerians and Babylonians, Arameans and Philistines, Phoenicians and pre-Islamic Arabs are examples of (one or more) *ethnies* with a degree of self-definition, myths of common ancestry, some shared memories and elements of common culture, usually a language and a cult, perhaps associated with particular terrains. But these communities were frequently subdivided into political units, such as city-states or tribes, and often lacked overarching laws and customs, or a public culture that embraced the whole population. Generally speaking, too, they had little sense of communal chosenness or ideals of destiny through mass sacrifice, and their memories of golden ages were muted and imitative, rather than energising.[17]

Nations in the Middle Ages

This same sense of common ethnicity seems also to have been more widespread among the various barbarian 'peoples' of early modern Europe from the later Roman empire to the empire of Charlemagne than authors like Patrick Geary allow. Certainly by the end of this period, we witness the rise of what Susan Reynolds terms barbarian *regna*, communities of law, language and common descent attached to a royal house, such as the Franks, Saxons, Lombards and Visigoths. Although some of these communities may have been precursors of later nations, it is straining our often scanty evidence to see in these ethnic kingdoms 'nations' at this early date, as the late Adrian Hastings claimed for late Anglo-Saxon England and its neighbours, and as some medievalist historians contend for the emergence of a French and a German nation in the tenth or eleventh centuries. This seems to me to confuse ethnicity with nationhood. Although we find in these cases a profusion of myths of descent, as well as symbols, memories and traditions of self- and other-defined communities, it is difficult to discern in these communities the spread of a distinctive public culture and a common legal system to the majority of their members, except among a small literate elite which had imbibed biblical models and saw their kingdoms as true successors of the ancient Jewish prototype.[18]

Only in the later medieval era is there growing evidence of nation formation in Western and Northern Europe. In England, Scotland, Wales and Ireland, France and Spain, Denmark and Sweden, as far back as the thirteenth and fourteenth centuries, several of the key processes may be discerned: clear-cut self-definition, cultivation of common myths, symbols, traditions and memories, especially myths of dynastic but also ethnic election, growing attachments to bounded homelands, the spread of a distinctive public culture and language among the elites, and a growing observance of common laws and customs. Of course, such observance of standardised cultures and laws was often patchy and intermittent, as was any sense of golden ages, let alone destiny through sacrifice, even within the elites; and the classic divide in agrarian societies between small, largely urban, elites and the mass of the peasant population to which Gellner attached such importance undoubtedly hindered the dissemination of a wider sense of common nationhood. But, then, there was, and there is, nothing inexorable about nation formation; nothing like a general or a specific evolution of nations, not even, as we have seen, a single social model of the ideal type of the 'nation-in-general' (see Gellner 1983: ch. 2).[19]

By the fifteenth and sixteenth centuries, on the other hand, the development and combination of these processes had, in some cases, reached the point where we can clearly discern an approximation to the ideal type of the nation. Not only can we chart the general processes of nation formation – marked self-definition, the cultivation of ethnic myths, symbols and memories, the growth of a single public culture, the occupation by a dominant *ethnie* of a bounded homeland, and the dissemination of distinctive but standard laws and customs. We also find some evidence of the specific cultural resources of national identity: a renewed conviction of ethnic chosenness, particularly after the return to the Old Testament encouraged by the Reformation, stronger attachments to homelands and a deeper territorialisation of memories, and a return to an ideal past and a yearning for lost golden ages – witness, for example, the rival Arthurian and Anglo-Saxon myth-memories in late medieval England, the alternative Trojan, Frankish and Gallic myths of origins in medieval France, the elevation of Arminius and the virile ancient Germanic tribes by German humanists, and the chronicling of resistance by the forest cantons of inner Switzerland and the legend of William Tell in the White Book of Sarnen and in Aegidius Tschudi's work (Poliakov 1974; MacDougall 1982; Beaune 1985; Im Hof 1991).

In Holland and England, in addition to these sacred cultural resources, a new note of commemoration of patriotic resistance and sacrifice in the face of enemy 'tyrants' like Catholic Spain is heard, again on the model of ancient Jewish proto-types such as Moses, Hezekiah, Josiah and the Maccabees, even if it has not yet been worked up into a mass cult. Sixteenth-century England, France, Spain, the Netherlands, Switzerland, Sweden and Russia may not be nations according to the modernist canon – the masses were excluded from politics and there was as yet no legitimating ideology of national*ism*. Yet, in many respects, these cultural and political communities conform closely to the generic ideal type of the nation; and certainly by the seventeenth century, a sense of nationhood and a belief in 'national character' were widely accepted among elites in much of Europe (Schama 1987: ch. 1; Greenfeld 1992: ch. 1).[20]

Modern nationalist nations

The rise of nationalism in the eighteenth century marks a watershed. Henceforth, as Charles Tilly points out, it became possible to create nations 'by design', according to the canons of cultural diversity and authenticity, simply by moulding populations into the format required by the ideologies of nationalism. This meant endowing them with a distinctive public culture, a glorious past and an equally splendid destiny. In the Western context, under the dominance of the Anglo-French model, it also meant giving the new nationalist nation 'natural' frontiers, uniform laws, citizenship, popular sovereignty and independent statehood – in effect, all the attributes of the specific civic-territorial nationalist conception of the nation, as it had been developed in Western Europe. Given the new role and growing political importance of intellectuals and professionals, and the influence of the national state model pioneered by some pre-modern European nations and codified in treaties between the European powers, it is hardly surprising that most present-day nations were created after the rise of national*ism*, the ideology and movement, if not necessarily wholly through its operation (Tilly 1975: Conclusion).

Undoubtedly, the French Revolution marked the 'breakthrough' to the dissemination of this new civic-territorial model of nationhood and its ideals of uniform public culture, citizenship and popular sovereignty. Important as the philosophical concepts and ideals of the German Romantics and their successors were, it was in and through the Revolution that the possibility of a territorially unified, autonomous and authentic nation of citizens fusing ethnocultural community with popular sovereignty was first fully realised, only to be carried across Europe by the armies of the Revolution and Napoleon. Doubtless, too, the causal chain postulated by the modernists, which sees nations as the creations of a nationalism which is itself in turn the product of modern conditions, was supported by the French and English examples, the French Revolution, in particular, being provoked by the fiscal and military crises of capitalist modernity, the revolt of the middle classes and the long wars with England, and in turn embodying a strong civic-nationalist impulse (See O'Brien 1988; Mann 1993: ch. 7).

But, even here, we need to exercise caution. Modernisation may have acted as a solvent of the *ancien régime* and a catalyst of the new national order, transferring sovereignty from unelected monarchs to the nation and its citizens, but it cannot explain the incidence and the shape of nations, their 'what' and 'where'. Here we need a different kind of approach, one that gives greater weight to the elements of continuity with older ethnocultural communities and earlier sacred traditions. Only an ethno-symbolic account that is prepared to see nations prior to both nationalism *and* modernity, exactly because it can trace the relationship of nations to *ethnies* and religious traditions in terms of the cultural and subjective components of society that both perennialists and modernists tend to omit, can do justice to the complex historical realities. Moreover, the likelihood that some nations antedated both nationalism and modernity tends to undermine the significance of modernity as a key epoch and as an explanatory model (see Hastings 1997: ch. 1).

Conclusion

It is clear from this brief survey that historical ethno-symbolism rejects the sweeping claims of perennialists and modernists alike, as well as the organic naturalism and the cultural or biological determinism of the primordialists. It finds in all three paradigms a lack of historical depth and sophistication in their treatment of the problems of dating and explaining nations. For primordialists history is largely decorative, a refinement on underlying biological drives or cultural givens. Perennialists, too, insofar as they regard nations and nationhood as ubiquitous, recurrent and immemorial, are unable to tell us anything about their historical development and periodisation. For modernists, on the other hand, history only begins in the eighteenth century, with modernisation and the rise of nationalism. Everything before that, Ernest Gellner tells us, is irrelevant to the task of explaining why nations and nationalism emerged. Nations do not need navels (Gellner 1996).

Ethno-symbolists, per contra, contend that in fact they do need navels, and that modernists here are confusing 'state' with 'nation'. States may not need navels, but nations as culturally unique and historically distinctive communities do. They need antecedent cultural resources and sacred foundations if they are to resonate among and mobilise the populations that recognise themselves (and/or are designated by one or other elite) as nationals. Here, then, we find an ethnosymbolist answer to both of our questions: the sociological enquiry into when is *a* nation, and the historical investigation of when is *the* nation. Nations need and draw on these cultural resources from antecedent ethnic symbols, memories, myths and values, and from the sacred traditions which they have inherited from earlier ages and peoples, and which they, like preceding generations, sift and reinterpret anew. This implies that the category of the nation emerged in stages over *la longue durée*, becoming visible in the historical record in parts of the ancient world and reappearing in the later Middle Ages and especially after the Reformation – with each stage contributing something to the next in terms of the selection and reinterpretation of ethnic myths, memories, traditions and symbols.

In this sense we may liken the nation to a kind of palimpsest, on whose parchment many different texts and messages from various epochs have been collated and written down, and which go on being written down to our own day and into the foreseeable future. The difference here is that older layers of writing are not wholly erased, and so it becomes our task to unravel and provide a nuanced understanding of its many symbols, texts and messages.

Notes

1 For a critical survey of modernist theories of nationalism, see Smith (1998: Part I).
2 Here I paraphrase the argument of such leading exponents of modernism as Elie Kedourie (1960), Ernest Gellner (1983), Eric Hobsbawm (1990) and John Breuilly (1993).
3 On the derivation of Western territorial nationalism in sub-Saharan Africa, see Hodgkin (1964). On the normative claims of civic-territorial nationalism, see Miller (1995).
4 These are not the features singled out by Hans Kohn (1967 [1944]), for whom 'Eastern' nationalisms are organic, authoritarian and often mystical, because they lacked a strong bourgeoisie to lead the movement and had to rely on small coteries of anxious and insecure intellectuals (cf. Kedourie 1960).
5 Modernists are happy with the emphasis on standardised law and public culture, but rather less so with attachments to the homeland and the cultivation of ethnic myths and memories.
6 This definition differs to some extent from my earlier attempts in, for example, Smith (1991: ch. 1), in emphasising self-definition *vis-à-vis* external others, and in dropping the insistence on a common division of labour throughout the territory, the latter being clearly a modern development (hence prejudging the issue of 'when is the nation') and a causal factor more than an element of the ideal type.
7 For a critique of the concept of popular resonance, and of ethno-symbolism in general, see Özkirimli (2003).
8 I have summarised the differences and similarities between *ethnies* and nations in Smith (2001: 13).
9 On the Slavophile understanding of 'Old Russia' and Muscovy, see Thaden (1964). On the return to the ancient chronicles of the Heian empire after 1900, see Oguma (2002).
10 For the *fêtes* of the French Revolution, see Herbert (1972); on Tilak's use of the cult of Kali, see Kedourie (1971: Introduction).
11 The literature on myths of ethnic election and covenantal ideals includes Nicholson (1988) and Novak (1995) on the ancient Israelite covenant, as well as Walzer (1985);

and, for comparative studies, Akenson (1992), Hutchinson and Lehmann (1994), and Smith (2003: chs 3–5).

12 On these *antemurale* ethnic kingdoms and their sense of mission, see Armstrong (1982, chs 2–3). On the development of a sense of ethnic, and imperial, mission in pre-Petrine Russia, see Milner-Gulland (1999: ch. 3).

13 For this sanctification of territory, see Smith (1999). For modern national shrines, see Mosse (1990).

14 For fuller discussions of ethno-history and 'golden ages', see the essays in Hosking and Schopflin (1997); and Smith (2003: chs 7–8).

15 The pioneering research into this cult was carried out by the late George Mosse (1975, 1990).

16 Grosby's seminal essays are collected in Grosby (2002); cf. Routledge (2003). On ancient Egypt, see David (1982).

17 On the energising role of such myths and memories, see Walzer (1985). Other examples of nation-forming processes in the ancient world could be cited. For example, in Assyria, we find processes of self-definition, myths, symbols and memories, and elements of a public culture, but Assyrian policies of deportation and mingling of peoples, their dependence on Babyloniam cultural models and their adoption of Aramaic as the lingua franca of their empire militated against their further develop-ment, and contributed to the rapid absorption of the Assyrian people after the swift demise of their empire in 612 BC. In Persia, an indigenous language, culture and (Mazdaic) religion had more staying power after the downfall of the Achaemenids, and experienced a conscious revival under the Sasanian monarchs. On the other hand, the number of different ethnic groups in Iran, the social and religious upheavals, and the later Arab Islamic conquest impeded the development of a Persian nation. See Liverani (1979) on Assyria, and Frye (1966, 1975) on Persia.

18 See Hastings (1997: ch. 2). For the barbarian *regna*, see Reynolds (1984: ch. 8). Geary's (2002) constructivist critique traces the 'toxic wasteland' of nineteenth-century nation-alism back to the influence of ancient authors like Pliny who failed to follow Herodotus' understanding of the fluidity of ethnicity and his refusal to objectify and rank ethnic communities. On some debates on national origins among medievalist historians, see Scales (2000).

19 Good examples of the development of nation-forming processes and the partial forma-tion of nations may be found in medieval France and England, on which see Beaune (1985) and Hastings (1997).

20 How far collective sentiments in France before the late seventeenth century were *national* is unclear, since the expression of the nation was tied to the dynasty and ruler, as in Russia. On the French myth of ethnic election, see the sources cited in Beaune (1985: 293–295); but cf. Bell (2001: ch. 1). On Russia, see Cherniavsky (1961).

References

Akenson, D. (1992) *God's Peoples: Covenant and Land in South Africa, Israel and Ulster*, Ithaca, NY: Cornell University Press.

Armstrong, J. (1982) *Nations before Nationalism*, Chapel Hill: University of North Carolina Press.

Beaune, C. (1985) *Naissance de la Nation France*, Paris: Editions Gallimard.

Bell, D. (2001) *The Cult of the Nation in France, 1680–1800*, Cambridge, MA: Harvard University Press.

Breuilly, J. (1993) *Nationalism and the State* (2nd edn), Manchester: Manchester University Press.

Campbell, J. and Sherrard, P. (1968) *Modern Greece*, London: Ernest Benn.

Cherniavsky, M. (1961) *Tsar and People*, New Haven, CT: Yale University Press.

Connor, W. (1990) 'When is a nation?', *Ethnic and Racial Studies*, 13(1), pp. 92–103.

David, R. (1982) *The Ancient Egyptians: Religious Beliefs and Practices*, London, Boston and Henley: Routledge & Kegan Paul.

Davies, W.D. (1982) *The Territorial Dimension in Judaism*, Berkeley, Los Angeles and London: University of California Press.

Eriksen, T. (1993) *Ethnicity and Nationalism*, London and Boulder, CO: Pluto Press.

Frye, R. (1966) *The Heritage of Persia*, New York: Mentor.

Frye, R. (1975) *The Golden Age of Persia: The Arabs in the East*, London: Weidenfeld & Nicolson.

Garsoian, N. (1999) *Church and Culture in Early Medieval Armenia*, Aldershot: Ashgate Variorum.

Geary, P. (2002) *The Myth of Nations: The Medieval Origins of Europe*, Princeton, NJ, and Oxford: Princeton University Press.

Gellner, E. (1983) *Nations and Nationalism*, Oxford: Blackwell.

Gellner, E. (1996) 'Do nations have navels?', *Nations and Nationalism*, 2(3), pp. 366–370.

Gershoni, I. and Jankowski, J. (1987) *Egypt, Islam and the Arabs: The Search for Egyptian Nationhood, 1900–1930*, Oxford and New York: Oxford University Press.

Greenfeld, L. (1992) *Nationalism: Five Roads to Modernity*, Cambridge, MA: Harvard University Press.

Grosby, S. (1991) 'Religion and nationality in antiquity', *European Journal of Sociology*, 33, pp. 229–265.

Grosby, S. (2002) *Biblical Ideas of Nationality: Ancient and Modern*, Winona Lake, Indiana: Eisenbrauns.

Hastings, A. (1997) *The Construction of Nationhood: Ethnicity, Religion and Nationalism*, Cambridge: Cambridge University Press.

Henze, P. (2000) *Layers of Time: A History of Ethiopia*, London: C. Hurst & Co.

Herbert, R. (1972) *David, Voltaire, Brutus and the French Revolution*, London: Allen Lane.

Hobsbawm, E. (1990) *Nations and Nationalism since 1780*, Cambridge: Cambridge University Press.

Hodgkin, T. (1964) 'The relevance of "Western" ideas in the derivation of African nationalism', in J.R. Pennock (ed.) *Self-government in Modernising Societies*, Englewood Cliffs, NJ: Prentice-Hall.

Hosking, G. and Schopflin, G. (eds) (1997) *Myths and Nationhood*, London and New York: Routledge.

Hutchinson, W. and Lehmann, H. (eds) (1994) *Many Are Chosen: Divine Election and Modern Nationalism*, Minneapolis: Fortress Press.

Im Hof, U. (1991) *Mythos Schweiz: Identität-Nation-Geschichte, 1291–1991*, Zürich: Neue Verlag Zürcher Zeitung.

Kedourie, E. (1960) *Nationalism*, London: Hutchinson.

Kedourie, E. (ed.) (1971) *Nationalism in Asia and Africa*, London: Weidenfeld & Nicolson.

Kohn, H. (1967 [1944]) *The Idea of Nationalism*, New York: Collier-Macmillan.

Levine, D. (1974) *Greater Ethiopia: The Evolution of a Multiethnic Society*, Chicago, IL: Chicago University Press.

Liverani, M. (1979) 'The ideology of the Assyrian empire', in M.T. Larsen (ed.) *Power and Propaganda: A Symposium on Ancient Empires*, Copenhagen: Akademisk Forlag.

MacDougall, H. (1982) *Racial Myth in English History: Trojans, Teutons and Anglo-Saxons*, Montreal: Harvest House, and Hanover, NH: University Press of New England.

Mann, M. (1993) *The Sources of Social Power*, Cambridge: Cambridge University Press, Vol. II.

Miller, D. (1995) *On Nationality*, Oxford: Oxford University Press.

Milner-Gulland, R. (1999) *The Russians*, Oxford: Blackwell.

Mosse, G. (1975) *The Nationalisation of the Masses: Political Symbolism and Mass Movements in Germany from the Napoleonic Wars through the Third Reich*, Ithaca, NY: Cornell University Press.

Mosse, G. (1990) *Fallen Soldiers*, Oxford and New York: Oxford University Press.

Nersessian, V. (2001) *Treasures of the Ark: 1700 Years of Armenian Christian Art*, London: The British Library.

Neusner, J. (1981) *Max Weber Revisited: Religion and Society in Ancient Judaism*, Oxford: Oxford Centre for Postgraduate Hebrew Studies.

Nicholson, E. (1988) *God and His People: Covenant and Theology in the Old Testament*, Oxford: Clarendon Press.

Novak, D. (1995) *The Election of Israel: The Idea of the Chosen People*, Cambridge: Cambridge University Press.

O'Brien, C.C. (1988) 'Nationalism and the French Revolution', in G. Best (ed.) *The Permanent Revolution*, London: Fontana Press.

Oguma, E. (2002) *A Genealogy of 'Japanese' Self-images*, trans. David Askew, Melbourne: Trans Pacific Press.

Özkirimli, U. (2003) 'The nation as an artichoke? A critique of ethno-symbolist interpretations of nationalism', *Nations and Nationalism*, 9(3), pp. 339–355.

Poliakov, L. (1974) *The Aryan Myth*, New York: Basic Books.

Redgate, A. (2000) *The Armenians*, Oxford: Blackwell.

Reynolds, S. (1984) *Kingdoms and Communities in Western Europe, 900–1300*, Oxford: Clarendon Press.

Routledge, B. (2003) 'The antiquity of the nation? Critical reflections from the ancient Near East', *Nations and Nationalism*, 9(2), pp. 213–233.

Roux, G. (1964) *Ancient Iraq*, Harmondsworth: Penguin.

Scales, L. (2000) 'Identifying "France" and "Germany": medieval nation-making in some recent publications', *Bulletin of International Medieval Research*, 6, pp. 23–46.

Schama, S. (1987) *The Embarrassment of Riches: An Interpretation of Dutch Culture in the Golden Age*, London: William Collins.

Smith, A.D. (1986) *The Ethnic Origins of Nations*, Oxford: Blackwell.

Smith, A.D. (1991) *National Identity*, Harmondsworth: Penguin.

Smith, A.D. (1998) *Nationalism and Modernism: A Critical Survey of Recent Theories of Nations and Nationalism*, London and New York: Routledge.

Smith, A.D. (1999) 'Sacred territories and national conflict', *Israel Affairs*, 5(4), pp. 13–31.

Smith, A.D. (2001) *Nationalism: Theory, Ideology, History*, Cambridge: Polity Press.

Smith, A.D. (2003) *Chosen Peoples: The Sacred Sources of National Identity*, Oxford: Oxford University Press.

Suleiman, Y. (2002) *The Arabic Language and National Identity*, Edinburgh: Edinburgh University Press.

Thaden, E.C. (1964) *Conservative Nationalism in Nineteenth-Century Russia*, Seattle: University of Washington Press.

Tilly, C. (ed.) (1975) *The Formation of National States in Western Europe*, Princeton, NJ: Princeton University Press.

Walzer, M. (1985) *Exodus and Revolution*, New York: Harper-Collins, Basic Books.

6 Ethnies and nations
Genealogy indeed

Pierre L. van den Berghe

It is a triple pleasure to respond to Anthony D. Smith's 'The genealogy of nations': first, because the clarity of his position makes the task easy; second, because the compatibility of our positions neatly circumscribes our areas of disagreement; and third, because the latter do not significantly affect the validity of what either of us is saying.

Basically, I see Smith's lifelong contribution to the study of ethnicity and nationalism as a valiant and erudite attempt to reconcile theory and historicism. I am firmly with him in holding that nations and nationalism antedate 'modernism', and have their roots in ethnicity. With Smith, I reject the fatuous presentism of the 'modernists'. Indeed, I find the very concept of 'modernity' one of the least useful in our analytical arsenal, precisely because it is so Euro- and temporocentric. Of course, nations are not a Western monopoly, nor were they born with the French Revolution. They have their roots in pre-existing ethnies.

The several book-length demonstrations by Smith (1986, 1991, 1998) of the rich, diverse and many-stranded paths to nationhood clearly constitute his lasting contribution to the literature. It is this historical detail and variety which makes Smith impatient of any attempt to reduce the scope of the concept of nation by arbitrary and ethnocentric definitions. Smith seeks to achieve a universal definition of nationhood that encompasses all the rich historical detail, and he largely succeeds. My disagreements with him, I hope to show, in no way detract from the historicist Smith, and improve on the theoretical Smith. Indeed, I propose a theory which is even more universalistic than Smith's.

The basic disagreement between Smith and myself is not one of substance but of epistemology. Smith is clearly in the idealist tradition of making culture (in his words, 'symbols, memories, myths and values') the prime mover of human history, whereas I am a materialist. I believe that the cultural superstructure grows out of a material structure, not vice versa. Furthermore, I take the additional reductionist step of anchoring the structure of human societies in our biological evolution as *Homo sapiens*, and thereby incorporate the study of human sociality in the neo-Darwinian synthesis of evolution by natural selection. This latter step is anathema to the vast majority of social scientists (including, I suppose, Smith) who, even when they are not in the idealist tradition, are still firmly committed to an anti-reductionist stance *vis-à-vis* the natural sciences.

In the spirit of Occam's razor, scientific theory construction is intrinsically a reductionist process: one seeks to explain as much as possible about a given phenomenon at the lowest level in the organisation of matter. One only turns to the next higher level if there is an unexplained residual which requires the introduction of emergent properties. This is not to say that the higher levels (notably the transmission of culture through symbolic language, in the human case) are unimportant or uninteresting, but simply that they are *derivative* of the subjacent levels. The nature of the explanandum largely dictates the most fruitful level of analysis, but each escalation in level of analysis involves a reduction in the scope of theory and a step towards historicist description. Theory construction is inherently reductionist, with the resulting loss of detail. Historicism captures all the richness of detail at the cost of scope. The two processes of knowledge acquisition are *complementary*, not mutually exclusive.

In human terms, there is much room for theory at the level I called the biological infrastructure; there is still considerable scope for theory at the level of social structure; but much of the cultural superstructure can only be apprehended in detail through a historicist approach.. The hierarchy between these levels is purely of *anteriority-posteriority*, not of superiority-inferiority. All levels interact, and the choice of focus is dictated by what one seeks to understand. There can be a general theory about, say, the universality of music in human culture, but there cannot be a meaningful theory about the Mozart sonata.

So much for epistemology. Here is not the place to demonstrate why a full understanding of human behaviour and sociality must be linked to the history of what kind of an animal we became. The gradual incorporation of the human social sciences as one-species specialties in the life sciences is gaining ground in developmental psychology, linguistics, neurophysiology, behavioural genetics, biological anthropology, population ecology and half-a-dozen other disciplines. My own modest contribution to that vast enterprise was made a quarter of a century ago (van den Berghe 1978, 1981), when I proposed that ethnicity was an extension of kinship, which, in turn, was based on the biology of nepotism. We favour fellow ethnics because, rightly or wrongly (but on the whole rightly), we believe that we are more closely biologically related to them than to people outside our ethny. (Parenthetically here, unlike Smith who uses the French *ethnie*, I anglicised the term in the belief that English should join the other main European languages in having a noun to designate 'ethnic groups'. Happily, in the plural form, it makes no difference.)

Ethnies are formed by groups of interacting individuals at the most elemental level: they mate and produce offspring on whom they lavish parental care. That is how we form the most basic unit of human society. Families of nuclear or extended kin tend to intermarry, if only because of spatial constraints, and, through several generations of endogamous marriage, form ethnies. Over time, the latter can subdivide in sub-ethnies, merge in super-ethnies, combine with others, disappear or dissolve. Ethnogenesis, fission, recombination and extinction are extremely flexible processes, but, basically, ethnies form through three or more generations of endogamy, fission through physical or political separation, combine through widening interaction, and dissolve through exogamy. These processes can take less than a century or last for millennia, but they are highly dynamic because, ultimately, they are based on thousands of individuals choosing mates, having children and thereby forming the basic human society: a group of people linked in a tight social fabric made up of the warp of kinship and the woof of marriage. Several generations of endogamy ensure that the ties of kinship and marriage overlap, and that is how ethnies form. The biology of human reproduction and heavy bi-parental care, and the ecological necessity to form minimum social groups made up of several nuclear families, has been the blueprint for hominid sociality for many millennia, but the actual composition of these groups has been in continual flux.

Ethnogenesis is thus at the very root of the kind of sociality for which our species evolved. It is an integral part of our system of mating and reproduction, with pair-bonding, heavy bi-parental investment in a few costly, highly dependent, slowly maturing young, co-operative hunting and gathering, food sharing and so on. But, of course, the story only *starts* there. As an ethny is in the formative process, it quickly develops an elaborate cultural superstructure around itself: a set of rules regulating marriage and filiation, a legal system adjudicating conflicts, an origin myth and so on. That superstructure in complex, stratified, state-level societies with which Smith is primarily concerned can loom so large that its behavioural, individualistic underpinnings become totally obscured. Indeed, it often seems to take on a 'life of its own' that appears only distantly related to the behaviours and choices of individuals. An understanding of the formation of any specific ethny must, of course, include an account of this cultural superstructure, and it is perfectly legitimate to state that all the unique interest of a particular ethny resides in that superstructure. However, it is equally true that, unless that superstructure remains linked to its underlying social structure of interacting individuals, the ethny ceases to exist, or becomes something else. That structure, based on the biology of human mating and reproduction, is *prior*. Ethnies have existed since the dawn of our evolutionary history.

We now turn to the relationship between ethnies and nations. For Smith, nations are ethnies with additional elements of self-consciousness, myth- and memory-making, territorialisation, a public culture, and legal standardisation. In short, for Smith, nations are ethnies with a particularly elaborate cultural superstructure. The problem with this definition is that all its elements are already present in many ethnies, including many stateless societies, such as the Nuer of Sudan described by Evans-Pritchard (1940). Furthermore, these criteria for nationhood are matters of degree with no clear test of whether they are present or absent. Indeed, many people use the concepts of ethny and nation interchangeably, a fact that was made clear to me on a recent visit to Greece. I was talking to the translator into Greek of my *Ethnic Phenomenon*, Manusos Marangudakis, who mentioned his difficulty in translating my term 'ethny'. What is wrong with 'ethnos', I naively asked him. In Greek, 'ethnos' means 'nation', he replied. He, too, had to coin a neologism.

The critical historical moment where some ethnies are transformed into nations is that of *state formation*. Nationhood is *politicised ethnicity*. This process, to be sure, is accompanied by the development of an ideological superstructure around the kingship, territory, symbols, and political and legal institutions, as Smith rightly says. It is also accompanied by a heightened self-consciousness of being a people distinct from its neighbours. But this is largely a result of the inter-ethnic conflicts that almost invariably arise during state formation.

This link between nation and state formation is especially clear in Africa where scores of states and nations arose in the century preceding European colonialism, and where state formation is so historically visible. The Zulu state under Shaka, and some of its derivative states such as the Swazi, Ndebele and Shangaan, are good cases in point. A generation of warfare and conquests in the early twentieth century transformed an insignificant, clan-based Nguni subgroup into a powerful nation, which, in a second phase, spawned several new nations to its north.

Of course, state formation is not a simple process of one ethny becoming one state. Sometimes, the conquerors intermarry with and quickly absorb their neighbours, thereby creating a new nation out of several pre-existing ethnies, as in the Zulu case. Alternatively, the conquering nation merely dominates its ethnic neighbours, but fails to absorb them, thereby forming multi-ethnic empires, or, indeed, multi-national states where the conquered were already nations when they became incorporated into larger states. The European colonial empires and the Ottoman empire are cases in point.

Another scenario is represented by multi-national states formed, not so much by conquest, as by the politics of dynastic succession, election or marriage, as was the case in so many European states such as Spain, Burgundy and the Habsburg empire. Within such states, ethnies often develop or revive a sense of separate nationhood. Sometimes a national consciousness occurs, à la Benedict Anderson (1983), through the spread of literacy and literature in a newly standardised language used by an educated elite to develop a new nation. This was a frequent scenario in the late colonial period in Asia and Africa. There is also the case of the multi-statal nation where a weakly constituted national state breaks up into several states, as in Germany and Poland. The German nation antedates Bismarck by a millennium, but, even there, the political institutions of nationhood were kept alive, however vestigially, in the triply misnamed Holy Roman Empire of the German Nation. Finally, ethnies can transform themselves into nations by seeking statehood out of splinters from several multi-ethnic states, as, for example, the Kurds and the Armenians.

The common denominator of all these processes of transformation of ethnies into nations is a political programme of seeking and/or achieving self-rule. The politics of state formation are at the core of this transformation, often aided and abetted by elaborate myths and ideologies to legitimate it. The only truly new feature of the French Revolution and its Jacobin ideology was the radical delegitimation of all states, except the nation-state. From then on, all other states, whether sub-national, multi-national or simply non-national, were on the ideological defensive.

Ironically, 90 per cent or more of the existing states since then have not been nation-states, nor are most of them clearly on a trajectory of becoming such.

Most simply pretend to be nation-states, and their ruling elites have a mutual interest in maintaining that fiction. Such is the foundation of the so-called United Nations, made up, in fact, in large part of squabbling states ruled by neo-colonial kleptocracies, corporate plutocracies or socialist apparatchiks. Even France and the USA, the leading heirs to the Jacobin ideal of the nation-state, took quite some time to come close to that model. A much smaller French nation has existed north of the Loire for at least 500 years, but it became nearly coterminous with the 'hexagone' only a century ago after a sweeping educational policy of linguistic ethnocide. As for the USA, slow processes of cultural assimilation are periodically reversed by waves of immigration, and it remains deeply split along racial lines. At the outset, of course, the creation of the USA was only made possible through brutal conquest, ethnic cleansing and land expropriation of hundreds of native ethnies and nations. Of the modern states, only Switzerland, it seems, sees no need to apologise for *not* being a nation-state, or to pretend to strive to become one. It seems quite happy to have escaped 'modernity'.

Let us recap. What I have proposed here is a universal model of ethnicity, based on the social structure of human kinship and marriage, and, ultimately, on the biology of mating and reproduction. My detractors have dismissed my approach as 'primordialist', and Smith appears to join them in his conclusion, although he does not name me. Indeed, I am a primordialist in that I believe the causal and temporal sequence goes from biology, to social structure, to cultural superstructure, while Smith puts the entire burden of explanation on 'symbols, memories, myths, and values'.

That said, I object to the construction put on primordialism by those who dismiss the approach without understanding it, a common combination unfortunately. First, most 'social constructionists' of ethnicity seem to assume that anything rooted in biology is frozen and static. This strange notion that 'biology is destiny' flies in the face of the theory of evolution, the most sweeping theory of change we have. Three or four generations of changing patterns of exogamy or endogamy can profoundly alter ethnic boundaries, fuse small groups into larger ones, create entirely new ones, or blur hitherto existing lines of cleavage.

Second, there is a curious asymmetrical intolerance at work in the ethnicity literature. The 'social constructionists' seem to assume that their categorical rejection of primordialism is reciprocated, when, in fact, it is not. Countless times, but to little avail, I reiterated that ethnicity is *both* primordial *and* socially constructed. Symbols and myths can and do alter the formation and dissolution of ethnies and nations. Indeed, they can lead to genocide. But these social constructions, however powerful, do not spring up like a *deus ex machina* in an ethnic vacuum where anything can be invented or imagined.

Let me use the example of 'race' in the USA. The USA is still a racial caste society because the government continues to institutionalise the 'one-drop rule' of who is 'black'. Any 'black' African ancestry defines one socially as 'black' in the USA, and that is the criterion used in the census, in race-based 'affirmative action', in reports of crime or educational statistics and so on. This is obviously a weird but powerful social construction. My guess is that firmly race-blind government policies, and deletion of 'race' from all government statistics and censuses would turn North America into a society resembling Brazil in a generation or so. Race would become a continuum rather than a dichotomy, and racial boundaries would become so blurred as to lose much of their social import.

In short, social constructions do matter a great deal, especially when the power of government is behind them. But 'race' in the USA, as well as in Brazil, Jamaica or Mexico, can only be understood within the context of the social structure of slavery from which these social constructions arose.

Let me conclude with two suggestions. The first is that any understanding of ethnicity must go back to *stateless* societies. Only then will the universality of ethnies become obvious. Smith's accounts, however erudite, almost always start with the highly complex, stratified, state-level societies of antiquity. Second, the problem of how and when some ethnies turn into nations is largely a *political* process, concomitant with the rise, expansion or dissolution of states. Nothing focuses one's ethnic consciousness faster or better than political conflict with or within states dominated by people who are ethnically different from oneself.

References

Anderson, B. (1983) *Imagined Communities*, London: Verso.
Evans-Pritchard, E.E. (1940) *The Nuer*, London: Oxford University Press.
Smith, A.D. (1986) *The Ethnic Origins of Nations*, Oxford: Blackwell.
Smith, A.D. (1991) *National Identity*, Harmondsworth: Penguin.
Smith, A.D. (1998) *Nationalism and Modernism*, London: Routledge.
van den Berghe, P.L. (1978) 'Race and ethnicity, a sociobiological perspective', *Ethnic and Racial Studies*, 1 (4): 401–411.
van den Berghe, P.L. (1981) *The Ethnic Phenomenon*, New York: Elsevier.

Question and answer III

Question 1

Prof Smith, you said at the outset that the modernist ideal type of nation is to be contrasted with the nation as such. This implies an objective existence for what is surely a deeply subjective sociological phenomenon. This raises a prior question: What is nation?

Anthony D. Smith

When I said that the modernist ideal type of the nation is to be differentiated from the ideal type of the nation as a generic concept, I did not imply an objective existence for the nation. Both are, after all, ideal types. The difference is that the modernist ideal type relates solely to the *modern nation*, and, as a product of eighteenth-century Western Europe, it is inevitably partial and restricted in range. What we need is an ideal type that covers the whole historical and geographical range of cases of nationhood, and a category that will differentiate the concept of the nation from other related categories (of ethnic group, tribe, religious community and caste).

On the other hand, I would not agree that the concept of the nation in this broader sense is a 'deeply subjective sociological phenomenon'. Certainly, among its main features are subjective elements; but we may also discern more 'objective' features, with the result that the ideal type of the nation consists of a balance of subjective and objective elements, as befits so complex a concept.

As to 'what is a nation', I would define it in ideal-typical terms as *a named and self-defined community whose members cultivate shared myths, memories, symbols and values, reside in and identify with a historic homeland, possess and disseminate a distinctive public culture, and create and disseminate common laws and shared customs.* In historical terms, the nation is a form of human community with a collective cultural identity, whose concrete manifestations vary with their historical contexts, but always within the parameters of the ideal type of the nation as a category of collective cultural identity.

This accords with the origins of the category of the nation and of particular kinds of nations as the products of certain general and recurrent processes: the growth of self-definition of human communities; the cultivation of a fund of social and symbolic elements (myths, memories, symbols, values, rituals and traditions); the territorialisation of communities, including their attachment to historic homelands; the creation of a distinctive public culture and education system for spreading it to the members of the community; and the dissemination of shared customs and common laws to the members of a community. The development and combination of these processes creates the conditions for the emergence of nations, as defined above.

Question 2

There is a remarkable agreement between Professor Smith, Professor van den Berghe and modernists on the idea that the nation is somehow associated with the emerging state or with the state. Under this circumstance there is first of all a growing body of empirical evidence that there is a significant number of nations that for a variety of reasons do not wish to have states and they are no less nations because of that and there are a significant number of states that share the number of nations and there are very good reasons for that to happen. Isn't it time that we have to take both of your very important and seminal arguments one step further and reach the point where we have to dissociate the idea of the nation from the idea of the state?

Anthony D. Smith

With regard to the question of nations and states, perhaps I was misunderstood; I don't think that nations or the growth of nations result entirely from the presence and the influence of states, though clearly that is an important factor in many cases. There are cases of groups that have not wished to have states of their own or have been prevented. We can talk about nations in that sense too. When I referred to the observance of customs and laws, for example, I've often been misunderstood as saying that there must be state structures for that. You can have that, for example, within a religious community and religions; churches have certainly provided a chrysalis if you like for the growth of nations out of one or more ethnic communities, so I would agree that we can and we certainly should separate the concept of nation from the state, but there is a complex relationship between state and nation and historically, of course, states have often been very important, particularly in the Western Europe prototypes.

Pierre L. van den Berghe

The state versus nation confusion and controversy is being perpetuated by people who keep hyphenating those two words 'nation-state' to refer to nations, all the way from the cases that clearly are nation-states, say, Swaziland, to states that are nothing of the sort such as Nigeria. Professor Walker Connor and I have spent the past thirty or forty years trying to untangle that. I think in many cases deliberate confusion of the two is perpetuated by elites of states, particularly in the Third World, that pretend to rule nation-states but in fact are ruling multi-national states. So, yes, about 90 per cent of 160-odd politically 'independent' states are not nation-states. Only about 10 per cent of them are nation-states by the criterion of 90 per cent or more of the population speaking a single language.

So we live, for the most part, not in nation-states, but in multi-national states. Some states, at least in the past, have been quite willing and happy to define themselves as multi-national states. The Habsburg empire quite happily described itself as one, and until the eighteenth century it was a perfectly respectable form of state. It only came on the defensive after the French Revolution when the multi-national state was no longer the way to go, but it is now being revived in the form of multiculturalism which becomes fashionable once more. The important thing for us as social scientists is to clearly differentiate between nation-states and multi-national states. It is also true that some ethnic groups do not want states of any kind. For example, the Hutterites, an extremely cohesive ethnic community of Anabaptists and Anarchists, would say, 'a plague on all states'. They are perfectly happy to be 'the City of God on Earth', and they don't want states of any kind. So not all *ethnies* strive to become states; many *ethnies* would rather not be part of any state. But if and when an *ethny* becomes a nation, by definition, it either has a state of its own or it strives to achieve one.

As for the ability of states to recognise, define and redefine ethnicity and 'race', I quite agree that the state has a very powerful role in defining or redefining what ethnic and/or racial boundaries are. For example, in the USA, the 'one-drop rule' of who is black and who is white is clearly a social construction imposed by the American state. The census asks questions about racial membership and this has had a powerful influence on racial conflicts in the USA. Affirmative action has been an attempt to remedy this racism, but the remedy is worse than the disease because it keeps re-enforcing the very categories on which the invidious distinctions are based. So, yes, I quite agree that the state can play an important role in defining and redefining those categories. The point is that states are typically unsuccessful at defining categories which are entirely unrelated to historical ancestry. It would have been very difficult for the American state to create out of nothing an ethnic category, say, of left-handed people, that did not share some kind of common history and ancestry. Thus state definition of race and ethnicity is always constrained by past history.

Question 3

What are the major differences between primordialism and ethno-symbolism?

Anthony D. Smith

'Primordialism' is a term which covers those theorists of ethnicity and nationalism who emphasise the 'primordial' ties which bind populations and which are not subject to rational calculation. For Edward Shils and Clifford Geertz, for example, such ties are prior, binding and overriding; they take priority over all other ties, and stem from the *assumed* cultural 'givens' of race, language, custom, territory and kinship, as these are perceived and felt by individuals.

At an even more basic sociobiological level, Pierre L. van den Berghe argues that ethnic, racial and national groups are ultimately forms of inclusive kinship. They are mainly formed by genetic reproductive drives and the desire of individuals to maximise their gene pools through such mechanisms as endogamy and nepotism, though reciprocity and coercion also play a part. What distinguishes ethnic groups and nations from races is the role of cultural signs such as dress, customs and language, as well as the presence of myths of shared ancestry, and, in the case of the nation, the emergence of the state. Common to both versions of 'primordialism' is the assumption that ethnic communities and nations are part of 'nature', that they are intrinsic and 'natural' to the human condition as such.

In contrast, ethno-symbolism holds that ethnic communities and nations are historical phenomena. They do not exist 'in nature', nor are they part of the human condition. They are, instead, characteristic of certain places and periods of history. More particularly, ethno-symbolists such as John Armstrong, John Hutchinson and Anthony D. Smith contend that most, if not all, nations are modern (after 1789), but that one can trace the origins of many of them to pre-existing, and often pre-modern, ethnic communities (or *ethnies*). For all the many economic and political changes, pre-existing *ethnies* are often linked to modern nations by ethnic myths, memories, traditions, values and symbols – as opposed to the genes or cultural givens of the two versions of 'primordialism'. But these symbolic and social links must be demonstrated rather than simply assumed, and demonstrated in and through the historical record. For this purpose, socio-symbolic analysis must be conducted over the *longue durée*, and must pay attention to the ways in which symbols, myths and memories resonate among the designated population.

Hence the major differences between primordialism and ethno-symbolism concern (1) the status of explanation, with much that is part of the explanation in ethno-symbolism being taken for granted by primordialists; (2) the 'naturalism' of primordialism as opposed to the historicism in ethno-symbolism and its respect for historical data; (3) the key distinction in ethno-symbolism between ethnic community (or *ethnie*) and nation, which is largely ignored by primordialists, though van den Berghe has supplemented his version with an account of the formation of nations under the aegis of the state, and (4) the status of social and symbolic elements in ethno-symbolism, as opposed to genes or cultural givens in primordialism, in explaining *ethnies* and nations.

Pierre L. van den Berghe

For me, the primordialism of ethnicity is rooted in the biology of nepotism. We have a biological predisposition to favour others to the extent that they are, or at least that we perceive them as, related to us by common descent. Nepotism advances our genetic interests by favouring the reproductive success of individuals to the degree that we share their genes. The ethno-symbolism that Smith and others talk about is simply the cultural superstructure which defines, activates and reinforces ethnic nepotism. Ethnic sentiments and behaviours, like everything we do as humans, have both a biological basis and an elaborate cultural construct erected on that basis. The two are interacting aspects of the same human sociality. The biology is primordial because, while one can understand nepotism without reference to culture (notably in many animals that do not have culture), one cannot, in my view, truly understand culture bereft of biology.

Question 4

I would like to ask both speakers if they can somehow give us an opportunity to reflect on the achievement of their synergetic added value of what has been substantially done in this field of research in comparison to the two giants, Hans Kohn and Ernest Renan, and several others. About the state of discipline, about the self-consciousness or some kind of guilt that might penetrate our thinking today should be rather healthy for the state of our disciplines.

Anthony D. Smith

Well, the question of achievements in the field since Renan and Hans Kohn. Renan wrote one very celebrated essay which is very important, but he wasn't exactly a student of nationalism as such. And for Hans Kohn, he was a student of nationalism and he wrote voluminously and excellently on ideology. I think that there have been many achievements since then. First of all there has been, since the Second World War, enormous interest in the sociology, the social structure of nationalism, social groups and their contribution. Second, there have of course been a vast number of historical case studies with regard to both the sociology and ecology, and the politics of nations, and third, there is the linkage of ethnicity to nationalism which I think is a very important factor and which of course forms the basis of my own approach. So here at least I think are three important areas; there's also been an explosion of the normative side of thinking about nationalism and the ethics of nationalism as such, philosophy of nationalism and I think that's been very interesting too. So, I'm sure we could list very many more achievements.

Question 5

Do you still hope that there is one general theory so comprehensive as to include all cases of nationalism?

Anthony D. Smith

In a word, no I don't, and I never have. I've never held to a single theory; mine is an approach, it's not a theory, and I think I can rest on that matter.

General discussion

Question 1

Where are the meeting points between the so-called modernists and primordialists? What can we explain with the nation? What is nationalism studies good for?

Steven Grosby

Many of the observations of the so-called modernists – that's not my vocabulary – have a great deal of merit to them. I've taken many of them for granted because, as part of our intellectual currency, we are raised in universities reading Tocqueville and what he has to say about equality. My own teacher wrote convincingly that the development of modern societies is characterised by a diminution of the distinction between centre and periphery. The periphery has greater access to the centre, for example, democratic elections. I have taken all of this for granted; and I have no particular axe to grind with writers, if I may group them together, such as Professor Breuilly and Professor Greenfeld. I welcome many of their arguments. None the less, I have been troubled by their arguments because of what I have at times viewed to be a superficiality to them. Too often they have not taken seriously what it has meant to be human, specifically human divisiveness. I'm not going to repeat my comments from this morning. Suffice it to say that I have considered what is powerful in the modernist arguments. None the less, I have observed occurrences in other periods of time that have led me to question many of their assumptions. How we go forward seems to me to be what the study of nationality says about what it has meant to be human. This is a very complicated question because the nation is by no means all that it has meant to be human. There have been empires; there have been universal aspirations. There is the universal community of science. There is monotheism. So this question has to be approached very carefully, very subtly.

Walker Connor

The entire matter of dividing analyses of nationalism into primordialist or modernist I find distasteful, arbitrary and misleading, little more than an exercise in academic name-calling. The term 'primordialist', in particular, is often used dismissively. Declare a scholar of the stature of Clifford Geertz a primordialist, as has often been done, and there is no need to consider further the rich lode of his ideas. Indeed, describing Geertz as a primordialist underlines the arbitrariness of such name-calling, for sociobiologists, with greater justification, describe him as an unbending critic of perennialist explanations of identity. Dichotomising studies into modernist and primordialist is misleading, and obscures a more insightful relationship. In terms of objective history, today's nations are indeed modern creations, but in the intuitive perceptions that people hold of their nation, it is eternal, beyond time; that is to say, primordialist. Most recent articles and books on nationalism have been written by those who describe themselves as modernists, social constructivists or instrumentalists, and thus ignore the more profound aspects of national identity. Moreover, most writers when they refer to nationalism mean thereby patriotism (civic identity and loyalty). It is a sad commentary on the state of the art that after forty years of lecturing on nationalism I still feel compelled to begin any public talk with 'I had better explain first of all what I mean by a nation'. Is our insight into nationalism progressing? I would rate those works of Carlton Hayes published before the Second World War as the most perspicacious treatises on nationalism to date. Most of the current literature is simply confused and confusing, and I am prepared to suggest that, just as disciplines have broken down into 'schools', those of us who distinguish between nationalism and patriotism and who basically agree that there is something much more to national consciousness and national identity than can be conveyed in any simple declaratory sentence such as 'the nation is a social construct', simply part company with the others. If we wish for real progress let us restrict our dialogues to one another and let the others do the same. I have friends in the audience in their sixties and seventies who I know share this same sense of frustration with things as they are. Let us do away with these conferences in which panellists discuss totally different phenomena while employing the same key terms, nations and nationalism. I urge you young Ph.D.s and Ph.D. candidates not to be sitting here forty years from now thinking we should have heeded Connor's advice. Otherwise, insight into nationalism will not have made the strides it should.

John Breuilly

I think if you want to get an answer to everything then you should be depressed because we haven't got the answer to everything. I certainly haven't but I feel there's been a lot of advance in the historical field. I feel that we have been sharpening questions about different kinds of fields, whether we're looking at the history of mentalities, or the history of political movements, whether we're using archaeology to try and work out cultural traces or much else. . . . I feel we've come on a lot since Carlton Hayes. He wrote marvellous books but I for one would not write about nationalism and national culture in those ways any more because so much more research has been done. It's such a rich field. I don't think we advance like physicists by reducing everything to a few laws; I think we simply advance by knowing more about diversity, and in that sense I'm not a reductionist. However, I do think we should try to relate the emergence of nationalism to a range of other conditions which I associate with modernity.

I don't think it's the job of the historian to try and instruct anybody dealing with difficult problems today about how they should set about it. However, I was struck while I was talking to Ephraim Nimni who has just published a translation of *The Question of Nationalities and Social Democracy* by Otto Bauer. Bauer confronted difficult problems about conflicting nationalities in the Habsburg empire. We could look profitably at how his ideas about federalism, developed in the multi-national empires of the late nineteenth and early twentieth centuries, might say something to us now as we confront multicultural, multi-faith or multi-ethnicity in our own societies. People like Bauer were smart and they were living with the problems, and they came up with a lot of good ideas. So it is not so much that we historians can instruct politicians and others confronting national questions today as that our histories might offer some illumination.

There is another area where historical examples might be helpful. I was giving a paper last week on ideas about civil society and voluntary associations and the roles that they can play. I think that at the moment there is a rather cuddly notion of civil society as a jolly good thing and that the more associations there are the better. Tell that to the Weimar Republic when the associations included bodies such as the Brown Shirts. Nevertheless I think there are a number of areas, such as how voluntary and autonomous associations can prevent the illiberal manipulation of national sentiments or how a multiplicity of cultural or ethnic or religious identities can be handled in the public sphere, where the historical record can provide some food for thought.

I would like to praise superficiality as well as variety. I think the more profound and unifying we try to be, the less informed and analytical we become. I think history in many ways is a superficial subject – it does not plumb philosophical or psychological depths – but it's a subject that can make advances in studying the things for which we've got some evidence and can analyse, and I really believe in breaking it down into distinct areas. My argument resembles Walker Connor's when he spoke of breaking nationalism down into a series of different fields, not so much in terms of approaches but in terms of subject matter. Studying the regulation of ethnic conflict, or national movements, or the pursuit of self-determination, or national cultures, or the intellectual history of ideas about nationality: these are different subjects and one of our problems is when we jump from one subject to another, promiscuously constructing artificial histories of a non-subject.

Just an observation on the issue of whether the USA may be described as a nation. Partly we can simply say we want to use the word 'nation' differently. For me the important question is not the use of words but how it is that people who are clearly not closely ethnically related have come together. There has been destruction of indigenous American-Indian societies and the subordination of African-Americans, but at the same time so many different ethnic groups have come together and partly through luck. Because if the Civil War had gone the other way, we might now be talking about two nations and constructing completely different history. But, partly through luck but also through a public culture, through a state system, through a common civic culture there has been a construction of a supra-ethnic sense of nationality. It is not adequate to describe this as convergence on an original Anglo-Saxon norm. Further, civic culture which is vital to this process does not fit into the civic/ethnic division. Identities formed through civic culture are clearly not voluntarist in the sense of the product of rational choice but they are clearly not ethnic in the sense of being based on blood and descent. Yet in most nationalisms I know something about, there has been a central role for civic culture, public culture, public institutions which habituate everybody to behave in the same way, so even if they detest each other they detest each other in the same kind of way and in that sense have a kind of affinity. In that sense I think it's interesting to see how the USA became a 'nation'. I find illuminating Professor Walker Connor's observations that by and large immigrants came in wishing to assimilate rather than wanting to remain distinct. In that sense attitudes are clearly important, but additionally you can't deny there is a public culture, a public ethic which shapes this process of coming together and which I want to say is national.

Anthony D. Smith

I don't think there are any meeting points between modernists and primordialists, except that both agree that particular ethnic groups and nations emerge and dissolve. Otherwise, for modernists, the nation as a general category emerges only with modernity, whereas for primordialists it is a natural and hence a universal category. I'm not sure that we can explain a great deal 'with the nation', except perhaps the importance of political expression for cultural diversity and social solidarity, where and whenever human beings feel the need for both. The study of nations and nationalism is useful for highlighting the importance of cultural diversity and cultural creativity, the fine line between diversity and exclusiveness, and the need for rigorous analysis of the causes and consequences of the interplay between culture and politics, including their potential for violence.

Eric Hobsbawn

Where is the debate going? I don't know. But if the debate is going to go anywhere, it will have to reflect what is happening in history today, particularly in the past fifty years when the nature of the world has changed more rapidly than it has ever before and it continues to change more rapidly than ever before with its implications for all sorts of things that we would consider nations or are linked with nations, local culture, group culture, language or whatever; and not least the state. We are finding, for instance, that in the past thirty years we've been living in a period of the gradual weakening and disintegration of the old territorial states, which had been increasing in power for about two hundred years before that, irrespective of ideology. Again, today we must ask whether language will continue to have the same significance in the future as it has at present, for then most people in the world will to some extent have returned to the multilinguality which was normal in situations such as those of sub-Saharan tribal society when most people who needed to could communicate in two or three languages. There are all sorts of questions like that. It seems to me that we don't start with the question of whether nations are modern or ancient but we start with what's happening in the world and what implications it has for our problem.

Question 2

What schools of thought answer best the questions of what is the nation, when is the nation and why is the nation, and what do they omit to ask or to answer?

Anthony D. Smith

I do not think any school of thought, or approach, has a monopoly on truth in this area. It depends very much on the question that is posed. For some questions (for example, why people are prepared to die for the nation), certain approaches such as primordialism or ethno-symbolism may yield better answers; whereas for other problems (for example, the impact of nationalism or the role of elites), other approaches (for example, the varieties of modernism) tend to offer more illuminating answers. And, naturally, each of these approaches has the limitations of its strengths, and they may fail to ask certain questions and miss some pertinent answers. This is the case with the present question: When is the nation? Some approaches do not address this question; others do, but are restrictive and arbitrary; still others are grappling with the problem, but like the rest do not possess a definitive answer.

Eric Hobsbawn

This could be the largest possible question. I don't want to answer the question, 'What is a nation', and I don't believe the question 'Why is a nation' has very much sense, but the question 'When is a nation' is after all the subject of our meeting today. May I refer you to what I think is one of the most brilliant pieces of work on the subject, namely the late Gwyn Alf Williams' essay 'When was Wales' which discusses exactly that problem. The term 'Welsh' itself, as a name for all the inhabitants of the principality, came from the Teutonic invaders, who did not bother to distinguish between the kinds of foreigners to the West and South to whom they gave this name. No doubt the inhabitants of Wales were all quite distinct in many ways, and knew themselves to be distinct from the Saxons, but when did these peoples begin to think of themselves as internally coherent or belonging together, which is quite different from seeing themselves as not being Saxons? Only history can answer that question. Incidentally, why don't we talk about Saxons anymore? All the peoples who came into contact with the Teutons in the past tended to call them Saxons, but this patently formidable people have disappeared from sight, except as a part of the administrative organisation of Federal Germany. So far as I know, they play no part in the debates of the theorists of nationalism.

John Breuilly

When, what, why is a nation? I want to use this question to smuggle in something else. Why is the nation? My answer is that the nation is there because of modernity and I just want to take issue with people who don't believe in modernity. What strikes me most is the otherness of the past, not just of ancient societies or stateless societies but ones much closer to us. At the moment I am reading Diarmaid MacCulloch's wonderful book on the Reformation and I can see that the people whom he describes cannot believe in the nation because they know that earthly history is going to end soon, and what matters is not what collectives we belong to in this world but what will happen to our souls in the next. Modernist is, by contrast, secular and this-worldly. Take another aspect of modernity. Most of us constantly have to work out how we relate to strangers. You can gauge the scale of this challenge just by counting the number of different surnames in the telephone directory. For in any country you can pretty much equate modernity with the number of different surnames. Pre-modern societies have a much smaller stock of family names. One could argue that the idea of the nation is basically the idea that a society of mutual strangers actually belong together as if they were not strangers. Such an idea has no function in a pre-modern world where strangers are marginal. The idea of the nation does not reflect or directly build upon pre-modern ethnicity, as sociobiologists would have us believe, but is a response to the breakdown of such ethnicity.

Steven Grosby

I have been preoccupied with the problem of why is the nation. I think that the work of scholars will be furthered if we stop running away from that question and consider it head-on. This is a problem of philosophical anthropology. I understand that the answers to this question will be contested. Maybe nothing definitive can be said about the problem. We will have arguments and differences over it, but I think it is a problem that should be confronted head-on. Why is the nation is the question that has been most on my mind, knowing full well the problems involved in answering this question. The pursuit of an answer to this question is most certainly not an excuse to avoid serious scholarly research about when or how is the nation. Those historical and sociological questions are obviously important.

Question 3

What sort of educational impact do the topics of nation, nationhood and nationalism have?

Eric Hobsbawn

There has been too much educational impact. After all, educational systems, including university education systems, have been deeply imbued with national-ism and nationalist ideas, or in the best of cases with resistance to nationalist ideas. I think at present that the main problem is precisely how we can emancipate education and higher education from this built-in nationalist virus, built in because educational systems are, as I pointed out, virtually congruent with national boundaries. I think that is a very, very important element.

John Breuilly

On the educational aspect I tend to be pessimistic. Academics don't get involved as much as they should do in school-level education but that's partly because in this country, school education has become so complex. I would reiterate the point that certainly, as far as history is concerned, history was formed as a discipline along with the nation-state, and it's very difficult to think historically outside of national tunnels. I make a distinction between national history and nationalist history. Nationalist history is easy enough to subvert as it so clearly is teleological and serves a political purpose. It is more difficult to subvert national history because you have to construct something else. It's partly being done in schools with local history-type topics, but to move towards transnational frameworks is hard. There are both people at this conference and elsewhere who know a lot about how history is represented in school textbooks. There are many interesting and recent examples of regime changes which will lead to a lot of rewriting of history, for example, in Eastern Europe. I was in South Africa a little while ago, and clearly Afrikaaner views of history are being challenged and displaced. Afrikaaners themselves, I was told, don't believe in history any more, a likely reaction when history no longer appears to be on one's side. Conversely, there is an upsurge in black national history. For example, Zulus are starting to take seriously such a site as the battlefield at Isandlwana where they won a great military victory over the British. Equally, however, we will witness an effort by the new regime to give historical backing to a multicultural ethic. The big question of course is: Is it good to have an educational system designed to produce a good end, a good identity (say, committed to multiculturalism) as opposed to an edu-cational system designed to produce a bad identity (say, an ethnic one)? Or should we perhaps try to think of an educational system with history books that doesn't have an identity end in view at all? And, of course, do such educational pro-grammes make an impact only when their audience is already receptive to the message being preached?

Anthony D. Smith

On one level, education has often suffered from an excess of nationalism to the detriment of dispassionate analysis, and has thereby encouraged one-sided and exclusive attitudes. On another level, the study of nations and nationalism can serve a useful corrective function – both to nationalist one-sided bias, and to naive and idealistic cosmopolitanism. How far such studies can be conducted at school level I'm not sure, as this demands considerable knowledge of history and other cultures, not to mention rigorous analysis. But I do not know what educational impact such studies have had in schools, and I do not know if any study of this has been conducted. We also do not know what educational impact such studies may have, or indeed have had, in a university setting. It would be extremely helpful to hold a conference of teachers of nationalism studies to begin to assess this impact, and the strengths and pitfalls of such studies.

Question 4

What kind of impact has social Darwinism had on studies of nations and nationalism?

Anthony D. Smith

I'm not sure that *social* Darwinism in the classical sense had any impact on studies of nations and nationalism, since in the late nineteenth century there did not exist a field of studies of nationalism. Its impact was nevertheless great, but on the politics and culture of nationalism. For social Darwinism helped to turn many nationalisms in Europe (and in America) towards a more racial formulation and even in some cases to racism (aided by other political, economic and ideological factors). If by social Darwinism we mean, more broadly, sociobiological intellectual approaches, then its impact has been surely significant but much more limited. We can see this in the addresses and exchanges at this conference, and I cannot add much to this. Sociobiological approaches have certainly forced scholars to think about the relations between kinship and biology on the one hand, and culture and politics on the other, even when they reject the reductionism of this approach. Yet, even if we concede the importance of kinship and of myths of descent for sentiments of ethnic solidarity and national cohesion, as I think we must, I am not sure how far studies of individual genetic reproductive drives and inclusive fitness can illuminate more specific but large-scale historical problems and phenomena of ethnicity and nations, including the question, When is the nation? At this point it becomes necessary to appeal to other factors such as the state, which are not derived from a sociobiological framework. And it is to such factors, rather than to sociobiological premises, that most scholars appeal today.

Steven Grosby

I have come to the conclusion that we must come to some kind of terms with neo-Darwinism. It can't be avoided. I have some differences with Professor van den Berghe. I'm not quite sure of the extent to which he really supports the things that he says. He says one thing one time and then he says another. If I try to pin him down and take the determinism seriously, important facts severely complicate, so it seems to me his understanding of nations. Presumably, according to the argument, nations must have something to do with inclusive fitness. We have the curious fact that when nations reach a high standard of living, they have declining growths in population. Now that's just an extraordinarily interesting fact, which presents an enormous difficulty of understanding the nation as a mechanism for furthering inclusive fitness. We really must think seriously about Darwin's work. I myself do not believe that there is a direct connection between biological mechanism and cultural expressions.

Pierre L. van den Berghe

Professor Grosby raises the old conundrum of how sociobiology can explain the decline of fertility in advanced industrial societies, and why, in those countries, those who can most afford children have fewest. I would need an hour to answer the question satisfactorily, but let me try in three minutes.

First, we have long evolved as an extreme 'K-selectionist' (i.e. as an organism in which both parents invest lavishly in very few, spaced, highly dependent, slowly maturing offspring). For a brief historical hiatus, the pasteurisation of cows' milk enabled us to become effective lacto-parasites and have a baby every year, thereby producing an unprecedented population explosion. We are now, in part, reverting to our more natural mode of producing a viable young every four or five years, as, indeed, do all our great ape cousins (chimpanzees, gorillas and orang-utans).

Second, we have developed a technology of cheap and reliable contraception which enables us to dissociate the reproductive and recreational aspects of sexual behaviour. We have long had sex for reasons other than reproductive, as shown by the fact that we are 'copulatorily redundant' (i.e. that many of us copulate thousands of times more often than we reproduce). We can have sex for fun, for power, for money, for companionship, for any number of resources, but, until recently, we could not reliably dissociate vaginal sex from reproduction.

Third, we are biologically programmed to have sex for its immediate sensory rewards, and only derivatively because we want to have children. As good hedonists, we now consciously and safely use sex for fun, even when reproduction is farthest from our thoughts.

Fourth, those of us who could afford most children (the educated, well-to-do) have fewest because we can best indulge in a multiplicity of other things worth living for (e.g. ballet lessons, Caribbean vacations, Ph.D.s).

As for my alleged propensity to say different things at different times, as Grosby suggests I do, I submit that it results from an aversion to false dichotomies. I spent much of my career arguing that both sides of a false dichotomy (e.g. between primordialists and social constructionists in the field of ethnicity) are correct. This only sounds like I am talking out of both sides of my mouth if one believes in the false dichotomy in the first place. The result, alas, is often a dialogue of the deaf.

To summarise, it is not culture *versus* nature – it is culture *in* nature. We are on a double evolutionary track which includes genetic evolution and cultural evolution. The two are in an intricate relationship, the specifics of which still need to be disentangled, but it is absolutely inconceivable to explicate culture except in reference to biological evolution. We can only come to that realisation by comparing our species to other species. If you accept as a minimum definition of culture the social transmission of learned behaviour, we are by no means unique as a cultural species. Scores of mammalian and avian species have been shown to have culture in the minimum sense of social transmission of learned behaviour. To me it has become axiomatic that one cannot understand anything about the specificity of human culture except on a comparative and evolutionary basis, but again I don't have the time to make that case here.

On the gender business, sociobiology is about the only theoretical model that gives both genders equal time except that we call it sex. It takes two to tango.

One final comment on modernity and nation. If the nation is a product of modernity, as many here, notably Hobsbawm, have suggested, perhaps we're rapidly becoming *unmodern*. The nation-state as a political ideal has clearly crested. We are at last in an age of denationalising the state, and for that matter of devolution of state power as a result of globalisation, the escalating role of NGOs, international capitalism escaping state control, the internet and so on. Personally I would like to see what I call a Luxemburgisation of the world. I would like to see a multiplicity of small, subnational states, basically municipalities and their immediate hinterland. Clearly, Europe is becoming denationalised. Nationalistic ideology is passé in contemporary Europe and I think this is all to the good. The Balkans, Africa and so on represent the rearguard of the nationalist age. So, if nationalism came in with modernity, does that mean we are becoming unmodern? I hope we are!

Eric Hobsbawm

Allow me a small remark on neo-Darwinism. Nobody is against neo-Darwinism. On the contrary. We have to take neo-Darwinsim and sociobiology as one of the important factors. The point is that it does not explain what we're talking about. Human history, by the standards of Darwinian natural selection, is extraordinarily brief. We are only a few hundred generations distant from the invention of agriculture and metallurgy, which is nothing by the standards of prehistory, palaeontology, let alone geology. It may have been long enough for a few, so to speak, Darwinian mutations in the human species such as the appearance of blondes and a number of other things like that, but essentially human beings have remained substantially unchanged genetically since the beginning of history except of course that we're bigger and heavier, but I think that's another matter.

Short as human history is by Darwinian standards, the speed with which things have been changing over the past five hundred years, even more in the past two hundred years, is quite dizzying. The accelerating speed is such that, however significant you believe the Darwinian patterns of selection for survival are for the formation of human nature, they are quite inadequate to explain why, say, modern populations live so differently from their prehistoric ancestors dug up in the bogs of Jutland. You have to have different kinds of patterns, cultural patterns, patterns which are specifically historical, and indeed my view is that the enormous advances in biology, the biological revolution which enables us through the use of DNA techniques to trace the chronology of human history, enables us also to identify the era of history within which Darwinian sociobiology isn't enough to explain it.

Part II

Case studies

7 When was the English nation?

Krishan Kumar

If we are to understand nationalism, it seems to me that we must look above all at what is distinctive in the modern world, rather than at what it shares with the past.

(Gellner 1998: 96)

History is indeed the key to the problem. It usually is. But it turns the lock only if allowed to confront what is truly distinctive about the English past as well as what is not.

(Wormald 2001: 3)

Claims that a nation existed prior to the late nineteenth century should be treated cautiously.

(Connor 1994: 224)

Forever England?

Remember, sir, my liege,
The kings, your ancestors, together with
The natural bravery of your isle, which stands
At Neptune's park, ribbed and paled in
With banks unscalable, and roaring waters,
With sands that will not bear your enemies' boats,
But suck them up to th' topmast. A kind of conquest
Caesar made here, but made not here his brag
Of 'came and saw and overcame.' With shame –
The first that ever touched him – he was carried
From off our coast, twice beaten; and his shipping,
Poor ignorant baubles, on our terrible seas
Like eggshells moved upon their surges, cracked
As easily 'gainst our rocks; for joy whereof
The famed Cassibelan, who was once at point –
O giglot fortune! – to master Caesar's sword,

Made Lud's town with rejoicing fires bright,
And Britons strut with courage.

(Shakespeare, *Cymbeline, King of Britain*, Act 3, Scene 1)

Everyone knows the famous paean to England delivered by John of Gaunt in
Shakespeare's *Richard II* ('this sceptred isle, this earth of majesty' . . . – as good an
example of the English/British confusion as we will find). Far fewer know the
equally majestic tribute paid to *Britain* by Shakespeare in his less well known and
infrequently performed play *Cymbeline*. Not just the tone but the coincidence of
theme and imagery is striking. Here Britain – unlike England – is truly an island,
proud and independent, defying the mighty Caesar and coming within an inch of
seeing him off (the play depicts another failed act of defiance of the Romans).
'Britain's a world/By itself,' says another character in the play, 'and we will nothing pay/For wearing our own noses' (Act 3, Scene 1). If there is nationalism here,
it is British, not English nationalism.

There have been several scholars who have championed the idea that it was in
Shakespeare's time – in the sixteenth and early seventeenth centuries – that
England truly came into its own. It was then with the Protestant Reformation, the
declaration of royal supremacy, an increasingly assertive and heavily Puritan
Parliament, and spectacular successes against Catholic Spain, the dominant
power of the time, that England broke away from its centuries-old continental
mooring and struck off on its own. Writers and poets celebrated England as the
'elect nation', God's chosen, like the Israelites of old.[1] The English, it is said,
became nationalistic – indeed, they invented nationalism (see esp. Greenfeld
1992: 29–87; and cf. Greenfield 2002: 80). Shakespeare's history plays have
always been included in the recital of items indicating this rise of nationalist
consciousness: they are, says Derek Hirst, 'central to the writing of England and
its destiny' (2002: 257), and Adrian Hastings refers to 'the nationalist message of
Shakespeare's histories from *Richard II* to *Henry V*' (1997: 56).[2] What indeed could
be more nationalistic than 'On, on, you noblest English', Henry V's speech before
the walls of Harfleur, which concludes with the ringing cry, 'God for Harry,
England, and Saint George', or the rousing speech – 'we few, we happy few, we
band of brothers' – before the battle of Agincourt (*Henry V*, Act III, Scene 1; Act
IV, Scene 3)?

Shakespeare is a treacherous guide in most areas, except perhaps the human
heart. What he gives with one hand he takes away with the other – this is the
famous 'negative capability' that Keats admired in him. We do not know – at least
from his plays, and there is not much else – whether he was Protestant or Catholic,
royalist or populist, nationalist or cosmopolitan. He seems capable of taking all
positions, and none. Nationalism indeed seems one of the most unlikely characteristics to attribute to him, from all that we know from his plays. Even in what
appears his most nationalistic of plays, *Henry V*, we find a chilling assessment of
the cost to the common people, in blood and money, of Henry's ambitions in
France (Act IV, Scene 1); while the prominent presence of Welsh, Scottish and
Irish figures, and what amounts to a running debate on ethnicity between them,

further reveals Shakespeare's clear awareness of a British dimension to the English question. There are many other indications of ambivalence and detachment in what are often taken to be Shakespeare's firmly held attitudes, whether towards royalty, religion, the family or the nation. Shakespeare is too often read solely through the lens of a particular period or age. In our case, and with special reference to nationalism, there has been a tendency to see him as one of the earliest, and in some ways the greatest, prophet of English nationalism. We can see this especially in the popular film versions of *Henry V* (1945) and *Richard III* (1955), suitably embellished by Laurence Olivier's athletic acting and William Walton's stirring music.[3]

At any rate, the existence of a 'British' theme in Shakespeare's plays, even if there were no other reasons, is sufficient warning that we would be wrong to see the uncomplicated celebration of England and Englishness as the leitmotiv either of his work or of Elizabethan and Stuart culture in general. It is well known that James I, when he linked the thrones of Scotland and England in 1603, attempted to promote Britishness throughout his new realm. His failure, on the whole, to do so, and the deferment of the formation of Great Britain to the union with Scotland in 1707, has led many people to write off this early attempt to create a British identity (see e.g. Levack 1987: 32–41; Wormald 1992). However, not only is the 'British idea' itself much older than this Stuart effort, with a genealogy stretching back into medieval times (Hay 1955–1956; Williamson 1983). As a policy it was energetically prosecuted by the Tudors, and received a considerable boost with the victory of the Protestant Reformation in Scotland in 1560. Moreover, James' vision of a union, not just of crowns but of hearts and minds among all the peoples of Britain, was shared by several prominent thinkers and artists of the time, among them the philosopher Francis Bacon and the poet Michael Drayton. England and Englishness, it is clear, did not occupy the field uncontested in the early seventeenth century; they were powerfully challenged by several alternative ideas, one of them being Britain and Britishness (Kumar 2003: 132–134).

It has been a notable feature of recent English historiography to find the English nation alive and well in some very remote periods indeed. The time of the Venerable Bede, in the eight century, is one such, or at least the late Saxon period before the Norman Conquest (Campbell 1995; Hastings 1997: 35–43; Wormald 1994). Others have seen a distinct English nationalism developing in alliance with the conquest of the Celtic nations and the creation of 'the first English empire' from the eleventh to the thirteenth centuries (Davies 2000; Gillingham 2000). More familiarly there is the fourteenth century, the time of Chaucer, as the period in which 'the Englishing of the nation' truly took place (Elton 1992: 52).[4] These earlier periods now take their place alongside the claim – actually quite a venerable one – that it was the early modern period, the time of the Tudors, that saw the birth of English nationalism (Pollard 1907: 26–78; Greenfeld 1992; and see Kumar 2003: 93–97). If we add to these claims for the seventeenth (Kohn 1940) and eighteenth centuries (Newman 1987; Lucas 1990), we can see that the student of English nationalism is spoilt for choice. This still leaves out the most obvious period, the nineteenth and twentieth centuries, when the ideology of nationalism, by the more or less unanimous agreement of scholars, became widespread, first in Europe and then in the rest of the world (see e.g. Hobsbawm 1992; Zimmer 2003). The English nation, in other words, like the bourgeoisie, is, it seems, always rising, if not always there (Black 1994: 91).

What are we to make of all these claims? How do we adjudicate them? What are their bases, and how do they relate to any general criteria we might lay down for the recognition of nationhood? It is not possible here to examine these claims in detail,[5] but some general observations might help us to assess them, and point us towards a plausible resolution.

Understanding the nation in time

The question, 'When was the English nation?', evidently falls under the more general rubric of nations and nationalism. At what time may we speak, with any degree of confidence, of 'the English nation', and what would we mean by that? When did the idea of the nation emerge, and to what extent does England conform to the general pattern? Can there be 'nations before nationalism', that is, the existence of a developed sense of nationhood before the creation, in the nineteenth century, of systematic ideologies of nationalism? Is England an instance of that?

Walter Bagehot, the great Victorian journalist and author of *The English Constitution* (1867), thought that nations are 'as old as history' (in Billig 1995: 26). This perhaps reflects the conviction and confidence of the age of nationalism. For many nineteenth-century people, nations were indeed natural, the primary and persisting units of political and social organisation that had existed time out of mind. These days we might call them 'primordialists' or 'perennialists'. They are opposed by the 'modernists', who think that nations are recent inventions, linked to the great modern developments symbolised by the French and Industrial Revolutions. One implication of the modernist view is that both the invention of nations and the ideology of nationalism occur in the same period and are, indeed, inextricably connected, since 'it is nationalism which engenders nations, and not the other way round' (Gellner 1983: 55). On this view, nations have no meaning, and perhaps no existence, outside their construction within an ideology of nationalism. Therefore there cannot be, strictly speaking, nations before nationalism.[6]

Anthony D. Smith [Chapter 10, this volume] proposes an 'ethno-symbolic' approach which avoids the ahistoricism of the perennialist approach – nations have always been and always will be – and the almost equally ahistorical view of the modernists that nations spring more or less full-blown from the processes of modernisation in the late eighteenth and nineteenth centuries [as Gellner (1998: 90–101) engagingly put it, most nations do not have or need navels]. Against these, Smith argues for a historical understanding of the development of nationhood in time and over time. Nations, he claims, emerge at different times and places, building upon the 'symbols, memories, myths and values' of long-existing *ethnies* or ethnic communities. Not only, then, can we separate *ethnies* from nations – unlike the perennialists, who conflate them, and the modernists, who regard ethnicity as more or less irrelevant to nationhood. We can also investigate the times and conditions in which *ethnies* take on the full trappings of nationhood, adding to their symbolic core such features as 'territorialisation' (the occupation by the majority of a historic homeland), the dissemination of a public culture, and the standardisation of laws and customs among members of the community.

This is an attractive proposal, which has the advantage not only of making sense of the various sightings of nations in the pre-modern period but also of separating the appearance of nations from the rise of nationalism as an ideology. There can be and have been, in other words, nations before nationalism, though Smith is suitably cautious about seeing this to any great extent before the fifteenth and sixteenth centuries (see also Smith 2003: 118–119). This more flexible approach puts Smith close to the equally persuasive view of Philip Gorski that nationalism itself is a more varied phenomenon than we like to admit, and that this means that the search for some unitary cause or origin, in the manner of the modernists, is likely to be fruitless:

> Nationalism does not have an origin or a single history; it has a genealogy, a ruptured and fragmented history whose only unity lies in the national category itself. Nationalism is not something that happened at a particular time and place; it is something that happens in many places and times, and in many different ways.
>
> (Gorski 2000: 1462; cf. Connor 1994: 219; Smith 2002: 12–14)

Disputes about nationalism, its origins and meaning, turn in most cases on differences in the understanding of that vexatious concept, the nation. Where one person sees a nation, another sees at best an *ethnie* or perhaps no more than a political community with a loosely defined ethnic component. There is probably broad general agreement, though, that a minimum definition of a nation would include some sense of shared membership, some idea of a common culture linking all members more or less equally such that all felt they were participants in the community. This does not mean that democracy in any formal sense is a condition of nationhood – that would make nations and nationalism very late developments indeed, later than most modernists accept. But it may mean that we must accept that some kind of populism is to be found at the heart of the national idea, some sense that rulers and ruled partake of the same 'national soul'.[7]

This, admittedly, is to be influenced by late eighteenth- and nineteenth-century concepts of the nation. But can we – perennialists, modernists, ethno-symbolists alike – avoid that? Was it not only in that period that the idea of the nation first came under scrutiny and achieved its most searching examination? Even those who are most convinced that there are nations before nationalism have to work with some definition of the nation, and it would be strange if that definition varied greatly from the classical definitions achieved in the nineteenth century. There is an inescapable irony here, that the prophets of nations before nationalism have to work with a concept of the nation elaborated most fully in nineteenth-century nationalism.[8]

But one consequence of accepting this situation is that it does put some very great obstacles in the way of those who want to see nations in the medieval or early modern period. If some kind of horizontal, populist solidarity is, in principle at least, a condition of nationhood, how likely are we to find it in societies in which monarchy, aristocracy and church hold sway? Democratic ideas did gain some kind of currency at various times – during the seventeenth-century English Civil War, for instance. But in England as well as elsewhere they went under-ground for a century or more before resurfacing in the American and French Revolutions. At most other times prior to the eighteenth century, the general principle of European society was hierarchy and difference – a principle to be found not only in society but also, as a God-given and God-sanctioned fact, in nature, as symbolised in the idea of 'the Great Chain of Being'. Royalty and even aristocracy could on occasions attempt to annex the national idea, as David Bell (2003) shows in the case of kings and *parlements* in eighteenth-century France. But in principle there was an irreducible opposition between the hierarchical principle of monarchy and aristocracy – supported in most instances by the Church – and the fundamentally egalitarian aspiration of the nation. If we take seriously the idea that nations and nationalism are mass, not elite phenomena, it is really difficult to argue for their rise in any significant way before the nineteenth cen-tury – perhaps even the late nineteenth century (see Hobsbawm 1984, 1992: 101–130; Englund 1992; Connor 1994: 224; Zimmer 2003: 27–49).

The imperial nation

Such general considerations must obviously affect our understanding of the par-ticular case of the English nation, not to mention that curious and elusive, almost un-English entity, English nationalism. Historians, like everyone else, respond to the *Zeitgeist*. British historians have not been immune to the great burgeoning of interest in nations and nationalism that has been such a marked feature of the intellectual scene over the past two decades. This has not been so surprising in the case, say, of Scottish or Irish historians, reflecting a long period of concern by Scots and Irish of English domination of the British Isles, but it has been suf-ficiently unusual among English historians to be the cause for public notice and comment.[9] Works such as Linda Colley's *Britons* (1992) and Norman Davies' *The Isles* (1999) have attracted attention and debate well beyond the scholarly community.

Not only has there been a renewed interest in nationalism among English historians and historically minded sociologists. Even more remarkable has been the rise of what we can only call a school of English nationalist historiography. It is they – scholars such as Patrick Wormald and Geoffrey Elton – who have made the claims for the early development of the English nation that we noted earlier. What makes their contributions noteworthy is the fact that English scholars have a long-standing indifference to questions of English nationalism, based on the conviction that there really is no such thing. 'English nationalism,' says Hugh Seton-Watson, 'never existed, since there was no need for either a doctrine or an independence struggle' (1977: 34); and John Breuilly remarks on 'the absence of any distinctive English nationalist ideology' (1993: 87; see also Kumar 2003: 18–21). Presumably the rise of an English nationalist historiography, matching that of almost all of England's continental neighbours, reflects the sense that there is now a need for a clear statement of English national identity. In a period in which the United Kingdom has come under intense pressure from nationalist movements in the 'Celtic' lands, and in which substantial devolution has been granted to Wales, Scotland and Northern Ireland, it has occurred to many of the English that they too need a national story to tell, and an English nation to define. Combined with concern about the integration of a significant immigrant population, the attempts to create a European identity to match and perhaps surpass national ones, and a general sense of a loss of power and influence in the world, it is hardly surprising that English nationalism, perhaps for the first time ever, now shows a distinct presence in English political life. Put another way, we might say that England is at last becoming a normal nation, a nation like others, at least in the West.[10]

If so, it has been a long haul. 'At what point in its development' asks Walker Connor (1994: 223), 'does a nation come into being?' In the English case, not only might we be tempted to say, 'not yet', but we are faced with a series of complexities and perplexities that makes the dating of English national consciousness unusually if not uniquely difficult. A familiar problem, though no easier to resolve, is the English–British elision and conflation (Langlands 1999). How to separate English and British developments, when for the English at least the confusion is so total, and so disarmingly admitted, as to render the distinction of identities virtually impossible (Condor 1996)? The Scots, Welsh and Irish do not have the same problem, certainly not to the same degree. This is because they have seen themselves, at various times and in various ways, as the victims of English aggression and imperial ambition. Their sense of themselves as Scottish or Irish has been formed to a considerable extent by their opposition to the English.

The problem for the English is the opposite. Insofar as they have a sense of themselves, it is as an imperial nation – in relation to their Celtic neighbours as much as to non-Europeans (Kumar 2003). The English were the creators of two different kinds of empire, each with its characteristic effect on English self-conceptions. They first built up an 'inner empire', what contemporaries as late as the eighteenth century called 'the empire of Great Britain'. This was a land empire, one created, as in the case of the Ottoman and Russian empires, by the expansion of imperial power into adjacent lands. Starting with the Norman Conquest, and continuing particularly under Henry II and Edward I, the English conquered Wales and Ireland and came within an ace of conquering Scotland. While Wales was comprehensively 'Englished', the Irish conquest remained patchy and incomplete until the more brutal conquest and colonisation of the seventeenth century; while it took a parliamentary union with the Scots in 1707 to pressure them into a united kingdom. Nevertheless, with the formal incorporation of Ireland in 1801, the 'British empire in Europe' – another contemporary term – was complete. Although this does not in several respects fit the 'internal colonialism' model proposed by Michael Hechter (1999) – partly because the Celtic regions shared in the spoils of the second, overseas, empire – there is no doubt of England's hegemonic position in that empire.

Imperial nations, especially in the case of land empires, have to be particularly careful about nationalism – their own, that is. As the dominant nation, they have to be sensitive to the susceptibilities of the subject peoples. They must not beat their own drum too loudly, or they are likely to find a threatening echo in the nationalist drums of their various subjects. Their rule is likely to be more efficient, and to last longer, if they play down their own nationalism, their own sense of themselves as the imperial power. Thus the Ottomans were quite content to take Christians, in large numbers, into the imperial bureaucracy, to the point where the Anatolian Turks – putatively the dominant people – could feel themselves discriminated against. So too could Russians, both in the Tsarist and the Soviet empires, feel some resentment as their rulers, in pursuit of the goals of Orthodoxy or communism, neglected or downplayed purely Russian interests while stimulating the cultures of non-Russian peoples and giving them a considerable role in imperial governance. The point at which Turks and Russians, in the late nineteenth century, began to flex their nationalist muscles was the point at which their respective empires revealed their weakness; it proved indeed to be the prelude to imperial extinction, though the Russians found a new imperial cause and inaugurated a new empire.[11]

The English were only following this politic pattern in their studied disavowal of official displays of English nationalism: allowing themselves, for instance, since medieval times, to be ruled by Welsh and Scottish, not to mention German, kings and queens; lacking their own distinctively named national cultural institutions, while allowing the Scots and Welsh to flaunt their own national museums and national galleries; even, in recent years, granting the Scots, the Welsh and the Northern Irish their own parliaments and national assemblies while resisting calls for a comparable English one. The English even, until very recently, lacked their own patron saint and flag. The Scots had St Andrew, the Irish St Patrick, the Welsh St David, with flags to match which were proudly displayed on festive and ceremonial occasions. The English made do with the Union Jack, in most cases unaware that this was not an English flag at all but an invention of James I in pursuit of his British dream. Only in recent years, with the growth of English nationalism, has there been the rediscovery of St George and the St George's Cross as English emblems, now seen in their thousands on the terraces at international football matches.

English indifference and even antagonism towards nationalism, at least on the part of rulers and elites, could be said in the early modern period to be shared by most of Europe's ruling dynasties, especially those who conceived of themselves in imperial terms. For what could be more contradictory than the principles of nation and empire? But there is a sense in which we may say that, though not fitting the standard models of nationalism very well, and perhaps in the end not even deserving of the name, imperial peoples do develop a form of self-consciousness and self-identity that we might call 'imperial nationalism'. Since this is generally tied to the putative 'mission' of empire, I have proposed elsewhere the alternative designation 'missionary nationalism' (Kumar 2000, 2003: 30–35; see also Smith 2003: 95–130). This suffers from a number of drawbacks, one major one being that it applies to empires that existed for centuries before the coming of nationalist ideologies proper in the nineteenth century. It may indeed be applied to what we might think of as the *ur*-instance of missionary nationalism, that of Rome from the first to the fourth centuries AD. It was Rome, both in its pagan and its Christian form, that gave to Europe the model of 'the civilising mission'; it was Rome that pioneered the policies of extending equal citizenship to all its subject peoples, and of suppressing its own identity, and that of Italians in general, as it converted itself into a 'world empire' with a world mission (see Pagden 1995: 11–28).

Nevertheless, suitably understood, the concept of missionary nationalism does seem to be a reasonably satisfying way of describing the self-conceptions of imperial peoples such as English and Russians. It has the advantage above all of highlighting the most characteristic feature of such a collective identity, which is the displacement of attention from the people – the 'nation' – to the mission or cause, be it Islam, Orthodoxy, Catholicism, Protestantinism or simply *la mission civilisatrice*, the form it took in the nineteenth century when religious goals lost their former importance. Missionary nationalism is the nationalism of people who have more to celebrate than merely themselves. It gives to such people a goal or purpose from which they derive their place in the world. This is far from conducive to modesty. But it does generally entail a disposition, born of a statesmanlike prudence, not to insist too stridently on the character and virtues of the people who know themselves to be the principal 'carriers' of the imperial mission.

The English recognised this in the case of their 'inner' land empire, perhaps more in later centuries than in earlier ones, when the tendency to stereotype and belittle their Celtic neighbours achieved something resembling a racist dimension (Gillingham 2000; Jones 1971). But they had an additional cause to do so as the builders of a second, worldwide, 'outer' empire, the more familiar overseas empire of Great Britain. Here was truly a missionary enterprise, no less than to spread what were seen as the benefits and blessings of English civilisation to every corner of the globe. At the height of its power, the British empire occupied more than one-fifth of the world's land mass and controlled a quarter of the world's population – the largest empire the world had ever seen (Barraclough 1978: 245).[12]

But this was indeed the *British* empire, to a far greater extent than the 'empire of Great Britain in Europe'. All parts of the United Kingdom participated in imperial rule, Scots, Welsh and Irish as much as English. Indeed, it has often been claimed that the Celtic nations, especially the Scots, did disproportionately well out of the overseas empire (Colley 1992, chs 3–4; Kumar 2003: 165–172). There was thus even less reason to stress English management of the empire, despite England's undoubted historic role in laying its foundations. With the obvious exception of the Irish Catholics – who showed their feeling by leaving the United Kingdom in 1921 – a common Protestantism linked all the peoples of Britain, giving them a common cause to promote at home and abroad. Later there was the British Industrial Revolution, and Britain's rise to worldwide industrial supremacy. Again this was a joint enterprise, in which merchants, industrialists, entrepreneurs and engineers from all parts of the isles played their part. English money may have oiled the works, but some of the most famous names – James Watt, Thomas Telford, John Macadam, Thomas Lipton – were Scottish. In the imperial army and police, the Irish – including Irish Catholics – and Scots were prominent in all ranks. Scottish missionaries and educators, such as David Livingstone and Mary Slessor, spread over the entire empire.

All these developments militated against a stress on Englishness and English national identity. The monarchy under Queen Victoria was encouraged to establish Scottish roots, a task to which Victoria and Albert took enthusiastically; statesmen such as Gladstone stressed their Scottish and Welsh connections; the Irish Wellesley brothers, above all the great Duke of Wellington, became national heroes – but of a decidedly British, not English, stamp. The empire in particular did much to establish an overarching British identity which, without suppressing consciousness of the differences between English, Welsh, Scottish and Irish, did much to mitigate them. This applied in particular to the role of the English. As Linda Colley says, 'if Britain's primary identity was to be an imperial one, then the English were put firmly and forever in their place, reduced to a component part of a much greater whole . . . and no longer the people who ran virtually the whole show' (1992: 130).

The relations between the English and the non-European components of the empire were naturally somewhat different. There was no question of admitting Indians, Africans, Burmese, Chinese and others on an equal footing with the British. But even here the missionary character of empire – with the due degree of hypocrisy – could lead to a playing down of ethnic or national superiority. This was especially aided by the fact that the British, unlike, say, the French, made little attempt to integrate the empire into the fabric of national politics. British imperial rule was to a large extent indirect, relying on the authority and leadership of native rulers. The official policy always remained that of preparing the colonies for eventual independence and self-rule. The role of the imperial ruler was tutelary (Mehta 1999). The civilising mission consisted in the spread of education, science, law and parliamentary government. Inevitably these would have an English or British inflection (Gikandi 1996; Viswanathan 1990). But, with some exceptions – Macaulay's notorious Minute on Education of 1835 being one[13] – the English drew back from the idea that they were imposing Englishness on the native populations and undermining native cultures. British missionaries, scholars and administrators in fact took the lead in the unearthing – sometimes literally – and the preservation of native cultures. There was indeed pride in the empire; but the pride resembled more that of craftsmen and architects in their creations than any kind of self-regarding ethnic or national pride.

With the end of empire in the 1950s and 1960s, along with the end of British industrial supremacy and generally of Britain's position as a world power, the whole British synthesis unravelled (McCrone 1997). The causes for which the two empires, inner and outer, stood – Protestantism, industrialism, Western civilisation – no longer made sense, or were taken up by others, notably the Americans. The British were thrown back upon themselves, one response being the revival of Scottish, Welsh and Irish nationalism. The protective layers that had cocooned the English, allowing them to regard nationalism as an alien force, inimical to the English way, fell away. The English were now forced to confront the question of their own national identity – and they did so without the benefit of any tradition of reflection on the matter.

Reluctant nationalists

English antipathy to nationalism is a well known and much commented on characteristic, from David Hume to George Orwell (Kumar 2003: 18–21). It may even be, as Hume was the first to suggest, that this antipathy in itself constitutes a central element of the English national character.[14] What is clear at any rate is that it reflects a central fact of English history. At the very time when nationalism was becoming one of the most powerful of European ideologies, the English found themselves governing the largest empire the world had ever seen. This, together with their experience as the superintendents of the British Isles, left them with an attitude of indifference towards nationalism. Nationalism was for other, (lesser), peoples. If they considered it at all, it was as a threat to the imperial system, whether in the United Kingdom or overseas. Engaged on what they considered more important and more pressing enterprises, the English had neither the time nor the interest to reflect on themselves as a nation.

It is this that gives such an air of implausibility to recent – and not so recent – claims to have found a strong English national consciousness, and even a vibrant English nationalism, at various points from the eight to the eighteenth centuries. On general grounds alone, as suggested earlier, we would have reason to be suspicious of these claims for an early English nationalism. There may be, to use Anthony D. Smith's distinction, a case for speaking of an English *ethnie* in these years but not an English nation. When we add to these general considerations England's own distinctive history as an imperial power since the Middle Ages, we have even more reason to be sceptical. Neither Bede's nor Chaucer's nor Shakespeare's England show either the need or the existence of a strong English nationalist consciousness (Kumar 2003, *passim*). No more does Johnson's England, the England of the eighteenth century, when ideas of nationhood were certainly being discussed in European societies. But this was also the time when England was consolidating its hold over the British Isles, and recommencing its imperial ventures overseas after the loss of the North American colonies. From the English point of view, the time could scarcely have been less propitious for raising the flag of English nationalism.

It is, as I have argued in detail elsewhere (Kumar 2003: ch. 7), not before the late nineteenth century that we first begin to discern the rise of anything that we can properly call an English national consciousness. Again, the causes may be seen as both general and particular. Generally, this is the period at which nationalism began to penetrate deeply into the consciousness of European societies. Every people, it was felt, had a 'national soul', the protection, strengthening and cultivation of which was a moral duty. Throughout the European continent, from West to East, intellectuals and statesmen set about discovering and, if necessary, inventing, such a national identity for their people. Moreover, unlike the more political or civic concept of nationhood that generally held sway in the first half of the nineteenth century, the popular nationalism of the second half was more distinctly ethnic and cultural. The soul of a nation was seen to lie essentially in its language, its religion, its musical and artistic culture, its folkways and folklore (Hobsbawm 1992: 101–130).

The British Isles were not immune from these currents, as is evident from the rise of Irish, Scottish and Welsh nationalism at this time. So too the English, spurred in part by nationalism in other parts of Britain, began to reflect on themselves as a distinct people. But there was an additional, more particular reason for this new-found self-consciousness on the part of the English. The late nineteenth and early twentieth centuries may be regarded, in one guise, as the high point of the British empire, certainly if we consider the scale of territorial expansion and the zealous promotion of official symbols and ceremonials, such as the great imperial jubilees and coronations of 1887, 1897 and 1901, and George V's Delhi Durbar of 1911. But, in another guise, it was also an age which saw the beginnings of a great anxiety about empire, a sense that, like Rome of old, the signs were showing of weakness and decadence. Certainly this was the mood of Rudyard Kipling's great poem 'Recessional' (1897), with its theme of the passing of glory and greatness (Cannadine 1984: 125, 2001: 106–112).

This too added to the new mood of sobriety and self-reflection. It seemed to require a searching of the national conscience, and of the national past, in the effort to discover and define what constituted England's true essence, what were the springs of national greatness – and perhaps, too, national failings. I have called this movement a 'moment of Englishness', to distinguish it from the more full-blooded nationalism that was developing elsewhere (Kumar 2003: 175). For if this was nationalism it was of a severely limited kind. The imperial and the British identities remained powerful and perhaps still ascendant. There was no talk of an independent English nation, distinct from the Scots, Welsh and Irish. There was no movement for 'English Home Rule'. What there was, however, was an attempt to define a certain cultural Englishness; and if this was tinged, as it sometimes was, with racial Anglo-Saxonism, this was not so much an expression of English nationalism – after all, Anglo-Saxonism encompassed the whole English-speaking world, including America – as an attempt to express what were thought to be characteristically English attitudes and values.

English thinkers and artists during these years discovered 'the Whig interpretation' of English history, the view that the English had had a peculiarly blessed history, allowing them to avoid the frequent civil upheavals of the French, for instance, and to progress by peaceful and orderly means towards parliamentary liberty. Complementing this was what Stefan Collini (1993) has aptly called 'the Whig interpretation of English literature'. English literary critics and historians canonised their men of letters, arguing for a great and glorious tradition of writing from Chaucer to the Romantics and beyond which expressed certain distinctively English values of sincerity, individuality, diversity and concreteness. Similar features, with the stress on empircism and pragmatism, were also seen to characterise English philosophy (thus enthroning utilitarianism as the national philosophy, to the detriment of the great early English metaphysical tradition) (Easthope 1999: 61–114). The English language itself was cleaned up and stand-ardised, as expressed in that 'great national project', the *Oxford English Dictionary on Historical Principles*, in the terms conceived by its founder James Murray (a Scot). In a series of influential books and reports, the teaching of English in the schools and universities was urged as the most efficacious way of instilling a sense of national consciousness in the young. 'Our language and literature,' said the Newbolt Report of 1921, 'are as great a source of pride and may be made as great a bond of national unity to us as those of France are, and have long been, to the French' (in Collini 1993: 366).

Poets, novelists, folklorists, musicians, architects and town planners made their equally important contributions to this moment of Englishness. A distinctive English musical tradition, drawing especially on the Elizabethan legacy, was elab-orated by composers such as Vaughan Williams, Delius, Holst and Elgar. Tudor was also largely the inspiration for the new 'vernacular' domestic architecture of E.F. Voysey and the Edwin Lutyens. Cecil Sharp and others embarked on the great enterprise to collect and record English folk music. Folklorists and musicians as well as town planners, with their new 'garden cities', frequently evoked the English countryside; and it was the countryside – particularly in its southern aspect – that was perhaps the central symbol of the new Englishness which was being discovered and defined in these years. 'England has become a garden', says Old Hammond in William Morris' utopian novel *News from Nowhere* (1890); and Morris' utopian vision of the southern English countryside was projected by a score of English writers and publicists of the period – even when, as in the novels of Thomas Hardy, a much darker vision was intimated by the authors themselves. Stanley Baldwin's passionate credo of 1924, 'to me, England is the country, and the country is England' (Baldwin 1926: 6), drew deeply on this wellspring of feeling for the English countryside that was cultivated so intensively in the previous decades.[15]

The vision of England created in the period from the 1880s to the 1920s has indeed been astonishingly long-lasting. It was powerfully evoked in the interwar period, when its nostalgic, backward-looking aspect seems to have particularly appealed to a generation traumatised by the horrors of the First World War (Light 1991). A.L. Morton called upon it in his popular travel book, *In Search of England* (1927), as did Joseph Priestley in his anti-industrial *English Journey* (1934). It con-tinued to serve in another World War with much the same therapeutic effect, as George Orwell noted while himself making use of it in his famous evocation of

England, *The Lion and the Unicorn* (1941). As late as the 1990s a Conservative Prime Minister, John Major, could still turn to it for his statement of the 'unamendable essentials' of Britain (*sic*) as 'a country of long shadows on county grounds, warm beer, invincible green suburbs, dog lovers and pools fillers and – as George Orwell said – "old maids cycling to Holy Communion through the morning mist" ' (*Guardian*, 23 April 1993).[16]

The longevity and continuity of this image of England is a tribute to the creativity of the artists and writers of the decades on either side of the First World War. It is also of course deeply problematic, insofar as it does not seem to equip the English particularly well in dealing with the demands of Europeanisation, globalisation, and the possible break up of the United Kingdom. It seems to ignore the experiences and concerns of large sections of the English population – women, especially working women, the urban working class, the new immigrant populations, the cosmopolitan young. While it may still appeal to those groups, vocal but relatively small in numbers, who wish to turn their backs on Europe and the wider world, it is unlikely to provide much of a guide for those in search of an England for the twenty-first century.

The trouble for the English is that this image is practically all they have. There have been very few attempts to create anything new, and where efforts have been made – as in New Labour's 'Cool Britannia' campaign – the results have usually been embarrassing. At the moment an English nationalism, if it does develop to any great extent, is likely to fall back on a very narrow base made up of selective components drawn from an often remote past and detached from the memories and experiences of the majority of the population. It is an England that is rural or small-town, white, male, middle or upper-middle class, and fearful of change and the challenges of a global, multicultural world. A work such as Roger Scruton's *England: An Elegy* (2001) reflects this vision with eloquence and intelligence, even as the author shows his awareness of its passing and the near-impossibility of reviving it.

The crisis of English national identity in the present fairly represents the history of English nationalism. The claims for its 'precocity', at any time from the eighth to the eighteenth centuries, are unbelievable both on comparative grounds – there seem to be no other instances of such early expressions of nationalism – and on the basis of England's own history as an imperial power, with every reason to discourage English nationalism. In earlier centuries – up to the fifteenth and beyond – English rulers engaged in the common European practice of creating empires and extending dynastic power within the whole continent (Bartlett 1994). Norman and Plantagenet kings swept beyond England into Wales, Scotland and Ireland. They competed for power with the kings of France, rightly seeing themselves as having equal claims to many French territories and indeed to the French crown itself. Only in the sixteenth century, with the loss of Calais, did English monarchs finally give up effective claims to France, though they continued to bear the French title right up to 1801. The early Hanoverians, like the Stuarts and 'Dutch William' before them, continued the continental interest and involvement; only with George III do we find anyone approaching the character of an 'English' king – by which time the monarchy was British and heavily implicated in a world that stretched well beyond England.

This was the second theatre in which English ambitions displayed themselves and which acted as a further restraint on nationalist consciousness of a purely English kind. England became the centre, the metropole, of a worldwide empire with responsibilities and concerns going far beyond the merely national. English nationalism, in such a complex, would have been petty and destructive. English elites were perfectly aware of that and so did almost nothing to stimulate English nationalist feeling. On the contrary, they went the other way and culti-vated British and imperial identities. These did not necessarily override ethnic identities and differences. The English were aware of themselves as a people with their own history and traditions, and if they ever lost sight of that, the Scots, Welsh and Irish were there to remind them of it. In the latter part of the nine-teenth century they went a considerable way towards systematic reflection on Englishness. But not only was this compatible with Britishness and a wider imperial consciousness; it never emerged as a movement of English nationalism on the scale and with the character of nationalist movements elsewhere.

The English have been reluctant nationalists. If they now see a need for nation-alism, they are severely handicapped by the lack of a tradition of reflecting on it. Moreover, they are attempting it in a global context that is vastly different from the period in which nationalism found its fullest expression and achieved its great-est victories. If one were in a position to advise, one might suggest that England would face its future better if it were to remember its historic global outlook.

Notes

1 It is probably worth noting that practically every nation with a Judaeo-Christian back-ground – starting of course with the Jews themselves – has seen itself at one time or another as an 'elect nation' or a 'chosen people', covenanted with God to fulfil his purpose in the world (see Gorski 2000; Smith 2003). There is nothing special about the English in this regard, which does not of course mean that they themselves may not feel that there is. But it does throw into question the idea – as advanced, for example, by Greenfeld (1992) – that this belief is what most qualifies the English to be seen as the inventors of nationalism. See further Kumar (2003: 108–114).

2 Cf. A.R. Humphreys: 'In a general sense, England is the hero of all the histories; Shakespeare writes of his country's fate. This is especially so in *Henry V* ('Introduction' to *Henry V*, in Shakespeare 1994: 672). But, as Humphreys himself indicates, the royal and dynastic character of the struggles chronicled makes the histories more – or less – than nationalist epics.

3 Baker and Maley remark on the 'iconic texts – "Shakespeare" – that were and are implicated in a hegemonic "Englishness" ' (2002b: 7). For some recent commentaries on Shakespeare, challenging especially the conventionally attributed attitudes on national-ism, ethnicity, patriotism, monarchy and so on, see Baker and Maley (2002a); Dollimore and Sinfield, (1985, 1986); Floyd-Wilson (2002); Greenfeld (2002); Holderness (1991: 81–91); Jordan (1997); Joughin (1997); Kastan (1982, 1999); McEachern (1996); Marcus (1988); Mikalachki (1995); Neill (1994); Parker (1998, 2002); Rackin (1990). On the film versions of *Henry V*, showing the radically different possibilities of interpret-ation, see Lewis (1995). On changing visions of Shakespeare across the centuries, see

Taylor (1991). The celebrations of the tercentenary of Shakespeare's death in 1916, occurring as it did in the midst of a World War which involved much of the British empire, revealed much about the ambiguities and ambivalences surrounding 'the poet of Englishness' who was at the same time supposed to speak to all peoples, of all times and nations. The standard resolution seemed to be to link Shakespeare to (the British) empire and so to the world at large. See Kahn (2001).

4 Claims for the medieval origins of English national consciousness – as for Scottish, French, German and even Italian national consciousness – were indeed common among a much earlier generation of historians, such as Marc Bloch, Johan Huizinga, and George Coulton, as Walker Connor (1994: 211–212) reminds us. A particularly favourite example was the Scottish Declaration of Arbroath (1320), as an early example of Scottish nationalism.

5 I have attempted this in Kumar (2003). See also John Breuilly's (2005) forthcoming essay, which examines especially the claims of the medievalists and early modernists. For a different view, see Smith (2002: 12–14).

6 For 'primordialism', 'perennialism' and 'modernism', see the chapters by Breuilly, Grosby and Smith in this volume. See also Smith (1998, 2002), Breuilly (1996), Zimmer (2003: 4–26).

7 See Nairn (2003: 89–90). And cf. Connnor (1994: 223): 'National consciousness is a mass, not an elite phenomenon'. For a questioning of this view, see Smith (2002: 9–12). Smith argues that 'nationalism may be described as a mass phenomenon . . . but there is no reason why the object of its endeavours, the *nation*, must also be constituted as a mass phenomenon' (2002: 10; emphasis in original). This brings us back to the possibility of 'nations before nationalism'. No one would deny that the language of nationhood pre-dates nationalism; the difficulty in almost all cases is knowing what to make of the notion of nation that is thereby invoked, especially as that varies so much as between, say, the 'nations' of medieval universities and the nation appealed to by *ancien régime* French kings or – differently again – *parlements*. While one cannot legislate on these matters, and there are indeed, as Ernest Gellner often conceded, ambiguous cases, it seems preferable to regard the modern idea of the nation as deriving from, if not entirely tied to, the discourse of nationalism that developed around the time of the French Revolution. This gives us a historical benchmark, a *terminus post quem*, which allows us to examine any particular earlier usage in the light of, and according to the understanding of, the full definition of nationhood as achieved in the language of nineteenth-century nationalism. With the relevant changes, the same could apply to the concept of 'national consciousness' – *in principle* a mass concept, if not always so in practice. If one wants to use it in relation to phenomena earlier than the advent of nationalism – say, of the English people at the time of the Spanish Armada, or of the Dutch at the time of the revolt against Spain – one would have to specify in what ways and to what extent it matched up to the later and more clearly recognisable expressions of national consciousness. The logic of this would be the familiar one of 'from the known to the less known'.

8 Pierre Nora speaks of the 'invincible tautology: one explains the nation by the nation . . . without ever breaking out of the circle and grasping the thing from without' (in Englund 1992: 316).

9 See, for instance, the correspondence in *The Times Literary Supplement* in March–April 2004.

10 See, on these developments, Kumar (2003: 239–273). From what is now a relatively large literature attempting to state the character of the English nation past and present, two good examples are Paxman (1999) and Scruton (2001).

11 For the Russian and Ottoman empires, and the comparison with the British empire, see Kumar (2000).

12 The Mongol empire of Gengis Khan was larger, but at its greatest extent very loosely integrated and very short-lived.

13 Even here, as Gauri Viswanathan (1990: 144–145) shows, Macaulay's purpose in advocating the English language and English education in India had a purely functional and utilitarian end; it was not meant to promote any idea of English moral or ethnic superiority. In that sense it could be held to be in line with the general British policy of advancement and 'modernisation' in the empire, rather than the promotion of 'Englishness' as a moral or cultural ideal.

14 'The English, of any people in the universe, have the least of a national character; unless this very singularity may pass for such' (Hume [1741] 1987: 207).

15 I have discussed the cultural developments of this period in Kumar (2003: 202–225). On the arts in particular, see Strong (2000: 561–601). John Lucas (1990: 9) makes the relevant point about the anti-industrial, anti-urban character of many of these contributions: 'By the end of the nineteenth century most English people lived in cities. To be English was not to be English'. See also Wiener (1981).

16 The propensity, as here and in many of Margaret Thatcher's speeches, to say Britain when they were really referring to England has been noted by many commentators: see e.g. Billig (1995: 102); Cannadine (1995: 13). This is an ironic reversal of the more common practice among the English of saying 'English' when they mean 'British'.

References

Baker, D.J. and Maley, W. (eds) (2002a) *British Identities and English Renaissance Literature*, Cambridge: Cambridge University Press.

Baker, D.J. and Maley, W. (2002b) 'Introduction: An Uncertain Union?' In Baker and Maley (eds), pp. 1–8.

Baldwin, S. (1926) *On England, and Other Addresses*, London: Philip Allan.

Barraclough, G. (ed.) (1978). *The Times Atlas of World History*, London: Times Books.

Bartlett, R.C. (1994) *The Making of Europe: Conquest, Colonization and Cultural Change 950–1350*, London: Penguin Books.

Bell, D.A. (2003) *The Cult of the Nation in France: Inventing Nationalism, 1680–1800*, Cambridge, MA: Harvard University Press.

Billig, M. (1995) *Banal Nationalism*, London: Sage.

Black, J. (1994) *Convergence or Divergence? Britain and the Continent*, Basingstoke: Macmillan.

Breuilly, J. (1993) *Nationalism and the State* (2nd edn), Chicago, IL: University of Chicago Press.

Breuilly, J. (1996) 'Approaches to Nationalism' in G. Balakrishnan (ed.) *Mapping the Nation*, London and New York: Verso, pp. 146–174.

Breuilly, J. (2005) 'Changes in the Political Uses of the Nation: Continuity or Discontinuity?' in O. Zimmer and L. Scales (eds) *Power and Nation in European History*, Basingstoke: Palgrave.

Campbell, J. (1995) 'The Late Anglo-Saxon State: A Maximum View', *Proceedings of the British Academy* 87: 39–65.

Cannadine, D. (1984) 'The Context, Performance and Meaning of Ritual: The British Monarchy and the "Invention of Tradition"', c. 1820–1977', in E. Hobsbawm and T. Ranger (eds), pp. 101–164.

Cannadine, D. (1995) 'British History as a "New Subject": Politics, Perspectives and Prospects' in A. Grant and K. Stringer (eds) *Uniting the Kingdom? The Making of British History*, London and New York: Routledge, pp. 12–28.

Cannadine, D. (2001) *Ornamentalism: How the British Saw Their Empire*, Oxford: Oxford University Press.

Colley, L. (1992) *Britons: Forging the Nation 1707–1837*, New Haven, CT: Yale University Press.

Collini, S. (1993) 'The Whig Interpretation of English Literature: Literary History and National Identity' in *Public Moralists: Political Thought and Intellectual Life in Britain 1850–1930*, Oxford: Oxford University Press, pp. 342–373.

Condor, S. (1996) 'Unimagined Community? Some Social Psychological Issues Concerning English National Identity' in G.M. Breakwell and E. Lyons (eds) *Changing European Identities: Social Psychological Analyses of Social Change*, Oxford: Butterworth-Heinemann, pp. 41–68.

Connor, W. (1994) 'When is a Nation?', in *Ethnonationalism: The Quest for Understanding*, Princeton, NJ: Princeton University Press, pp. 211–226.

Davies, N. (1999) *The Isles: A History*, New York: Oxford University Press.

Davies, R.R. (2000) *The First English Empire: Power and Identities in the British Isles 1093–1343*, Oxford: Oxford University Press.

Dollimore, J. and Sinfield, A. (eds) (1985) *Political Shakespeare: Essays in Cultural Materialism*, Manchester: Manchester University Press.

Dollimore, J. and Sinfield, A. (1986) 'History and Ideology: The Instance of *Henry V*' in J. Drakakis (ed.) *Alternative Shakespeares*, London: Methuen, pp. 206–227.

Easthope, A. (1999) *Englishness and National Culture*, London and New York: Routledge.

Elton, G. (1992) *The English*, Oxford: Blackwell.

Englund, S. (1992) 'The Ghost of Nation Past', *Journal of Modern History* 64(2): 299–320.

Floyd-Wilson, M. (2002) 'Delving to the Root: *Cymbeline*, Scotland, and the English Race' in Baker and Maley (eds), pp. 101–115.

Gellner, E. (1983) *Nations and Nationalism*, Oxford: Blackwell.

Gellner, E. (1998) *Nationalism*, London: Phoenix.

Gikandi, S. (1996) *Maps of Englishness: Writing Identity in the Culture of Colonialism*, New York: Columbia University Press.

Gillingham, J. (2000) *The English in the Twelfth Century: Imperialism, National Identity and Political Values*, Woodbridge: The Boydell Press.

Greenfeld, L. (1992) *Nationalism: Five Roads to Modernity*, Cambridge, MA: Harvard University Press.

Greenfield, M. (2002) '*1 Henry IV*: Metatheatrical Britain?', in Baker and Maley (eds), pp. 71–80.

Gorski, P. (2000) 'The Mosaic Moment: The Early Modernist Critique of Modernist Theories of Nationalism', *American Journal of Sociology* 105(5): 1428–1468.

Hastings, A. (1997) *The Construction of Nationhood: Ethnicity, Religion and Nationalism*, Cambridge: Cambridge University Press.

Hay, D. (1955–1956) 'The Term "Great Britain" in the Middle Ages', *Proceedings of the Society of Antiquaries of Scotland* 89: 55–66.

Hechter, M. (1999) *Internal Colonialism: The Celtic Fringe in British National Development*, (2nd edn), New Brunswick, NJ: Transaction Books.

Hirst, D. (2002) 'Text, Time, and the Pursuit of British Identity', in Baker and Maley (eds), pp. 256–266.

Hobsbawm, E. (1984) 'Mass-producing Traditions: Europe, 1870–1914', in Hobsbawm and Ranger (eds), pp. 263–307.

Hobsbawm, E. (1992) *Nations and Nationalism Since 1780: Programme, Myth, Reality* (2nd edn), Cambridge: Cambridge University Press.

Hobsbawm, E. and Ranger, T. (eds) (1984) *The Invention of Tradition*, Cambridge: Cambridge University Press.

Holderness, G. (1991) ' "What ish my nation?" Shakespeare and National Identities', *Textual Practice* 5: 74–93.

Hume, D. [1741] (1987) 'Of National Character' in E.F. Miller (ed.) *Essays, Moral, Political, and Literary*, Indianopolis: Liberty Classics.

Jones, W.R. (1971) 'England Against the Celtic Fringe: A Study in Cultural Stereotypes', *Journal of World History* 13: 155–171.

Jordan, C. (1997) *Shakespeare's Monarchies: Ruler and Subject in the Romances*, Ithaca, NY: Cornell University Press.

Joughin, J.J. (ed.) (1997) *Shakespeare and National Culture*, Manchester: Manchester University Press.

Kahn, C. (2001) 'Remembering Shakespeare Imperially: The 1916 Tercentenary', *Shakespeare Quarterly* 52(4): 456–478.

Kastan, D.S. (1982) *Shakespeare and the Shapes of Time*, Hanover, NH: University Press of New England.

Kastan, D.S. (1999) *Shakespeare After Theory*, London: Routledge.

Kohn, H. (1940) 'The Genesis and Character of English Nationalism', *Journal of the History of Ideas* 1: 69–94.

Kumar, K. (2000) 'Nation and Empire: English and British National Identity in Comparative Perspective', *Theory and Society* 29(5): 575–608.

Kumar, K. (2003) *The Making of English National Identity*, Cambridge: Cambridge University Press.

Langlands, R. (1999) 'Britishness of Englishness? The Historical Problem of National Identity in Britain', *Nations and Nationalism* 5(1): 53–69.

Levack, B.P. (1987) *The Formation of the British State: England, Scotland and the Union 1603–1707*, Oxford: Clarendon Press.

Lewis, A. (1995) '*Henry V*: Two Films' in M.C. Carnes (ed.) *Past Imperfect: History According to the Movies*, New York: Henry Holt, pp. 48–53.

Light, A. (1991) *Forever England: Femininity, Literature and Conservatism Between the Wars*, London and New York: Routledge.

Lucas, J. (1990) *England and Englishness: Ideas of Nationhood in English Poetry 1688–1900*, Iowa City: University of Iowa Press.

McCrone, D. (1997) 'Unmasking Britannia: The Rise and Fall of British National Identity', *Nations and Nationalism* 3(4): 579–596.

McEachern, C. (1996) *The Poetics of English Nationhood, 1590–1612*, Cambridge: Cambridge University Press.

Marcus, L. (1988) *Puzzling Shakespeare: Local Reading and Its Discontents*, Berkeley: University of California Press.

Mehta, U.S. (1999) *Liberalism and Empire: A Study in Nineteenth-century British Liberal Thought*, Chicago, IL, and London: University of Chicago Press.

Mikalachki, J. (1995) 'The Masculine Romance of Roman Britain: *Cymbeline* and Early Modern English Nationalism', *Shakespeare Quarterly* 46(3): 301–322.

Nairn, T. (2003) *The Break-up of Britain: Crisis and Neo-Nationalism* (3rd, expanded, edn), Altona, Victoria: Common Ground Publishing.

Neil, M. (1994) 'Broken English and Broken Irish: Nation, Language, and the Optic of Power in Shakespeare's Histories', *Shakespeare Quarterly* 45(1): 1–32.

Newman, G. (1987) *The Rise of English Nationalism: A Cultural History 1740–1830*, London: Weidenfeld & Nicolson.

Pagden, A. (1995) *Lords of All the World: Ideologies of Empire in Spain, Britain and France, c. 1500–c. 1800*, New Haven, CT, and London: Yale University Press.

Parker, P. (1998) *Shakespeare from the Margins: Language, Culture, Context*, Chicago, IL: University of Chicago Press.

Parker, P. (2002) 'Uncertain Unions: Welsh Leeks in *Henry V*' in Baker and Maley (eds), pp. 81–100.

Paxman, J. (1999) *The English: A Portrait of a People*, London: Penguin Books.

Pollard, A.F. (1907) *Factors in Modern History*, New York: G.P. Putnam.

Rackin, P. (1990) *Stages of History: Shakespeare's English Chronicles*, Ithaca, NY: Cornell University Press.

Scruton, R. (2001) *England: An Elegy*, London: Pimlico.

Seton-Watson, H. (1977) *Nations and States: An Inquiry into the Origins of Nations and the Politics of Nationalism*, London: Methuen.

Shakespeare, W. (1994) *Four Histories: Richard II, Henry IV Part 1, Henry IV Part 2, Henry V*, London: Penguin Books.

Smith, A.D. (1998) *Nationalism and Modernism: A Critical Survey of Recent Theories of Nations and Nationalism*, London and New York: Routledge.

Smith, A.D. (2002) 'When is a Nation?', *Geopolitics* 7(2): 5–32.

Smith, A.D. (2003) *Chosen Peoples: Sacred Sources of National Identity*, Oxford: Oxford University Press.

Strong, R. (2000) *The Spirit of Britain: A Narrative History of the Arts*, New York: Fromm International.

Taylor, G. (1991) *Reinventing Shakespeare: A Cultural History from the Restoration to the Present*, Oxford: Oxford University Press.

Viswanathan, G. (1990) *Masks of Conquest: Literary Study and British Rule in India*, London: Faber and Faber.

Wiener, M.J. (1981) *English Culture and the Decline of the Industrial Spirit 1850–1980*, Cambridge: Cambridge University Press.

Williamson, A.H. (1983) 'Scotland, Antichrist and the Invention of Britain', in J. Dwyer, R.A. Mason and A. Murdoch (eds) *New Perspectives on the Politics and Culture of Early Modern Scotland*, Edinburgh: John Donald Publishers, pp. 34–58.

Wormald, J. (1992) 'The Creation of Britain: Multiple Kingdoms or Core and Colonies?', *Transactions of the Royal Historical Society* (6th series) 2: 175–194.

Wormald, P. (1994) '*Engla Lond*: The Making of an Allegiance', *Journal of Historical Sociology* 7(1): 1–24.

Wormald, P. (2001) 'The Eternal Angle', *The Times Literary Supplement*, 16 March: 3.

Zimmer, O. (2003) *Nationalism in Europe, 1890–1940*, Basingstoke: Palgrave Macmillan.

8 When was the first new nation?

Locating America in a national context

Susan-Mary Grant

Citizens, by birth or choice, of a common country, that country has a right to concentrate your affections. The name of 'American,' which belongs to you, in your national capacity, must always exalt the just pride of patriotism, more than any appellation derived from local distinctions.

(George Washington's *Farewell Address*, 1796)

A Nation is born.

(Charles Sumner, 1867)

. . . the ones who crossed the ocean, who brought with us to America the villages of Russia and Lithuania . . . how we struggled, and how we fought, for the family, for the Jewish home, so that you would not grow up *here*, in this strange place, in the melting pot where nothing melted. . . . You do not live in America. No such place exists.

(Tony Kushner, *Angels in America*, 1992)

Introduction

Does America represent 'the first new nation'? The phrase is Seymour Martin Lipset's, but the driving force behind it lies in America's apparently unique development, in its birth as a modern nation at the dawn of the modern age, the only nation, according to America's most famous visitor, Alexis de Tocqueville, 'in which it has been possible to witness the natural and tranquil growth of society' from its inception. American author Henry James once observed that '[t]here is no doubt that nothing could be well more characteristic of our nationality than the sight of a group of persons more or less earnestly discussing it. We are the only people,' he continued, 'with whom such a question can be in the least what the French call an actuality.' Americans, however, have to date been debating their nationality in something of a scholarly vacuum, since this 'first new nation' remains notable by its absence from studies of nationalism. In the American case, indeed, the question more often revolves around whether there ever was, or is, any such entity as the American nation, making any further query as to when this might have emerged somewhat redundant. Although some attempt has been made to review American nationalism in the light of much of the work done in recent years by Eric Hobsbawm, Ernest Gellner, Walker Connor and, of course, Anthony D. Smith, America remains an awkward element in the scholarship, too frequently receiving only a cursory mention. America, it seems, does not readily fit into any of the main theoretical frameworks of nationalism studies.[1]

Modernists such as Benedict Anderson acknowledge the radical break with the past that America *qua* nation represented at the instant of its conception, but those elements that encouraged and reflected the development of a coherent national identity over time have proved rather more elusive (Anderson 1992: 192–193). The perennialist approach, such as that taken by Connor, perceives America's immigrant origins as a barrier to nationalism, certainly to 'instinctive' nationalism. Does this mean, however, that, as Conner has argued, Americans 'are not a nation in the pristine sense of the word'? (Connor 1978: 381). Approaching the subject from a rather different intellectual perspective – and writing about a rather different nation – the historian Linda Colley took issue with 'those who are accustomed to thinking of nations only as historic phenomena characterised by cultural and ethnic homogeneity'. By restricting the definition of a nation in this way, she observed, 'we shall find precious few of them available in the world either to study or to live in'. Most nations, she argued, 'have always been culturally and ethnically diverse, problematic, protean and artificial constructs that take shape very quickly and come apart just as fast'. On those grounds, she averred, 'we can plausibly regard Great Britain as an invented nation superimposed . . . onto much older alignments and loyalties' (Colley 1994: 5). The parallels with the American case – as indeed with many others – are obvious. The American people, comprising, by the nineteenth century, a heterogeneous population of relatively recent immigrants both voluntary and involuntary in origin together with Native Americans, established under a federal system which encouraged state and local as well as national loyalties, of necessity approached the idea of the nation in a multitude of ways.

As far as sociological theories are concerned, the ethno-symbolist approach offers perhaps the most useful framework for our understanding of American nationalism. It provides scholars with the concepts necessary to construct an affirmative response to the question 'was the nation?', in America's case, allowing them to pursue the related query of when it was and what it involved (and involves). As Anthony D. Smith has argued, America represents the 'model for the plural concept of the nation. The historic dominance of its white Puritan Anglo-Saxon culture and language, coupled with its messianic myths of origin and foundation, have provided a firm ethnic base for its subsequent experiment in cultural pluralism' (Smith 1995: 107–108). For 'primordialists, perennialists and ethno-symbolists', he has stressed, 'ethnic identity and community is a major point of reference and a vital building block for theories of nations and nationalism' (Smith 1998: xiii). Of course, America's 'ethnic base' has been contested ground since the outset, although this again should not – but perhaps does – exclude America from the general debate over nationalism. The purpose of this chapter is to place American nationalism firmly within the general theoretical debates over the subject, exploring it in turn from each of the three theoretical positions under analysis in the volume – perennialism, modernism and ethno-symbolism – in order to show how different aspects of America's national identity may be approached from these perspectives and why America's ethnic perspective was, and remains, 'a major point of reference' for America as a nation.

Modernism: a nation so conceived

On the face of it, dating the American nation is a straightforward matter. America was created at the point where the break with Britain was finalised. With a decisiveness that would delight undergraduates, the title of at least one textbook makes it clear that the American Revolution represented *Nationhood Achieved* (Ward 1995). Jon Butler's recent study of colonial society in the New World is similarly titled, not becoming *American*, but *Becoming America* (2001). This is far more than a distinction without a difference: it highlights the crux of the problem in any discussion of America as a nation and of American nationalism as a valid expression of identity to compare with European variants. By announcing the emergence of a nation, but avoiding the issue of whether there was such an entity as nationalism involved, scholars run the risk of making America seem like a hollow gourd: the ultimate civic nation in form, but no nation at all in function. For most nations, national identity has been 'the product of a long process of historical evolution involving common ancestors, common experiences, common ethnic background, common language, and usually common religion' (Huntington 1981: 23). America had none of those. Instead it had a 'proposition', as Abraham Lincoln put it in the midst of America's Civil War, 'that all men are created equal'. The Civil War was the ultimate test of 'whether that nation, or any nation so conceived . . . can long endure'. Lincoln was neither the first nor the last to ask this question, which preoccupied Americans from the time of the Revolution until long after the Civil War. This should give scholars pause; if the subjects under scrutiny expressed concerns over the validity of America's republican experiment, then perhaps such concerns were justified. Perhaps the Revolution had not, in fact, created the nation, at least, not in any sustainable form.

It may reasonably be asked to what extent any proposition could have been expected to have engendered the kind of national sentiment necessary to embark on a new experiment in government in the late eighteenth century in colonies notable for their diversity. 'By 1770 Britain's mainland settlements contained a polyglot population of English, Scots, Germans, Dutch, Swiss, French, and Africans', Butler observes, and out of this mix emerged a 'surprisingly modern' society. The colonies, he shows, 'became ethnically and nationally diverse, not homogeneous'. Sustained by an economy that was transatlantic in outlook, their 'politics looked ahead to the large-scale participatory politics of modern societies' and their 'religious pluralism . . . dwarfed the mild religious diversity found in any early modern European nation'. The result, Butler concludes, 'was America in its aspirations, its flaws, and its achievements' (Butler 2001: 2). Was it, however, in any sense national in its outlook? Recent scholarship suggests that it was. Nationality was part of the baggage that the first emigrants brought with them. When 'the peoples of Europe landed in the New World,' Tocqueville observed, 'their national characteristics were already formed.'[2] Whatever the British colonies lacked, it was not nationality – Greenfeld is clear on that point – but it was not yet American nationality. 'The *nationality* of American identity and consciousness does not demand an explanation,' Greenfeld asserts.

> The English settlers came with a national identity; it was a given. They necessarily conceived of the community to which they belonged as a nation; the idea of the nation was an American inheritance. *National* identity in America thus preceded the formation not only of the specific American identity (the American sense of uniqueness), but of the institutional framework of the American nation.
>
> (Greenfeld 1993: 402)

The idea of the nation may have been an American inheritance, but the form this idea took was the product of the colonial experience. Intercolonial trade, the postal service, the religious outburst and levelling impact of the first Great Awakening of the 1720s and, above all, warfare against the French and the Indians pulled the colonists together and reinforced their ties to Great Britain. Historians are, on the whole, agreed that it was the colonists' sense of Britishnesss, their self-perception as 'free-born Englishmen' that underpinned their growing opposition to the British Crown. Warfare was a constant in colonial America, with four major European conflicts – King William's War (the War of the League of Ausburg, 1689–1697); Queen Anne's War (the War of the Spanish Succession, 1702–1713); King George's War (the War of the Austrian Succession, 1744–1748); and the French and Indian War (the Seven Years' War, 1756–1763) – all played a part in both inculcating a sense of involvement in British affairs and, simultaneously, a growing feeling of resentment at such involvement. This was most obviously expressed by the fact that the colonists had their own name for these wars, indicating that they regarded them as essentially foreign conflicts into which they had been unwittingly and unwillingly conscripted. A significant marker on the road to American independence from the historians' perspective is the Treaty of Paris of 1763, which formally ended the Seven Years' War and assured British control over the colonies. With the French removed from the colonial game, the settlers could give their full attention to their increasingly fraught relationship with the mother country. The Stamp Act crisis of 1765 brought this to a head, but even then, opposition to British tax policies was expressed in the language of the political rights of British citizens. Increasingly, however, colonial newspapers were beginning to use the word 'American' to describe the colonies, indicating that a fledgling, and separate, sense of national identity distinct from Britishness was emerging (Bridenbaugh 1975; Greenfeld 1993: 413–416; Merritt 1966: 182; Ratcliffe 2000: 5).

The language of the Declaration of Independence gave expression to the idea that there existed a distinct, and singular, 'people' who had taken the decision 'to dissolve the political bands which have connected them with another'. Yet from the outset, Americans were conscious that the singular noun disguised a hetero-geneous population which shared hardly anything that could be termed a common identity. 'Aware of the need for outward expressions of this identity,' Ratcliffe notes, 'Americans everywhere adapted traditional street celebrations into rituals that legitimised the new order; the toasts – initially always thirteen in number – offered at public festivals expressed national rather than provincial pride.' The task of inculcating a genuinely national outlook was facilitated by the newspapers of the day, which provided a national perspective on local events. Indeed, Ratcliffe suggests, 'we might argue that the sense of American nationality gained deep roots so quickly because the binding thread of a common "print-language," so essential for creating an awareness of sharing a communal identity, was not restricted to an upper class, since literacy was already widespread and newspapers extraordinarily numerous' (Ratcliffe 2000: 5–6; Waldstreicher 1997: 11–12, 43–44). Although America is not the focus of his analysis, Anderson's description of the ways in which the national community is created, and the importance of both print capitalism and popular linguistic nationalisms, fits the American case very closely. 'In their rituals and their rhetoric,' Waldstreicher argues, 'the American revolutionaries created a new public called the "nation" '(Anderson 1992: 37–40; Waldstreicher 1997: 53).

Usefully for modernist theorists, this new nation was able to express its political ideals and civic identity in a language comprehensible to all; it was not only the traditions of public celebrations that Americans inherited from Britain, but the language to describe them. As Tocqueville observed, the American settlers 'all spoke the same language; they were all children of the same people'.[3] That this should have been the case was not a given. The first Pilgrim arrivals struck lucky in finding, half-way across the globe, Natives who could speak English, and this undoubtedly facilitated their own survival in the New World. By the Revolution-ary era, however, Benjamin Franklin was concerned at the linguistic impact of the large German community in Pennsylvania, and 'feared that America would fragment into a variety of speech communities'. That this did not happen, Bryson argues, rests on three factors: the physical movement of the population 'militated against the formation of permanent regionalisms'; their interaction required the development of a lingua franca; and most significantly, 'the desire for a common national identity encouraged people to settle on a single way of speaking' (Bryson 1990: 160–162). Language was, in a very real sense, the *sine qua non* of American political and civic discourse, and deserves more detailed analysis in the development of the American nation than it has so far received. Not that speaking the same language in a linguistic sense meant that the new Americans were speaking it in a political sense. At 'the moment of independence,' Greenfeld notes,

> one could easily think of thirteen American nations. Thus the very nation-ality of the American identity, the uncompromising commitment of Americans to the purified principles of civic nationalism, for a long time to come was bound to hinder the formation of a consensus regarding the geo-political

referent of American national loyalty, leaving open the question of what was, or whether there was, *the* American nation.

(Greenfeld 2003: 423)

That Americans neither entered nor exited the Revolution with a uniform sense of civic identity is hardly surprising. As Connor observes, 'nation-formation is a process, not an occurrence', a point which Smith reinforces, in a slightly different context, with his argument that the process of national construction is never 'a once-for-all affair', but is taken up anew by each generation (Connor 2004: 45; Smith 1993: 206). The American Revolution may be regarded as the beginning of that process, although the evidence that some version of nationalism pre-dated the emergence of America as a separate nation is compelling. As far as American nationalism is concerned, scholars are in a rather chicken-or-egg situation. Some argue, as Boorstin does, that the American nation was really a 'by-product of the assertion of each colony's right to govern itself', while others, such as Waldstreicher, propose that 'Americans practiced nationalism before they had a fully developed national state' or, in John Murrin's memorable phrase, the American nation was initially a 'roof without walls' (Boorstin 1988: 400–401; Murrin 1987: 344; Waldstreicher 1997: 112–113). Whichever came first – the nation or its national-ism – the years following the Revolution were 'overcast by a federal vagueness' that was not dispelled until the Civil War (Boorstin 1988: 401). That each state regarded itself as a discrete entity was made clear in the Articles of Confederation, which described their relationship as 'a firm league of friendship', voluntarily entered into and respectful of the sovereign rights, freedom and independence of the individual state. However, the desire to improve on the Articles, to create, in the words of the Constitution, 'a more perfect Union', does rather suggest that a degree of national identity was already fixed in America. The ensuing debates between Federalists and Anti-federalists were 'over the meaning of the Constitution, not its legitimacy' (Ratcliffe 2000: 8).

Americans may have developed a political language at least with which to articulate their civic ambitions, but they were nevertheless acutely conscious of the precarious nature of their republican experiment, so much so that during the early years of the republic the prediction that the Union could not last was 'a standard conversational gambit'. It 'was the persistence of union which excited surprise rather than recurring secessionist sentiment' (Kerber 1983: 34). George Washington was only the most famous American to remind his countrymen that they were 'Citizens, by birth or choice, of a common country' which 'has a right to concentrate your affections. The name of "American", which belongs to you, in your national capacity,' he stressed, 'must always exalt the just pride of patriot-ism, more than any appellation derived from local distinctions.' Quite how this American character was to be created and sustained, however, was not clear. The lack of any identifiable external threat seemed, ironically, to pose a difficulty for a new nation in search of a valid identity. Britain obliged once again in the War of 1812, the so-called second war for independence, after which the American Secretary of the Treasury Albert Gallatin enthused that the war had 'renewed and reinstated the national feelings which the Revolution had given and which were daily lessened. The people have now more general objects of attachment with which their pride and political opinions are connected. They are more American; they feel and act more like a nation.' Of course, the attempt by New England Federalists to effect a dissolution of the Union at the Hartford Convention in 1814 rather diluted Gallatin's exuberance, and the years that followed saw over-confidence in the American democratic experiment co-existing alongside deep-rooted fears over the validity and viability of the nation (Grant 2000b: 338). By the antebellum era such concerns had reached a peak. Writing in the 1830s, in the wake of the Nullification Crisis when South Carolina sought to nullify federal tariff legislation, Tocqueville observed that the 'Union is a vast body, which presents no definite object to patriotic feeling'. The states, by contrast, were 'identified with the soil; with the right of property and the domestic affections; with the recollections of the past, the labours of the present, and the hopes of the future. Patriotism,' he concluded, 'is still directed to the state and has not passed over to the Union.' In a similar vein, in 1848 the famous educator, Horace Mann, noted that it 'may be an easy thing to make a republic, but it is a very laborious thing to make republicans'. By the mid-nineteenth century, it seems, America had in place the political, bureaucratic and state apparatus of nationhood. It looked like a nation; it even sounded like a nation; but from the perspective of the time, it was not yet a nation.[4]

Primordialism and perennialism: the (ethnic) ties that bind

The modernist perspective, if applied to American nationalism, is invaluable in describing how that nation emerged in response to the political imperatives of the time. It aids our understanding of how the language of natural rights defined the sovereignty of the people and was used in the construction of a civic discourse designed to express, and to strengthen, the republican ideals of the nation's founders. It describes how such ideas were promulgated throughout a largely literate society that already had at its disposal not only a tradition of nationality but of 'revelry and rights' inherited from Britain (Greenfeld 1993: 402; Waldstreicher 1997: 43). The modernist perspective is excellent for understanding the development of the national apparatus, but not, perhaps, the ideas upon which it was predicated. Most significantly, it fails to explain the exclusion of certain groups – notably but not exclusively Native and African Americans – from the civic polity. Although most primordialists reject the idea of America as a nation, it did have many of the necessary – from their perspective – accoutrements of nationhood: a common language and territory, a sense of collective belonging and, oddly, perhaps, for a nation of immigrants, a sense of common ancestry. This last is the most significant element. Connor has defined the nation as 'the largest group that shares a common ancestry . . . the largest group that can be influenced/aroused/motivated/mobilised by appeals to common kinship. . . . Is there a Basque, Polish, or Welsh nation' he asks, and answers in the affirmative; but he denies absolutely that there is 'an American, British, or Indian nation' (Connor 2004: 37). Americans quite clearly do not share a common biological ancestry, yet the American population is quite capable – more obviously so than most nations – of being motivated by the invocation of a common ideological ancestry. Blood, it seems, is no barrier to belonging in America. That is the ideal of America; the reality of Americans, of course, is rather different.

Americans have always been conscious of their mixed – and relatively recent – origins, and of the intermingling of peoples that created their nation. As early as 1782, Hector St John de Crèvecoeur posed his now famous question: 'What, then, is the American, this new man?' His answer was that an American was, in fact, a European, but with a difference. '*He* is an American,' asserted Crèvecoeur, 'who, leaving behind him all his ancient prejudices and manners, receives new ones from the new mode of life he has embraced, the new government he obeys, and the new rank he holds.' The American was already, at this early stage, viewed as a conglomeration of national types, a 'strange mixture of blood, which you will find in no other country' Crèvecoeur observed, proud of the fact that he 'could point out to you a man, whose grandfather was an Englishman, whose wife was Dutch, whose son married a French woman, and whose present four sons have now four wives of different nations'. Even so, such apparently easy assimilation had to have some support, some means of making *unum* out of *pluribus*. Abraham Lincoln believed it was the Declaration of Independence that constituted the 'electric cord' which held the nation together. In the course of his famous debates with Stephen A. Douglas in 1858, he had addressed the thorny question of national identity in a nation of immigrants. Reflecting on the importance of the Fourth of July to Americans whose ancestors had won American independence, he noted that many Americans could not trace their blood lineage back to the Revolutionary generation. 'We have besides these men – descended by blood from our ancestors – among us perhaps half our people who are not descendants at all of these men, they are men who have come from Europe – German, Irish, French and Scandinavian,' Lincoln noted, and they had no 'connection with those days by blood.' Nevertheless, Lincoln argued, through the power of the Declaration of Independence American nationality could be achieved: the moral sentiment of the Declaration, Lincoln asserted, 'is the father of all moral principle in them, and . . . they have a right to claim it as though they were blood of the blood, and flesh of the flesh of the men who wrote that Declaration'.[5]

From Lincoln's perspective, blood was not the sole criterion of belonging to the American nation. Nearly one hundred years later, with America on the verge on entering the Second World War, Lincoln's words found an echo in a short but densely packed volume entitled *The Pocket Book of America*, which was distributed to American servicemen and to non-combatants in order to remind them both of the cause for which they were fighting and, more importantly, of their uniquely American heritage. In the volume's Introduction, it was observed that in 'times of great crisis, nations, like individuals, have to rediscover what it is they live by'. Wars, it went on, 'are made by men, and won or lost by men, and men are what they think, and feel, and believe'. It was acknowledged that no single volume 'could crowd between two covers the sum total of the American tradition', but the representative sample it offered was revealing. Almost half the volume was devoted to speeches, addresses and poetry produced during, or inspired by, the Civil War. The volume opened with Edward Everett Hale's famous morality tale, 'The Man Without a Country', and offered the Emancipation Proclamation, the Gettysburg Address, some of Walt Whitman's poetry and the 'Battle Hymn of the Republic' alongside the Declaration of Independence, the Constitution, varied population statistics and detailed instructions on how to fold the American flag. Together, this material represented, according to the Introduction, the unique ancestry of America, an ancestry 'not of the blood, but of the mind'. In an apparently unconscious echo of Abraham Lincoln's sentiments regarding the Declaration of Independence, it was asserted that such 'ancestry can be claimed by every American . . . all he needs to do is claim [it] and prove it by living in that tradition'.[6]

Yet the American tradition was not open to all, and Lincoln's overtly religious interpretation of the Declaration of Independence as the communion bread and wine through which access to the national host might be achieved needs to be placed in the context of his time. Nineteenth-century Americans had a quite specific understanding of race and nationalism. Both were perceived as dividing 'individuals into groups', but nationality was seen as 'a major divisive force for humanity in general' as well as a 'subdivision of race, a subgrouping with more subtly defined inherent characteristics'. Foreign nations were 'useful foils for the American', Elson notes, and school books introduced the concept of distinct national traits that, to varying degrees, had influenced America, singling out Scotland and Switzerland as 'prototypes for American character and civilization' (Elson 1964: 101–105). Oliver Wendell Holmes famously described Americans as 'the Romans of the modern world – the great assimilating people', but Americans did not assimilate indiscriminately. As Henry James mused to a friend a few years after the Civil War, Americans 'have exquisite qualities as a race, and it seems to me that we are ahead of the European races in the fact that more than either of them we can deal freely with forms of civilization not our own, can pick and choose and assimilate and in short . . . claim our property wherever we find it. To have no national stamp has hitherto been a defect and a drawback,' he concluded, but no longer. His views found support a few years later when Thomas Wentworth Higginson, the former abolitionist and colonel of the first black regiment in the Civil War, turned his attention to 'Americanism in Literature'. Contrasting the American national character with that of the English, Higginson suggested that the 'Englishman's strong point is a vigorous insularity which he carries with him. . . . The American's more perilous gift,' he continued, in an almost direct echo of James, 'is a certain power of assimilation, through which he acquires something from every man he meets.' It was not immediately obvious to men such as James or Higginson, however, how this attribute that each had identified could provide a strong foundation for a uniquely American nationalism. Higginson noted the tendency among his countrymen to believe that 'the war and its results have made us a nation, subordinated local distinctions, cleared us of our chief shame, and given us the pride of a common career'. What the war had clearly not done, in Higginson's view, was to have established an American national identity. 'It seems unspeakably important that all persons among us . . . should be pervaded with Americanism', he asserted, but as far as he was concerned, that lay in the future.[7]

As the nation prepared to celebrate its Centennial, the question of their nationalism still preoccupied Americans. Two years prior to the Centennial, the poet and travel writer Bayard Taylor took up the challenge of assessing the state of American national identity. He summarised the nature of immigration to America up to that point, singling out the English, French, Irish and Germans and noting that 'all these are European and Christian'. 'Which of these elements,' Taylor enquired, 'represents the American, the citizen of the United States, or enters most largely into his composition? How far do they combine to form a national character?' Taylor also acknowledged that America had 'the native red Indian and the imported African,' but concluded that these 'may be set aside as practically out of court.' There was more than a degree of irony here, since it was Taylor who penned the 'National Ode' for 4 July 1876, and claimed for his nation that 'No blood in her lightest veins/Frets at remembered chains,/Nor shame of bondage has bowed her head'. 'By the time of the centennial,' Lyn Spillman argues, 'Americans were celebrating a century of formal sovereignty, but an uneven and contested cultural unity.' The celebrations, when they got underway, did little to even things out, and were notable for what they avoided as much as for what they celebrated. Immigrants and African-Americans were hardly mentioned, and Native Americans were represented by a Smithsonian exhibit that acknowledged their existence as a colourful aboriginal presence in the USA but kept them firmly out of the imagined national community, portraying them, indeed, as 'an interior other to national identity' at that time (Spillman 1997: 25, 37, 43–45, 71–72). Although, by the turn of the twentieth century, America had in place several of the crucial components of nationhood, the ideological ethnic ties that been created were not especially strong. Americans spoke in familial metaphors, invoked the 'Fathers' of the nation, and frequently referred to an ancestry that was ideal rather than real, but the nationalism that this produced remained exclusionary and limited.

By identifying 'acceptable' national traits among the European nations alone, Americans had from the outset created a nationalism of exclusion that had distinct ethnic overtones and that denied, implicitly, the stated ideals of their own founding document. As one group of New England slaves pointed out forcibly in 1773, 'We have no property! We have no wives! No children! We have no city! No country!' During the War of 1812 the future president Andrew Jackson obviously perceived no irony when he rallied black troops to America's cause with the words: 'As sons of Freedom you are now called upon to defend your most estimable blessings. As Americans, your country looks with confidence to her adopted citizens.' By the time of the Civil War, many African-Americans were confident that their military involvement would result in their acceptance into the nation. As Frederick Douglass famously put it, 'once let the black man get upon his person the brass letters U.S., let him get an eagle on his button, and a musket on his shoulder and bullets in his pocket, and there is no power on earth which can deny that he has earned the right to citizenship in the United States.' In the middle of the war, one black soldier echoed Douglass' sentiments when he pointed out that African-Americans had 'suffered and died in defence of that starry banner which floats only over free men', while a white private expressed his belief that white Americans should give blacks 'a share in *our* nationality, if God has no separate nationality in store for them'. In theory, the civic nature of American national identity ought to have presented no obstacle to African-Americans seeking full membership of the nation, especially after the Civil War. There were individuals, such as Senator Thomas Hendricks of Indiana, who argued that black and white were 'not of the same race. We are so different that we ought not to compose one political community', but the civic nature of American national identity could easily have invalidated such arguments. 'Throughout American history,' Foner argues, 'wars have been a vital force in expanding the boundaries of the nation's "imagined community."' The same might be said of most other nations, but that is not the point. The fact is that the Civil War, the most dramatic conflict for the American nation in many ways, did not manage to push back the boundaries of America's imagination as far as it might have done (Foner 1999: 97).[8]

The primordialists' emphasis on the centrality of ethnic ties goes some way towards explaining why this was so, why the nation did not live up to its stated ideals of equality for all. The sense of collective belonging that America as a nation managed to inculcate in the first century of its existence was predicated on a set of origin myths – the Puritans' 'errand into the wilderness'; the 'City on a Hill'; the political vision of the Founding Fathers – and ethnic constructions – the 'Noble Savage'; the black slave; the 'free-born Englishman' – that positioned white against red and black. By the time of the Second World War the situation was hardly much better. As late as the Vietnam War African-Americans were struggling to achieve equality, and to acquire a full share in a nationalism predicated on the assertion that all men are created equal, but sustained by the fact that some were clearly more equal than others, while Native Americans had pretty much abandoned the idea of merging with the nation at all, had they ever even entertained it. Race, Germaine Greer reminds us, 'is a contested category, perhaps not even a genuine category, and offers no rational basis for the building of a state' (Greer 2004: 25). Yet the American nation had used race in exactly that way since the colonial period, not only in the racial constructions of blackness that the colonists had inherited from Britain's Elizabethan past, but fundamentally in the way they structured their political discourse and their society. Bacon's Rebellion in Virginia in 1676 is only one of the most obvious episodes in colonial history to reveal the lineaments of America's future ethnic constructions. As Morgan argues, for 'those with eyes to see, there was an obvious lesson in the rebellion', which had begun as an attack on Indians, but 'ended as a series of plundering forays' against the colony's leaders. 'Resentment of an alien race,' he noted, 'might be more powerful than resentment of an upper class' (Morgan 1975: 269–270). The American nation was, from the outset, circumscribed by ethnic constructs that denied citizenship to non-white peoples in order to create and sustain the idea of collective belonging among whites. This ethnic base grew alongside – indeed was an essential component of – the republican ideology at the heart of the nation. Unfortunately, it also worked against the development of a cohesive and lasting American nationalism. Primordialists and perennialists high-light the significance of ancestry, be it real or fictitious; the American case shows that paying too careful attention to where people come from can actually obscure where a nation is going. The truly 'ethnic' nation is not only clearly not America, it is actually no nation at all.

Ethno-symbolism: the once and future nation

The modernist paradigm offers the best means of dating the American nation – not that the date of its emergence as a nation on to the word's stage is in any doubt – and confirms its position as 'the first new nation' that arose out of the shifting political and ideological sands of the mid- to late eighteenth century. Although France and Britain, more specifically England, 'have provided the litmus test of the antiquity of the concept of the nation and the nature of national sentiment', it is time for scholars to add America into the equation, since its development relied to a great degree on developments in both France – the ideology – and England – the populace and the nature of its collective identity (Smith 1998: 172). Together, France, England and America form a valuable and mutually reinforcing triumvirate representing the various elements and stages of the nation-building process. To understand American nationalism itself, however, requires a broader and more nuanced approach, which only ethno-symbolism can offer. Historians are more interested in relating the sociological paradigms to what people in the past actually said and did. Although America clearly was a new nation, the first experiment in republican government, it is important to focus on what eighteenth- and nineteenth-century Americans themselves believed about their nation and, as already noted, prior to the Civil War they were not confident of its future. Some saw an opportunity in the nation's newness, while others regarded this as problematic for national development.

'Nationalist movements often require traditions,' Waldstreicher observes, 'inventing them out of whole cloth, if necessary. But the American revolutionaries already had a tradition,' and it was English. This proved problematic for a nation in the process of severing its ties with England. 'For the American patriots after 1776 . . . the more unprecedented everything appeared, the better. Appropriating the oldest English commemorative rituals and rhetoric, celebrants of the nation struggled to keep the character of a first celebration by always celebrating the *future*' (Waldstreicher 1997: 43). New England radical divine Theodore Parker was enthused by the fact that America was 'one of the few great nations which can trace their history back to certain beginnings; there is no fabulous period in our annals, no mythical centuries'. As a consequence, however, historian Agnes Repplier suggested that Americans, unlike other peoples, had to work hard at their nationalism, and needed to 'create artificially the patriotism which is the birthright of other nations'. By the antebellum period, Parker's position was the unusual one. Many Americans felt the lack of tradition keenly; however hard they focused their gaze on the future, they were conscious of the need for a past (Grant 1997: 90–92). The very modernity of their nation was its weakness, and so a process was begun – had begun in the immediate aftermath of the Revolution, in fact – to provide America with the unifying symbols and myths necessary for the creation 'of a strong sense of nationhood in a hurry' (Grant 1997: 93–95; Zelinsky 1988: 21).

In analysing the myths constructed around nationhood, Smith proposes that:

> it is possible and useful to distinguish myths that cite *genealogical* ancestry from those which trace a more *ideological* descent, between 'biological' and 'cultural-ideological' myths. In the former, filiation is the basic principle of myth construction: the chroniclers and poets trace generational lineages and rest their claims for high status and power on a presumed biological link with a hero, a founder, or even a deity. The community, according to this mode of myth-making, is descended from a noble and heroic ancestor, and for that reason is entitled to privilege and prestige in its own and other people's estimations. The biological link also ensures a high degree of communal solidarity, since the community is viewed as a network of interrelated kin groups claiming a common ancestor, and thereby marking them off from those unable to make such a claim.

An 'equally important set of generational linkages,' he asserts, 'rest on a cultural affinity and ideological "fit" with the presumed ancestors. What counts here are not blood ties, real or alleged, but a spiritual kinship, proclaimed in ideals that are allegedly derived from some ancient exemplars in remote eras.' Most significantly, he concludes, 'within given ethnic communities . . . both kinds of national myth-making emerge and persist in an often contrapuntal relationship. They thus both divide, and unite, the communities whose identity and consciousness they underpin' (Smith 1999: 57–58).

At first glance, the 'cultural affinity' model seems to apply most obviously to America, but we must bear in mind that Washington – as quoted above – cited both birth *and* choice as the criteria for belonging to the American nation. It is important to remember that those who fought for American Independence had not arrived the previous day: by the time of the Revolution, colonial society was established, and, as events would prove, divided, not least over the issue of the nation. Thus both the biological and the cultural criteria were present at the creation of the American nation, but what of the idea of founders, or heroes? Again, the Founding Fathers themselves seem to fulfil this function very neatly, but we should not overlook those who came before. Going back almost as far as we possibly can in terms of European settlement, we encounter the figure of Columbus – a contested figure now, certainly, but how was he understood in the nineteenth century? Cynthia Koch has argued that 'Americans in the new United States looked to Columbus as the prophet, even amidst the corruption and ignorance of the Old World, of their national independence'. She cites an 1819 schoolbook lesson in which

> 'Columbus . . . saw, once more, bright Del'ware's silver stream/And Penn's throng'd city cast a cheerful gleam.' The explorer is imagined as a heavenly figure sitting in benevolent judgment as Randolph, Washington, Franklin, Lee, and the whole founding panoply gather in sanctified political assembly leading a wronged people to reluctant Revolution.

The story of Columbus, Koch shows, 'was interpreted through a lens focused solely on the birth of the North American republic', and which pushed aside the opening up of both the West Indies and South America at that time. '[W]ith the benefit of considerable hindsight,' she argues, nineteenth-century Americans 'saw as inexorable the "progress of civilization" leading directly from Columbus to Washington.' In time, too, Columbus underwent a sex-change: 'feminised into the allegorical Columbia' s/he now represented 'the new land, the exotic wilderness of America', and acted as a 'symbolic counterpart to George Washington' who brought masculine order and republican government to the new nation. In his historical as opposed to his allegorical guise, however, Columbus acquired a strong moral and patriotic meaning, which Koch likens to that of 'an Old Testament patriarch . . . Columbus as the new nation's Moses,' she suggests, 'unfolded in tales of the struggles entailed in the voyages of discovery.' In true biblical style, the mantle of Columbus the prophet fell, in due course, on to Washington's shoulders, and it was his character that 'became iconographic for national character . . . his successes [that] signified heavenly approval for the national enterprise he came to symbolise' (Koch 1996: 32–33, 45).

Civil War-era Americans gave little obvious thought to Columbus, but a great deal to Washington. The Civil War generation was fixated on the war preceding the war preceding its own: namely the Revolution (the Mexican War and, arguably, the war of 1812 preceded the Civil War). The Revolution, however, bequeathed a divided legacy to America, not least in the matter of race. This issue goes to the heart of the problem of American nationalism. The Revolutionary generation had lacked the courage of its (stated) convictions. The Civil War generation simply lacked the conviction. Both North and South looked to the Revolution for guidance. In the end, they could no more right its wrongs than they could betray the memory of their comrades who had died. In focusing on the bravery of black soldiers and yet extolling white death as the better part of valour, the Civil War generation were the true inheritors of the Revolution. Washington acted as prophet, and as justification, for both sides in the conflict: one seeing him as the 'Father of his Country', as the man who had warned his fellow countrymen to beware of local attachments and to revere the whole; the other saw him as a slaveholder, as historical justification for a cause that, frankly, dared not speak its name in the Confederacy. The banner of states' rights was the arras behind which slavery lurked – and Confederates were unwilling to look behind it for the duration of the conflict. Yet the national future depended, increasingly, on the subject being addressed, by the North if not by the South. Yet Emancipation, when it came, came about with apparent reluctance. The political exigencies of the day did not allow for any sustained debate on the subject, to the great detriment of both black and white. Indeed, the divisions between black and white widened, as black spokesmen such as Frederick Douglass called for a rededication of the nation to the ideals of the Declaration of Independence, whites too frequently sought a return to the status quo antebellum.

By using Smith's theories on collective identities, historians may be able to see the Civil War debate over race from a new angle. Black and white divided at that point in America's history in a fundamental way; many members – by no means all, however – of the black community invoked the 'cultural affinity' criteria for inclusion in the American nation. They called for America to make good its promises of freedom and equality for all, and sought inclusion in the nation by virtue not just of cultural affinity but of military sacrifice – a traditional way of establishing legitimacy in the nation. The African-American vision of the nation was the more expansive, the more challenging and the more forward-looking. It was also, it must be said, the more realistic. As Frederick Douglass put it, 'the destiny of the colored American, however this mighty war shall terminate, is the destiny of America. We shall never leave you.' But Douglass also said this: 'I am an American citizen. In birth, in sentiment, in ideas, in hopes, in aspirations, and responsibilities. I am an American citizen ... I am not only a citizen by birth and lineage. I am such by choice.' In this address, Douglass harked back to Washington's definition: birth *and* choice, and placed the African-American squarely at the centre of American nationalism. So where and why did it all go wrong for Douglass? Why were his calls 'for something beyond the battlefield' in Civil War memory increasingly dismissed? I would suggest that it was because a fundamental shift took place during the Civil War as far as America's nationalism was concerned.[9]

Up to the Civil War, African-American citizenship was not merely denied by judgements such as Taney's 1857 Dredd Scott decision but, had it been recognised, it would have failed the test of voluntarism that seemed to define American nationalism. African-Americans were not Americans by choice but by compulsion. The black community had little use for Columbus, or for Washington, come to that, since these quasi-mythical figures did not feature in their version of the American story. That they came to have significance was due to the African-American demand for inclusion in the aspirational nationalism of America in the mid-nineteenth century. But the Civil War brought change. Now it was no longer African-Americans, north or south, who were unwilling members of the nation; it was white Southerners. The mantle of unbelonging, if you will, passed to them. By taking arms against the nation, white Southerners disinherited themselves from the nation. The years after the war witnessed a long struggle on their part to reacquire the inheritance they had tried so hard to discard. In doing so, they turned to the past: to the immediate, Civil War past, certainly, but also to the more distant past, the past of Columbus, Washington and the Revolution. In invoking this past, they re-established common ground with the North, and in that ground they buried the African-American dream of a more inclusive nationalism. It is often said that Americans compensate for their brief history by looking to the future; the tragedy of the Civil War and the Union's failure to live up to its own purported ideals lies in the fact that at that moment, as African-Americans looked forward, white Americans looked backwards, and sought reunion in what had been, rather than in what could possibly be.

From a historian's perspective, the Civil War story is one of ever-decreasing circles, as black hopes were dashed in the face of white intransigence, and as white combatants wrote their own version of the war's history in which black troops, never mind freed slaves, were almost wholly expunged. Both kinds of national myth, I would argue – the biological and the ideological – existed in mid-nineteenth-century America: the tragedy was that at that particular histor- ical juncture, different groups adhered to them, and so they served to divide, not unite, the nation. Yet the Civil War remains the central focus of American nationalism. It was at that point that both northerners and southerners believed that they finally had a nation (Grant 2000a: 15–152). New York diarist George Templeton Strong had consistently harboured doubts about the viability of American nationality long before his worst fears were realised. Scornful of the American tendency to 'venerate every trivial fact about our first settlers and colonial governors and revolutionary heroes', Strong nevertheless understood what this craving for history revealed. 'We are so young a people,' he argued, 'that we feel the want of nationality, and delight in whatever asserts our national "American" existence. We have not, like England and France, centuries of achievements and calamities to look back on; we have no *record* of Americanism,' Strong emphasised, 'and we feel its want.' When secession made Civil War between North and South inevitable, Strong shamefully concluded that Ameri- cans were 'a weak, divided, disgraced people, unable to maintain our national existence . . . impotent even to assert our national life'. The war's outcome found him in a better frame of mind. 'The people has,' he wrote '. . . just been bringing forth a new American republic – an amazingly big baby – after a terribly pro- tracted and severe labor, without chloroform.' Birth metaphors were clearly the order of the day. Addressing a group of young Republicans some two years after the end of the conflict, the radical politician Charles Sumner took as his subject the question 'Are We a Nation?' Sumner had no hesitation in answering it in the affirmative. 'Even if among us in the earlier day there was no occasion for the word Nation,' he observed, 'there is now. A Nation,' he confidently asserted, 'is born.'[10]

Conclusion

From an ethno-symbolist perspective, the American nation dates not from the Revolution but from the Civil War. It was the war that answered, definitively, the question of whether 'a nation so conceived could long endure', that finally resolved – if inadequately – the issue of slavery in the land of the free, and that reinforced the belief in America as the New Israel, Americans as a chosen people, through the blood sacrifice in the nation's name 'to save it from destruction and assure its sacred destiny' (Smith 1999: 43). Writing in 1910, William James suggested asking

> all our millions, north and south, whether they would vote now . . . to have our war for the Union expunged from history, and the record of a peaceful transition to the present time substituted for that of its marches and battles, and probably a handful of eccentrics would say yes. Those ancestors, those efforts, those memories and legends, are the most ideal part of what we now own together, a sacred spiritual possession worth more than all the blood poured out.[11]

As the Civil War became the source of heroes closer than Columbus, Americans turned to it for verification of all that they were. Its central image, perhaps, was the Gettysburg Address, in which Lincoln established the importance of the nation over the Union and invoked the ancestors of the nation, the 'fathers', in his attempts to make an internecine conflict meaningful. Indeed, Garry Wills argues,

> [o]ne cannot intelligently discuss Lincoln's attitude toward 'the fathers' unless one grasps this most basic fact about his use of the term: for him, the fathers are always the begetters of the national idea. The founders of the nation founded it on that. The fighters for the nation fought for that. The drafters of the Constitution tried to embody as much as they could of that idea. The sons of the fathers are sons only so far as they accept and perpetuate that idea. The fathers are always relevant because the idea is never old. It is life-giving every time new Americans are begotten out of it. Americans are intellectually autochthonous, having no pedigree except that idea. . . . The Declaration of Independence . . . has replaced the Gospel as an instrument of spiritual rebirth. The spirit, not the blood, is the *idea* of the Revolution, not its mere temporal battles and chronological outcome.
>
> (Wills 1992: 86)

The evidence suggests, however, that Americans may not be as autochthonous as Wills proposes. Although Greenfeld also argues that as a 'nation of self-made men, America was a self-made nation', she provides a wealth of evidence to the contrary (Greenfeld 1993: 480) Tracing the roots of American nationalism to English precedent, she shows how Americans struggled to achieve a different kind of nation from all that had gone before, a struggle which the ethno-symbolist paradigm reveals to be similar to that in many other nations. The Civil War was the conclusion of a process begun in the colonial era, a process that brought a new world out of the traditions of the old. It is the process itself that is of interest, since no single period can be defined as the moment when the American nation fully emerged. Each paradigm – the modernist, the primordialist, the ethno-symbolist – has a fresh perspective to provide on American national development, but America fits none of them exactly. Nor, it must be said, do other nations. American nationalism has always been a process of challenge and debate, reconception and reassessment, a breaking of old traditions and attachments and the forging of new ones, but always structured around a flexible but fairly consistent set of myths and memories through which Americans sought to interpret their nation and justify it to the world. These myths and memories have always revolved around the perennial questions of what the nation is, who belongs in it and what it stands for, questions that are more relevant today than ever.

Notes

1 Alexis de Tocqueville, *Democracy in America*, trans. Henry Reeve, ed. Phillips Bradley, 2 vols (1835, 1840, reprint: New York: Vintage Books, 1945), vol. I: 28; Henry James, 'Americans Abroad', *The Nation*, Vol. 27, No. 692 (3 October 1878), pp. 208–209.

2 Tocqueville, *Democracy in America*, p. 28.

3 Ibid.: 29.

4 *Washington's Farewell Address*, 1796; Albert Gallatin quoted in Dangerfield 1965: 3–4; Tocqueville, *Democracy in America*, pp. 401–402; Horace Mann, 'Twelfth Annual Report of the Secretary of the Board of Education of Massachusetts', in Mary Mann and George C. Mann (eds), *Life and Works of Horace Mann*, 5 vols (1865, reprint: Washington, DC: National Education Association, 1937), Vol. 3, pp. 682–683.

5 J. Hector St John de Crèvecoeur, Letters from an American Farmer (1782, London: Penguin, 1983): 69–70; Abraham Lincoln, 'Speech at Chicago', 10 July, 1858, in Roy Basler (ed.), *The Collected Works of Abraham Lincoln*, 11 vols (New Brunswick, NJ: Rutgers University Press, 1953), Vol. II: 484–502, quotations 499–500.

6 *The Pocket Book Of America* (New York: Pocket Books, 1942): v–xii.

7 Oliver Wendell Holmes, *The Autocrat of the Breakfast-Table* (1858): 18; Henry James to Thomas Sergeant Perry, 20 September 1867, in Leon Edel (ed.), *Henry James: Letters, Vol. I, 1843–1875* (London: Macmillan, 1974), p. 77; Thomas Wentworth Higginson, 'Americanism in Literature', *The Atlantic Monthly*, Vol. 25, No. 147 (January 1870), pp. 56–63, quotations pp. 56–57.

8 Andrew Jackson quoted in Mullen 1973: 15; New England slaves quoted in Foner 1999: 34; Frederick Douglass quoted in James M. McPherson, *Marching Towards Freedom: The Negro in the Civil War* (New York: Alfred A. Knopf, 1967): 68; Henry S. Harmon, Corporal, Co. B, 3rd USCI, Morris Island, South Carolina, in the *Christian Recorder*, 23 October 1863; the letter appeared in the paper on the 7 November; Edwin S. Redkey (ed.), *A Grand Army of Black Men: Letters from African-American Soldiers in the Union Army, 1861-1865* (New York and Cambridge: Cambridge University Press, 1992): 36; Charles Ray Brayton to his father, 13 September 1863, in Nina Silber and Mary Beth Sievens (eds), *Yankee Correspondence: Civil War Letters between New England Soldiers and the Home Front* (Charlottesville and London: University Press of Virginia, 1996): 103; White Private Henry T. Johns quoted in Leon F. Litwack, *Been in the Storm So Long: The Aftermath of Slavery* (1979, reprint: New York: Knopf, 1980): 70; Hendricks quoted in Foner 1999: 107.

9 Frederick Douglass, 'The Black Man's Future in the Southern States', an Address delivered in Boston, Massachusetts, 5 February 1862, in Louis P. Masur, *The Real War Will Never Get in the Books: Selections from Writers During the Civil War* (New York and Oxford: Oxford University Press, 1993): 109–111.

10 George Templeton Strong diary entries for 8 November 1854, 11 and 12 March 1861 and 1 June 1865, in Allan Nevins and Milton Hasley Thomas (eds), *The Diary of George Templeton Strong* (New York: The Macmillan Company, 1952), Vol. II, *The Turbulent Fifties, 1850–1859*: 196–197; Vol III, *The Civil War, 1860–1865*: 109; Vol. IV, *Post-War Years, 1865–1875*: 2; Charles Sumner, 'Are We a Nation? Address of Hon. Charles

Sumner before the New York young men's Republican union, at the Cooper Institute, Tuesday evening, Nov. 19, 1867' (New York, 1867): 4–5.
11 William James quoted in John Pettegrew, 'The Soldier's Faith: Turn-of-the-century Memory of the Civil War and the Emergence of Modern American Nationalism', *Journal of Contemporary History* 31 (1996): 49–73, quotation p. 49.

References

Anderson, B. (1992) *Imagined Communities: Reflections on the Origin and Spread of Nationalism* (1983). Reprint, London: Verso.

Boorstin, D.J. (1988) *The Americans: The National Experience* (1965). Reprint, New York and London: Cardinal.

Bridenbaugh, C. (1975) *The Spirit of 1776: The Growth of American Patriotism Before Independence, 1607–1776.* New York and Oxford: Oxford University Press.

Bryson, B. (1990) *Mother Tongue: The English Language.* London: Penguin Books.

Butler, J. (2001) *Becoming America: The Revolution Before 1776* (2000). Paperback reprint, Cambridge, MA: Harvard University Press.

Colley, L. (1994) *Britons: Forging the Nation, 1707–1837* (1992). Reprint, London: Pimlico.

Connor, W. (1978) 'A Nation is a Nation, Is a State, Is an Ethnic Group', *Ethnic and Racial Studies* 1(4).

Connor, W. (2004) 'The Timelessness of Nations', *Nations and Nationalism* 10 (1/2): 35–47.

Dangerfield, G. (1965) *The Awakening of American Nationalism, 1815–1828.* New York: Harper & Row.

Elson, R.M. (1964) *Guardians of Tradition: American Schoolbooks of the Nineteenth Century.* Lincoln, NE: University of Nebraska Press.

Foner, E. (1999) *The Story of American Freedom* (1998). Reprint, New York: Picador.

Grant, S-M. (1997) 'Myth and the Construction of American Nationhood', in G. Hosking and G. Schöpflin (eds), *Myths and Nationhood.* London: Hurst and Company, pp. 88–106.

Grant, S-M. (2000a) *North Over South: Northern Nationalism and American Identity in the Antebellum Era.* Lawrence, KS: University Press of Kansas.

Grant, S-M. (2000b) 'From Union to Nation?: The Civil War and the Development of American Nationalism', in S-M. Grant and B.H. Reid (eds), *The American Civil War: Explorations and Reconsiderations.* Harlow, Essex: Longman, pp. 333–357.

Greenfeld, L. (1993) *Nationalism: Five Roads to Modernity* (1992). Paperback reprint, Cambridge, MA: Harvard University Press.

Greer, G. (2004) *Whitefella Jump Up: The Shortest Way to Nationhood.* London: Profile Books.

Huntington, S.P. (1981) *American Politics: The Promise of Disharmony.* Cambridge, MA: Harvard University Press.

Kerber, L. (1983) *Federalists in Dissent: Imagery and Ideology in Jeffersonian America* (1970). Reprint, Ithaca, NY, and London: Cornell University Press.

Koch, C.M. (1996) 'Teaching Patriotism: Private Virtue for the Public Good in the Early Republic', in J. Bodnar (ed.), *Bonds of Affection: Americans Define their Patriotism.* Princeton, NJ: Princeton University Press, pp. 19–52.

Lipset, S.M. (1979) *The First New Nation: The United States in Historical and Comparative Perspective.* New York: Norton.

Merritt, R.L. (1966) *Symbols of American Community, 1735–1775.* New Haven, CT: Yale University Press.

Morgan, E.S. (1975) *American Slavery, American Freedom: The Ordeal of Colonial Virginia.* New York and London: W.W. Norton.

Mullen, R.W. (1973) *Blacks in America's Wars: The Shift in Attitudes from the Revolutionary War to Vietnam*. New York: Monad Press.

Murrin, J. (1987) 'A Roof Without Walls: The Dilemma of American National Identity', in R. Beeman, S. Botein, and E.C. Carter II (eds), *Beyond Confederation: Origins of the Constitution and American National Identity*. Chapel Hill, NC: University of North Carolina Press, pp. 333–348.

Ratcliffe, D. (2000) 'The State of the Union, 1776–1860', in S-M. Grant and B.H. Reid (eds), *The American Civil War: Explorations and Reconsiderations*. Harlow, Essex: Longman, pp. 3–38.

Smith, A.D. (1993) *The Ethnic Origins of Nations* (1983). Reprint, London: Blackwell.

Smith, A.D. (1995) *Nations and Nationalism in a Global Era*. Cambridge: Polity Press.

Smith, A.D. (1998) *Nationalism and Modernism*. London: Routledge.

Smith, A.D. (1999) *Myths and Memories of the Nation*. New York and Oxford: Oxford University Press.

Snyder, L. (1990) *Encyclopedia of Nationalism*. Chicago, IL, and London: St James, Press.

Spillman, L. (1997) *Nation and Commemoration: Creating National Identities in the United States and Australia*. Cambridge: Cambridge University Press.

Waldstreicher, D. (1997) *In the Midst of Perpetual Fetes: The Making of American Nationalism, 1776–1820*. Chapel Hill and London: University of North Carolina Press.

Ward, H.M. (1995) *The American Revolution: Nationhood Achieved, 1763–1788*. New York: St Martin's Press.

Wills, G. (1992) *Lincoln at Gettysburg: The Words that Remade America*. New York: Simon & Schuster.

Zelinsky, W. (1988) *Nation into State: The Shifting Symbolic Foundations of American Nationalism*. Chapel Hill and London: The University of North Carolina Press.

9 When, what and how is the nation?

Lessons from Greece

Anna Triandafyllidou

Introduction

Theories on nation formation may be roughly divided into two main schools: modernists and perennialists. The former claim that nations and nationalism are socio-political phenomena characteristic of the modern era (e.g. Anderson 1991; Gellner 1983; Kedourie 1992, among others); the latter sustain that nations have always existed albeit in different social or political forms than that characterising modern nations (Armstrong 1982; Hastings 1997; Smith 1986; for a more general critical discussion of the relevant theories, see Smith 1998). Different theorists provide for different definitions of the nation and, on the basis of these, try also to pinpoint the moment of birth of different nations. They try to specify the historical moment when an ethnic or cultural community may be said to have become a nation.

In this chapter I will first recast the main points of these two strands of theories regarding the definition and hence timing of the nation following the theoretical debate opened in Part I of this volume. It is my contention that it is possible to specify the moment of birth of a nation. However, this kind of research exercise risks being misleading. National identity, like any form of identity, is dynamic and constantly in evolution. The content of national identity and the borders of the national community are renegotiated, reorganised and reaffirmed repeatedly during the life of the nation. Paying too much attention to *when* is the nation risks obscuring *what* and *how* is the nation, both important research questions that cast more light on the character and historical processes of nation formation than the dating of the nation's birth.

I will adopt here a working definition of the nation following the main lines of the ethno-symbolist approach advocated by Anthony D. Smith. Taking Greece as an example, I will discuss when the modern Greek nation came into being and the important role the Greek nation-state played in this process. After reviewing briefly the main lines of the official and dominant national(ist) discourses in Greece immediately before and after the birth of the Greek nation, I will turn to two recent challenges to the Greek national self-definition: the 'Macedonian question' and the issue of co-ethnics' migration to Greece. I will investigate how the nation-state, the political elite and the media (all well-recognised and important players in nationalist struggles and discourses) have redefined the content of the national identity and the membership to the national community in response to these two challenges. I will thus analyse how earlier dominant nationalist discourses have been reorganised. My aim is thus to show that the nation as any type of collective identity is constituted in interaction, by reference to inspiring or threatening Significant Others (Triandafyllidou 2001, 2002). Hence, in order to better understand the phenomena of nation formation and nationalism, we need to question the relationship between the definition of the nation at the moment of its birth and at different points in time during the life of the nation. We may argue that the nation is symbolically reborn after successfully facing a new challenge to its 'unity' or 'authenticity' because it reaffirms the vitality and symbolic power of the national identity and culture.

Greece is a relevant and interesting case to test these arguments because of the strong ethnic perennial connotations that characterise political and partly academic debates on the Greek nation, defining the latter as an essential, quasi-organic entity and neglecting many of the historical and relational factors that have shaped the nation's self-definition. Many Greek nationals would consider the answer to the 'when is the Greek nation' question as self-evident. They would argue that the Greek nation 'has always existed', since time immemorial. They would even conceive of themselves as natural and legitimate 'heirs' of the ancient Greek culture and civilisation (Kokosalakis 2003; Triandafyllidou *et al.* 1997). At the same time, when faced with less glorious and more difficult questions such as whether co-ethnics from Albania belong to the Greek nation, they might reconsider their ethnic definition of the national in-group and introduce a civic or territorial criterion to it. Thus ethnic Greek Albanians would be seen as culturally or genealogically Greek but of a 'lesser' kind than Greek citizens born and bred in the country and socialised into the Greek public education system, the national economy and political culture (Triandafyllidou 2001; Triandafyllidou and Veikou 2002). By contrast, when considering the existence and legitimacy of the Slavomacedonian minority in northern Greece they would be likely to emphasise the subjective and ethnic definition of the nation (Greek Helsinki Monitor and Minority Rights Group 1998; Karakasidou 1993, 1997). Members of that minority might be considered as 'less' Greek than their majority fellow citizens because they are seen as 'national traitors' endangering the unity and authenticity of the national in-group and its culture. In sum, even though most Greek nationals would not hesitate to point to antiquity as the moment of birth of the Greek nation, they would have considerable difficulties in maintaining consistency in their ideas when confronted with contemporary challenges to the Greek nation and nation-state.

My analysis will focus on the dominant national(ist) discourses in Greece at different historical periods with a view to highlighting the dynamic and fluid character of the nation as a form of collective identity. Concentrating on the moment of 'birth' of the nation may be misleading, putting too much emphasis on when the nation is formed and obscuring the fact that the nation is a moving target. The Greek nation-state maintains and enhances the emotive and symbolic power of membership to the nation, through tackling new challenges to its 'purity' or 'authenticity' and clarifying its membership and boundaries. Any attempt to fix a historical moment when a nation comes into being risks overlooking the dynamic nature of this process and indeed the power of the nation as a specific type of collective identity.

In the following sections, I shall define the moment of birth of the modern Greek nation and briefly outline the main tenets of Greek national identity formation in the early years of its 'life'. My focus will be on the dominant state and elite discourses, even though I shall also provide evidence of popular support of such views where this is available. Keeping the focus on state, elite and also media discourses on the nation, I shall also analyse in more detail two recent challenges to Greek national identity, notably the 'Macedonian question' and the distinction between immigrants of Greek descent and aliens in the Greek state and elite discourse in the late 1990s, with a view to highlighting how these reconsider the boundaries and essence of the nation. It is my contention that such processes are ongoing and point to the importance of analysing what and how the nation is and not only when it is.

Theories of nationalism and the when is the nation issue

Asking 'when is the nation?' presupposes a set of analytic or descriptive criteria according to which a group, community or other collectivity may be recognised as one. The problem is not simple, not least because a great variety of different types of groups have asserted their nationhood during the past two centuries. In this section, I shall classify the definitions of the nation provided by the main theorists in the area and examine the extent to which one may answer the 'when is the nation' question from their different perspectives.

Definitions of the nation (see also Uzelac 1999) may be of an *objective* or *subjective* type (Hobsbawm 1990: 5–7). The former establish objective criteria, namely a set of features a collectivity should have to qualify as a nation, while the latter define the nation in relation to its members' sense of belonging. A similar distinction is introduced by Gellner, who proposes two provisional definitions: the *cultural*, which views a shared culture as the main feature for identification of two individuals that belong to the same nation, and the *voluntaristic*, according to which 'two men are of the same nation if, and only if, they recognise each other as belonging to the same nation . . . nations are the artefacts of man's convictions and loyalties and solidarities' (Gellner 1983: 7). Seton Watson (1977: 5) emphasises the collective aspect of the voluntaristic notion: 'the nation exists when a significant number of people in a community consider themselves to form a nation, or behave as if they formed one.' The subjective nature of the nation (i.e. the fact that it does not consist of a set of specific features that characterise fellow nationals but rather refers to their sense of solidarity and common belonging) is pointed out by several well known scholars (Bauer cited in Nimni 1991: 148; Connor 1978: 377–399; Habermas 1992: 2; Ha'am cited in Smith 1986: 11; Renan 1990: 8–22).

These two different types of definition provide for two kinds of answer to my question. According to the objective or cultural view, the nation comes into being when it satisfies a set of criteria and, in particular, that of a common culture shared by a given population. Subjective definitions, in contrast, would assert that a nation exists if and when the members of one collectivity perceive themselves as members of that nation, or, which is almost the same thing, share a feeling of belonging to it.

Anthony Smith, in one of his most quoted books (1991: 14), provided for a combined definition of the nation providing for a list of criteria that should be satisfied for a group to be recognised as a national community: 'a named human population sharing an historic territory, common myths and historical memories, a mass, public culture, a common economy and common legal rights and duties for all members.' Even though Smith's definition is essentially of the objective kind, it includes a subjective element to the extent that a shared culture, a single economy and a common set of rights and duties entail a certain degree of awareness of membership to the group. More recently, however, Smith (2002: 15) has modified his definition to 'a named community possessing an historic territory, shared myths and memories, a common public culture and common laws and customs', thus downplaying the importance of common legal rights and duties, a common economy and a public culture of a mass character (see also Guibernau 2004). None the less, Smith's definition essentially retains its composite nature which brings together both objective (such as common laws and customs) and subjective elements (shared myths and memories, for instance).

It may seem logical, within either the subjective or the objective definition of the nation, that a historical moment, which may be defined in space and time, exists when it can be said that a nation is formed. Regardless of whether the nation emerges from a pre-existing ethnic group, as primordialists would argue, or it is awakened from its lethargy, as the perennialist view would sustain, or it is formed to respond to the needs of men and women in the modern era, as modernists may suggest, there seems to be an implicit agreement that there is a moment when nationhood comes into being (see also Breuilly, Grosby and Smith in this volume). It would then follow that this threshold, this moment of realisation of the national potential could be located in time and space, if one investigated the relevant historical and sociological parameters.

In my view, however, addressing this analytical question risks disguising the true nature of nations. A student of nationalism may privilege one or other definition of the nation, operationalise its specific elements or criteria and classify human collectivities in accordance to these. But the nation is a form of collective identification, bounded historically, that is, however, in a process of constant mutation, reaffirmation or transformation of its character, including the redefinition of the features that bind fellow nationals together, the scope of the nation and/or its past. This is not to say that the nation is an artificial product of human will. It is not a mere artefact of social or political engineering. The nation is inscribed into a pre-existing matrix of cultural and social organisational forms, including their material aspects that characterise a given population. It is, however, a collective identity, and as such it is not a static social object but a dynamic process: for the sense of belonging to the nation to survive, national identity has to preserve its symbolic and affective power towards the members of the nation.

In order to cast light on my argument I shall explore the dynamics of the formation of the Greek nation. I shall first discuss the moment of birth of the modern Greek nation and the main elements that characterised it as a collective identity. The focus of my analysis will then move to the present, addressing in more detail the ways in which the Greek nation-state has redefined national membership and the content of national identity as a response to what has been perceived as an external – the 'Macedonian question' – and an internal – recent immigration to Greece – challenge to its existence. The implications of these processes of redefining the nation for the theoretical question on when is the nation will be discussed in the conclusion to this chapter.

When is the Greek nation: a view into history

Following Smith's ethno-symbolist approach to nations and his definition of the nation (2002: 15) as 'a named community possessing an historic territory, shared myths and memories, a common public culture and common laws and customs', I contend that the modern Greek nation came into being in 1831 at the moment of the declaration of independence of the Greek nation-state. Following the national struggle of the previous decade (1821–1831), the existence and independence (even if under the tutelage of Britain, France and the Ottoman Empire) of the Greek nation-state was recognised with the signature of the London Protocol in 1831. At that moment, we can argue with a high level of certainty that the Greek nation was 'a named community', it possessed a historic territory, and a relatively large part of the population living in this territory shared common myths and memories relating to their existence as an ethnic community, their life under the Ottoman rule and the myths of liberation of the nation and of its historical capital Constantinople (see also Kitromilides 1990; Tsaousis 1983). The formation of the nation-state created the necessary preconditions for the population to have common laws and customs and a common public culture. Naturally the common public culture should be seen as in the making, at least during the early years/decades of the life of the new state. Greek society at the time was traditional, rural and deeply religious, but the new state had democratic Western-type institutions from the moment of its creation following the influence of the Greek enlightenment movement in the late eighteenth century (Kitromilides 1990: 25–33; Veremis 1983: 59–60). Actually the two elements were combined in the new state's nationalist discourse which brought together common ancestry (Kitromilides 1983; Veremis 1983, 1990), culture and language (Kitromilides 1990: 30) with the civic and territorial elements of the new state.

During the nineteenth century, the state and political elite's definition of the Greek nation emphasised the *irredenta*, namely the regions[1] inhabited by Greek-speaking Christian Orthodox populations that had not been included in the Greek state at the moment of its creation. The 'Great Idea' (*Μεγάλη Ιδέα*) (i.e. the cultural, political and ultimately military project of integrating these territories into the Greek state) represented the political expression of the ethnically, religiously and culturally linguistically defined Greek nation. It also played an important part in unifying a traditional and internally divided society and transforming it into a nation-state. Greece thus became the national centre, the political and cultural basis for the Greek populations living in the Near and Middle East as well as in the Balkans (Kitromilides 1983).

The Western institutions transplanted into the newborn Greek state, although alien to the traditional Greek society of the early nineteenth century, could be said to mark the continuity between classical and modern Greece. The official state discourse as well as that of intellectuals affirmed the importance of the 'ancient glorious past' in the conception of the modern Greek nation. The construction of Greek identity was completed through the integration of the Byzantine period into the historic trajectory of the nation.[2] The 'invention' of such a united and unique community was pursued throughout the nineteenth century through the state educational and cultural policies.

The integration of the Byzantine past into national consciousness led to the gradual identification of the flock with the nation. Even though this identification was problematic due to the contradiction between the particularistic claims of Greek nationalism and the universalist tendencies of the Christian Orthodox religion (Kitromilides 1990: 51–59), the separation of the Greek church from the Patriarchate of Constantinople in 1833 confirmed the intricate link between members of the nation and the faithful. Thus the political and religious elites' discourse based Greekness on an amalgamate of presumed common ancestry, shared cultural traditions and a common religion. This triple boundary distinguished Greeks from the non-Christian populations of the Ottoman empire and from the South Slavs of Christian denomination living in the Balkan peninsula, who, however, could not raise a claim to classical Greek culture.

The construction of a common legal and political system within the independent Greek state, the existence of a national economy and, most importantly, of a national army, the improvement of mobility within the national territory and also the creation of a common public education system influenced significantly the nature of Greek national identity, adding to it a set of territorial and civic features. In the early twentieth century, the Greek nation-state acquired new territories extending its borders to the West (Ionian islands), East (Aegean islands), South (Crete) and to the North (Macedonia, Epirus and Thrace), and eventually both the elites and the citizens largely abandoned the irredentist discourse and the irredentist conception of the nation in favour of a stable but 'small' Greece (see also Triandafyllidou and Paraskevopoulou 2002). None the less, Greekness continues to be defined as a transcendental notion in Greek public discourse (Tsoukalas 1993).

In this section, I have defined the moment of birth of the modern Greek nation as that of the formation of an independent Greek nation-state. I have also briefly discussed the definition and boundaries of the nation and how these were shaped during the nineteenth and early twentieth centuries. In the following sections,

I shall turn to the present to discuss how recent challenges to the Greek nation have been dealt with in the dominant nationalist discourse leading to a reconsideration of both its membership and boundaries. My focus in this chapter is on the outbreak of the 'Macedonian question' in the 1990s (Roudometof 1996; Triandafyllidou *et al.* 1997) and on the (doubtful) incorporation of immigrants of Greek ethnic origin into the nation-state in the late 1990s. I will thus try to show how the state policy and the elite and media discourses redefined on two occasions the Greek nation, its borders and its content, shifting its contours in important ways.

The Macedonian question

The phrase 'Macedonian question' has been widely used over the past century to refer to a political conflict and warfare in the Balkan peninsula focusing on the geographical region of Macedonia. The use of this phrase here, however, is confined to the contemporary issues raised by Greece after the proclamation of independence by FYROM in 1991. The dispute between the two countries over the name of the new Republic is part of a 'global cultural war' (Featherstone 1990: 10) that the two states fought over the control of symbols, traditions and glorious ancestors.[3] The name 'Former Yugoslav Republic of Macedonia' (FYROM) has been assigned by the United Nations to the new state, despite the discontent of the latter. Indeed, this was the first time that an independent state has not been able to use its symbols and its name as it wishes in order not to offend the national sentiments of another country. These decisions have resulted from an international diplomatic rally the Greek government engaged in and which included a veto within the European Union. The quest was that the 'Republic of Skopje', as Greeks call it, would not be recognised as 'Macedonia' *tout court.*

The complexity of the Macedonian question is due to the intertwining of cultural with geographical and political issues. There is a Greek part of Macedonia, whose capital is Thessaloniki and which forms an integral part of the Greek state and the Greek nation. According to Greek historiography, the inhabitants of this region define themselves primarily as Greeks (Christides 1949; Martis 1984). Moreover, this region is identified with the dynasty and the accomplishments of origin of Alexander the Great. Therefore, Greeks consider the symbols, myths and traditions relating to Alexander as part of their cultural heritage.

By contrast, according to the government of FYROM, there can be no such historic claim regarding the nationality of Alexander the Great; he was certainly not Slav, but neither was he Greek or Bulgarian in the modern sense of the concept. Therefore, all parts of the geographical region of Macedonia (the ex-Yugoslav, the Bulgarian and the Greek section) have equal rights to refer to Alexander since his cultural heritage is shared by the entire territory. Thus, if Macedonian tradition is not the 'property' of the Greeks, there can be no veto raised on the use of its name and/or its symbols.

As Bourdieu (1991: 236) argues, naming is a fundamental expression of political power. To name something means to bring it into existence. As if to confirm

Bourdieu's argument, the Greek state has strongly opposed the use of the name 'Macedonia' by the new Republic. According to the claims of the Greek government, the use of the name implied the overall appropriation of the symbols, traditions, myths and even the territory associated with the name 'Macedonia'. It is worth noting that the 'Socialist Republic of Macedonia' existed previously as a federal state within Yugoslavia. After the dismantling of the Yugoslav federation and in accordance with the will of the people living in the Republic, as this was expressed in the referendum of 8 September 1991, an independent and sovereign state was established. Thus the name 'Macedonia' came to describe not a political unit subordinated to a federation, but a nation-state.

In accordance with the nationalist perspective, Greece had also opposed the use of the flag of FYROM, because it carried the image of the 'star' of Vergina. This 'star' or 'sunburst' was discovered in the mid-1970s at Vergina, where the ancient Macedonian capital 'Aegai' was located, at the south-west of Thessaloniki, and is considered to be the emblem of the empire of Alexander the Great. The Greek government pointed to the oddness of a flag which represents the national identity of a people (i.e. the 'Macedonians') by evoking the national tradition and cultural heritage of another nation, namely the Greeks. The argument is based on the specific political role assigned to cultural symbols within the nation-state. These are supposed to represent the continuity and unity of the national community through history. Therefore, the flag and the very name of the new state were judged contradictory by the Greek government.

During the crisis period of the 'Macedonian question' in the mid-1990s, political parties manipulated the nationalist feelings of the population during election campaigning, using the issue as a means of discrediting one another while keeping the voters' attention away from internal economic and social problems. A conservative government initially and later a socialist government stimulated nationalist sentiments and, simultaneously, acted to disorient the electorate in a period of economic and political crisis. National pride was systematically emphasised in a political discourse that concentrated on the 'injustice' caused by 'foreigners' (i.e. FYROM or the international community). Thus, as often happens, the glories of the past were used to compensate for the failures and dissatisfaction of the present.

Such manipulation has marked the political history of Greece since the beginning of this century. The example of the *Megali Idea*, i.e. the idealistic conception developed by the Greek state up to the expedition in Asia Minor in the 1920s, according to which all the territories in which people of Greek origin lived were to be incorporated into one powerful and independent Greek state, is an obvious case in point (Mavrogordatos 1983). The final scope was certainly not reached, yet Greece succeeded in dramatically increasing its territory and population as a result of its participation in the Balkan wars and the First World War, while shortly afterwards in the early 1920s it had to abandon all its remaining irredentist claims and reconcile the reality of the nation-state with the ethno-cultural vision of the nation as an entity much larger than the former (Triandafyllidou and Paraskevopoulou 2002).

Concerning the 'Macedonian question' in the 1990s, a rigid nationalist position was initially adopted by the conservative government of Mr C. Mitsotakis, leader of *Nea Demokratia*.[4] The governing party, which held a parliamentary majority of merely one seat, seems to have tried to increase its electoral appeal through the use of nationalist propaganda. The government undertook a number of cultural initiatives against the recognition of the 'Republic of Macedonia'. Roundtables, workshops and public debates with the participation of the academic community and the media were organised. Furthermore, the National Tourism Agency launched an advertising campaign promoting cultural trips to the North of Greece, in the regions of Macedonia and Thrace. Nationalist messages written in English were stamped on T-shirts and stickers: 'First learn history' and 'The spirit of Alexander the Great is universal but his homeland Macedonia has been Greek for the past 3,000 years'.

The government's initiatives were successful in mobilising Greeks at home and abroad. An enormous public rally took place in Athens in December 1992. Although organised in a rather informal way, this rally gathered approximately one million people. It seems that collective mobilisation occurred quite spontaneously due to the perceived importance of the matter at stake. Another public demonstration was organised in Thessaloniki a few months later, as were others in most of the Greek diaspora communities in the USA, Canada and Australia (Danforth 1995).

The adoption by Mr Mitsotakis of a more flexible attitude with regard to the Macedonian question during the summer of 1993 was regarded as behaviour that was 'nationally dangerous' and led a small number of MPs from his party to withdraw their support from the government. Moreover, a new party called *Politiki Anixi* was created under the leadership of the ex-Minister of Foreign Affairs, Andonis Samaras. A small number of conservative deputies abandoned *Nea Demokratia* and joined forces with the ex-Minister, claiming that Mr Mitsotakis was acting against the national interest, particularly with reference to the Macedonian question. Nationalist fervour dominated the pre-election campaign in autumn 1993 and was widely promoted by the opposition parties, both *Politiki Anixi* and the Socialist party PASOK,[5] in their campaigning discourse.

The Macedonian question remained a major policy issue for the socialist government and its leader, Mr A. Papandreou, who won the election of October 1993. After the election, the socialists and Mr Papandreou took a more rigid position than that adopted by the previous government. The situation reached a moment of particular tension during the Greek presidency of the European Union in the first semester of 1994. The Greek government upheld its position and refused to raise the embargo it had imposed on FYROM in November 1993. In fact, any proposal for compromise regarding the name 'Macedonia' and the symbols associated with it seemed likely to provoke a strong popular reaction and called into question the legitimacy of the government itself.

Diplomatic and economic relations between Greece and the FYROM were restored in September 1995 after the intervention of the USA, which put pressure on both countries to reach a compromise. Indeed, the 'star' of Vergina, royal symbol of Alexander the Great and his accomplishments, was removed from the flag of FYROM, while Greece lifted the embargo it had imposed on the country in 1993. The administrations that succeeded Mr Papandreou's withdrawal from politics in January 1996 made clear their wish to find a compromise, and so did the government of FYROM. None the less, negotiations over the name question are still on course and a number of alternatives have been discussed but no final decision has been made; both sides are extremely cautious in accepting a solution that could in any way provoke the national sentiments of their populations. For the time being, the country has been recognised by the United Nations, the Council of Europe and other international organisations with the name FYROM, even though in common parlance and in the media – outside Greece – it is now increasingly referred to as 'Macedonia' *tout court*.

Regardless of the eventual outcome of the name issue, this dispute shows that faced with a challenge over its ethnic and cultural myths, the Greek nation-state has had to redefine the nation in ways that responded to both the political and symbolic aspects of the challenge. While, at the early stages of emergence of the independent Greek nation-state, there were contradictory views with regard to the 'hellenicity' of the heritage of Alexander and his dynasty, the 'Macedonian question' challenge made of Alexander the Great a core element of the classical heritage. The state, intellectuals and laypeople discourses converged to reinforce the importance of Alexander in the Greek national history and genealogy. The whole 'Macedonian' issue led, unfortunately, to the revival of a defensive Greek nationalism that emphasised the ethno-cultural basis of the nation at the expense of its civic and territorial features. This tendency was further reinforced when Greece, again during the 1990s, faced the challenge of incoming migration from Central Eastern Europe and the Third World.

The immigration challenge

Greece, traditionally a country of emigration, has faced a large influx of immigrants from Central-Eastern European, Asian and African countries since the late 1980s. In this chapter, I am not concerned with the overall issue of recent immigration towards Greece nor about the overall development of Greek immigration policy. Rather I want to discuss how, in developing an immigration policy (and policy discourse) that would respond to the new international context and the de facto presence of several hundreds of thousands of undocumented immigrants in Greece, the national authorities introduced a distinction between immigrants of Greek descent and aliens, redefining once more the boundaries and identity of the nation.[6]

Over half a million immigrants reside legally in Greece today while the total immigrant population (including undocumented foreigners) is estimated at about 650 to 700,000 (Fakiolas 2003: 540), or approximately 6 per cent in a total population of 11 million. As in other EU countries, in Greece there is extensive support for restrictive immigration policies for third country nationals (Eurobarometere 1997, report 47.1, p. 7).[7] Already in the mid-1990s, Greek citizens felt that there were too many foreigners in their country (Triandafyllidou and Mikrakis 1995:

170–171). Regarding the relationship between the nation(-state) and immigrants, the prevalent discourse justifies discrimination delegitimising the position of the immigrant in the host society on the basis of ethnic and cultural arguments (Triandafyllidou 2001).

My aim here is to show how, in its efforts to control and manage immigration through the development of appropriate policy measures, the Greek nation-state has developed a policy and public discourse (accompanying and legitimising the related policy measures) that distinguishes between immigrants of Greek descent, in particular Pontic Greeks and Greek Albanians, from 'other' immigrants. According to dominant definitions of the nation, Greek Albanian immigrants do not entirely belong to the in-group because despite their Greek origins, they remain citizens of another state. Pontic Greeks, in contrast, have been recognised as entirely Greek and were granted Greek citizenship upon their arrival to Greece. The creation of a living space in Greek society for these two groups, as well as the range of possibilities and solutions found in practice, have depended to a large extent on their claim to Greek ethnicity. Their 'Greekness' became an issue of claim and negotiation, related to its potential in securing not only an easier entry into Greece but also a better reception and acceptance.

A large part of the migration patterns towards Greece correspond to pre-existing ethnic ties. A number of immigrants coming from ex-communist states claim Greek ethnicity and choose Greece as their resettlement destination on the assumption that a presumed common cultural past should allow an easier integration. Another important reason that attracts 'co-ethnics' to Greece is that according to the Greek Constitution, people from the Greek diaspora are entitled to a favourable legal status in Greece. To be granted this legal status, immigrants have to officially claim and prove their Greek origin (Article 1, par. 3 and Article 108 of the Constitution). According to this Article, immigrants of Greek origin are recognised as de facto refugees or *Ομογενείς* (co-ethnics). Fakiolas (2003: 540) states that 103,000 Pontic Greeks were naturalised in the period 1990 to 1999 and estimates the total number of ethnic Greeks from the former Soviet Union at 110,000. He also estimates that about 40 to 60,000 ethnic Greeks from Albania live in Greece and were registered at the last census (2001), although he calls for caution in assuming these estimates to be correct (real numbers may be higher).

Immigration law 1975/1991 dealt, in a separate section, with a specific category of foreigners, the so-called 'co-ethnics' (provided they do not have Greek citizenship), further identified as Vorioepirotes (*Βορειο-Ηπειρώτες*) and Pontic Repatriates (*Πόντιοι Παλλινοστούντες*) – carrying all the ideological connotations that these names signify[8] – who are differentiated from 'other' immigrants, the aliens, because of their Greek ethnic origins. The law did not provide a conceptual definition of who qualifies as 'co-ethnic'. According to the decision of the State Council[9] no. 2756/1983, the legitimate criterion for one to be characterised as a co-ethnic is 'to belong to the Greek Ethnos'. That is 'to have Greek national consciousness', which is 'deduced from characteristics of personality which refer to common descent, language, religion, national traditions and extensive knowledge of the historical events of the nation'. The decision presumably refers to unifying features based on religion, language and origin, which provide the grounds for social identity ascription. Another judgement of the State Council no. 2207/1992 also attempted to provide a description of the status of immigrants especially those of Greek origin coming from Albania: 'co-ethnics from Albania are the people that descend from Greek parents and their place of birth (theirs or their parents) is Vorios Epirus (*Βόρειος Ήπειρος*).'

The criteria of Greekness set out in these decisions replicate and reinforce the ethnic-cultural-religious definition of the Greek nation. The boundary between insiders and outsiders is defined by a combination of ethnic and religious features. This issue is particularly relevant for Albania, the major sending country for Greece, where people who are Christian Orthodox and have Greek names are given preference over Muslim Albanians.

The official policy discourse of the Greek government is somewhat differentiated towards each of these groups. Pontic Greeks are defined by the Greek state as members of the diaspora community[10] who 'return' – even though most of them had never lived in Greece before – to their 'homeland', and are therefore given full citizen status and benefits aiming to facilitate their integration into Greek society.[11] As regards Greek Albanians, law 1975/1991, on the basis of Article 108 of the Greek Constitution, provided them with a preferable legal status as people without the Greek citizenship but with the Greek nationality (Article 17). The preferential status of ethnic Greek Albanians in Greece is reiterated in law 2910/2001. In practice the Greek state avoids naturalising ethnic Greeks from Albania – as it did with Pontic Greeks – but instead issues special identity cards giving them all the rights of Greek citizens except the right to vote.

The special policy provisions concerning Pontic Greeks and the semi-formal preferential treatment of Greek Albanians were reflected also in the media and political discourse on immigration. The press adopted a favourable attitude towards Pontic Greeks and their return and integration into Greek society (Mikrakis and Triandafyllidou 1994: 799). Their Greek identity and the fact that they have preserved their Greek habits, their national consciousness and their Christian Orthodox religion in foreign lands were emphasised,[12] despite the fact that a large part of the Pontic Greek population, for instance, did not speak Greek, at least not when they first arrived in the country.

Genealogical descent was a prevalent dimension of the press discourse on immigration in the early to mid-1990s (Triandafyllidou 1998, 2001, ch. 6). Ethnic origins were emphasised in order to differentiate between immigrants of Greek descent and 'others'. Pontic Greeks were welcomed, as were Greek Albanians, even though the Greek authorities had not conceded them Greek citizenship. The distinction between these last and 'other' Albanians was prominent. The alleged rise of violence and criminality, for instance, was attributed to Albanian immigrants (Pavlou 2001). Greek Albanians, in contrast, were presented as their victims. The headings of the newspapers were often explicit: 'Albanians kill and rob people from northern Epirus',[13] 'Albanian criminals kill rob and rape . . . they have transformed neighbourhoods of Athens and entire provincial cities into ghettos'.[14] Ethnic Greek Albanians were confronted with a different spirit: 'Greece

is also their homeland . . . they have a right to come.'[15] A number of interviews
with Greek Albanians were published in the newspapers. Their inhuman living
and working conditions, the hostility they were often confronted with and their
exploitation by domestic employers were criticised. Any illegal actions they committed were justified as actions of despair and need. The situation of deep poverty
in which they lived in Albania and the inimical attitudes of ethnic Albanians
towards them were also emphasised.[16]

Similarly to the press, social actors involved in immigration policy and politics
expressed favourable attitudes towards both groups. The Greekness of either
group was considered a matter of (presumed) common ethnic origin and historical ties with the Greek culture and language. However, for matters of foreign
policy of the Greek state, or as it was eloquently stated by both NGO representatives and public administrative employees 'for matters of national interest',
Pontic Greeks were given full rights and Greek passports while Greek Albanians
were treated as guest workers. In other words, Greek Albanians were 'also a bit
like Greeks' but their Greekness was not recognised because it was in 'Greece's
interests' (i.e. the interests of the state, which represents Greek citizens) that they
remained in Albania to keep alive the Greek minority there. Not one of the
informants challenged the legitimacy of this view. Even though the Greek state
defines Pontic Greeks as Greek citizens, their Greekness was contested by some of
the interviewees. While a trade union representative acknowledged that Pontic
Greeks 'are not Pontic, they are Greeks', other informants, mainly from the
public administration, differentiated between Pontic Greeks and '*normal* Greeks'
(emphasis added) or '*ντόπιοι*' (locals).

The distinction between Pontic Greeks, Greek Albanians and aliens prompted
among the informants a reflection on Greek nationhood. With regard to the
former, the answer provided by most interviewees was straightforward: Greek
nationality was defined on the basis of ethnic descent, language, common historical memories and/or links with historic homelands and culture. Their Greekness
was derived from their 'Greek consciousness'. Even though most of these features
characterised Greek Albanians too, their Greekness was not recognised. Eventually, as an employee of the Labour Ministry argued: 'Each state has the discretion
of treating people of the same ethnicity in a different way [than aliens] if it wishes
to do so.'

As this analysis shows, the contradictions of the policy design and the ambivalence of the public discourse towards different groups of immigrants of Greek
origin were rationalised and accommodated through the creation of multiple
levels of inclusion–exclusion. Our informants conceptualised Greekness in con-
centric circles: 'real Greeks', i.e. citizens of the Greek state, of Greek ethnicity and
Orthodox religion, belonged to the inner circle, legal aliens to the outer circle
while Pontic Greeks and Greek Albanians stood in-between.

The preferential treatment of both groups was based on a redefinition of Greek
nationality and citizenship that emphasised the ethnic basis of either, building on
presumed genealogical and cultural ties between the incoming populations and
the native Greek citizens. Having said this, it is difficult to explain the outright

preferential treatment of Pontic Greeks as opposed to the overall insecure and ambivalent status of Greek Albanians on the basis of mere ethnic origin. The analysis of the policy framework and the public discourse showed that the 'Greekness' of the different groups was subject to an implicit, and sometimes also explicit, hierarchy. Thus, although populations of Greek ethnic origin and culture were recognised as (potential) members of the Greek nation, the (perceived) 'interests'[17] of full-fledged Greeks (i.e. the Greeks of Greece as opposed to the Greeks of the diaspora) as a nation prevail over the interests of such populations. According to this logic, Pontic Greeks had the right to 'return' to their 'homeland' because they were ethnic Greeks and because this did not in any sense contradict the interests of the Greek nation(-state). Likewise, their planned settlement in regions where there is a strong presence of the Turkish Muslim minority (Thrace) was meant to serve precisely these interests. Similarly, the Greek policy towards Greek Albanians was guided by the overall principle of an ethno-cultural definition of the nation but was further subordinated to the political interests of the Greek nation(-state) to maintain alive the Greek minority in Albania (Veikou 2001). These contradictory considerations were and still are reflected in the ambivalence of the legal and administrative provisions concerning this group which, although preferentially treated, at the informal level in particular, did not see its citizenship rights recognised.

Faced with the necessity to deal with immigration in a long-term perspective and integrate at least part of the immigrant population to the Greek society, the Greek state opted for a policy legitimised by a discourse of ethnic preference. Given the fact that the influx of Pontic Greeks had by the end of the 1990s been completed and regarded as a relatively small portion of the total foreign population, the net was cast more widely to the forgotten 'children' of Greece, the Greek Albanians. In adopting this view, the Greek authorities have taken into account the ethnic and cultural ties of these people with Greece, which could render their integration quicker, smoother and less costly for the host society than if they were aliens. Moreover, Greek Albanians, just like Pontic Greeks, were not considered as a 'threat' to Greek cultural homogeneity because of their ethnic origins and religion. In contrast, their inclusion offered a good excuse for rejecting those who do not belong, namely Muslim Albanians and 'other' immigrants.

In conclusion, I have shown here how the distinction between immigrants of Greek descent and aliens has involved a redefinition of the boundaries of the national community. State authorities, supported also by the media and elite discourses, have strategically used history, ethnicity and culture to include the newcomers in the national community.

Conclusions

In this chapter, I have used the case of Greece to illustrate how a nation's essence and boundaries may be redefined many times after the nation is born and often by the very same agents (nation-state, elites, intellectuals, media) that were involved in its 'birth'. I have briefly surveyed the dominant nation-state discourses regarding the content and boundaries of the nation in the early nineteenth century when the Greek nation was 'born'. I have then highlighted how the national myths, the history and genealogy of the nation and even its membership are redefined in the face of new challenges. Concentrating on the last decade of the twentieth century, I have illustrated how two recent challenges to Greek national identity, notably the controversy between Greece and the FYROM with regard to the latter's claim to the ancient Macedonian heritage (a heritage that Greece considered its own 'cultural property') and the public and policy discourse on immigration (in response to the large numbers of incoming migrants) involved the redefinition of the origins and boundaries of the nation. The nation was thus each time 'born anew' – not politically but symbolically – renewing its vitality in the eyes of its members.

In response to the 'Macedonian question' dispute, the country's cultural and ethnic unity was emphasised, and any political or territorial features that might reveal discontinuities of the national past – in particular the fact that the Greek region of Macedonia was incorporated into the independent Greek state only at the beginning of this century (Clogg 1992) – were downplayed. The origins of the nation were reinterpreted in the public and political discourse with a view to fully integrating Alexander the Great into the ancient Greek legacy.

The distinction between immigrants of Greek descent and complete aliens responded to the necessity of an at least partial integration of the undocumented immigrant population that has resided in Greece during the 1990s. The development of a state policy based on Greek ethnicity resonated with the dominant discourse on the Greek nation while also partly redefining its contours, taming an integral policy of ethnic preference to pragmatic considerations of the presumed interest of the Greek state and its citizens.

In conclusion, the Greek nation appears to be in full evolution, under the pressure of new internal and external challenges, despite its nearly two centuries of existence. Thus, while many Greek nationals and probably some scholars would argue that the Greek nation was born in antiquity and/or the modern Greek nation-state in the early nineteenth century, I want to stress that although either point may be acceptable – depending on the theoretical definition of the nation that one endorses[18] – it is more important to remember that this is only part of the story of nations and nationalism. Investigating the processes of reaffirmation and transformation of nations and national identities may be a more fruitful strategy for understanding the historical character and analytical status of nations as collectivities. In my view, insisting on a definite answer to the question 'when is the Greek nation' risks obscuring the dynamic character of national identity in general and of the Greek nation in particular.

Notes

1 The *irredenta* included all territories inhabited by ethnic Greeks, ethnicity (which for Greeks is coterminous with nationality) being defined in terms of language, culture, historical memories or religion. The *irredenta* extended to the north and included

Macedonia, Thrace and even farther northern Balkan regions south from the Donau. To the east the irredentist claims referred to territories of the Ottoman empire, notably the Aegean islands, Cyprus, Crete, Minor Asia and also parts of Anatolia (Kitromilides 1990: 43–45).

2 See, for instance, the (in)famous dispute between the Greek historian Constantine Paparigopoulos and the Austrian historiographer Jacob Philipp Fallmerayer. The latter claimed that Byzantine chronicles provided historians with sufficient proof to argue that the Slavic invasions of the sixth century in the Byzantine empire adulterated the Greek blood that the inhabitants of the Greek peninsula presumably had (Dimaras 1985, 1986; Skopetea 1999).

3 The analysis of the 'Macedonian question' presented in this section borrows heavily from Triandafyllidou *et al.* (1997). Excerpts presented here are reprinted with the kind permission of *Sociological Research Online*.

4 *Nea Democratia* is the major conservative party in Greece. It was in office from 1974 to 1981 and again from 1990 to 1993. Recently (March 2004), it was re-elected in government under the leadership of Mr K. Karamanlis.

5 PASOK (Hellenic Socialist Movement) is currently the second largest party in Greece and has been in office between 1981 and 1989 and again from 1993 until 2004.

6 The discussion of the distinction between ethnic Greeks and aliens in Greek immigration policy borrows heavily from Triandafyllidou and Veikou (2002). Excerpts included here are reprinted with the kind permission of *Ethnicities*.

7 See http://europa.eu.int/comm/public_opinion/archives/ebs/ebs_113_en.pdf

8 The 'Vorioepirotes' were, according to the dominant Greek political view, 'Greek enslaved brothers' who suffered in the past under 'the yoke of a foreign ruler'. Equally, the term 'Pontic Repatriates' signifies a specific kind of bond with the 'motherland', implying that Pontic Greeks 'return' to, although they had never actually lived in, Greece before. These views, supported by the ideological mechanisms of the state and other non-governmental institutions, spread in a rather large part of the domestic population and contributed to the shaping of a relatively positive attitude towards Greek Albanians and Pontic Greeks.

9 State Council is the Supreme Administrative Court of Justice in Greece.

10 With regard to Pontic Greeks see also *Journal of Refugee Studies* (1991, Special Issue, 4, 4).

11 For more details on the policies of the Greek state towards Pontic Greeks and ethnic Greek Albanians, see Triandafyllidou and Veikou (2002).

12 See, for instance, Athens newspapers *To Vema* (16 June 1991; 9 September 1991); *Kathimerini* (19 May 1991); *Tipos tis Kiriakis* (9 September 1992).

13 Headings from articles published in the national daily press: *Eleftherotipia* (14 December 1991); *Apogevmatini* (21 January 1993); *Mesimbrini* (11 February 1994).

14 Abstract from five-column article published in the Athens right-wing daily newspaper *Eleftheros* (11 January 1993). The article included a list of crimes committed during 1992 and emphasised the supposedly tight link between Albanian immigrants and the rise of violence and criminality throughout the country.

15 *Apogevmatini* (27 April 1993).

16 *To Vema* (16 June 1991); see also King *et al.* (1998).

17 Here we refer to the 'interests' of the Greek nation(-state) as these have been defined by successive governments and not to our personal views on the matter.

18 See also *Nations and Nationalism* (2004, Special Issue 10, 1–2).

References

Anderson, B. (1991) *Imagined Communities* (2nd edn), London: Verso.

Armstrong, J. (1982) *Nations before Nationalism*, Chapel Hill: University of North Carolina Press.

Bourdieu, P. (1991) *Language and Symbolic Power*, Cambridge, MA: Harvard University Press.

Christides, C. (1949) *The Macedonian Camouflage in the Light of Facts and Figures*, Athens: The Hellenic Publishing Company.

Clogg, R. (1992) *A Concise History of Modern Greece*, Cambridge: Cambridge University Press.

Connor, W. (1978) 'The nation is a Nation, is a State . . .', *Ethnic and Racial Studies*, 1(4): 377–399.

Danforth, L. (1995) *The Macedonian Conflict: Ethnic Nationalism in a Transnational World*, Princeton, NJ: Princeton University Press.

Dimaras, K. (1985) *Greek Enligthenment*, Athens: Ermis (in Greek).

Dimaras, K. (1986) *Konstantinos Paparigopoulos*, Athens: Morfotiko Idryma Ethnikis Trapezis (in Greek).

Fakiolas, R. (2003) 'Regularising undocumented immigrants in Greece: procedures and effects', *Journal of Ethnic and Migration Studies*, 29(3): 535–561.

Featherstone, M. (1990) *Global Culture: Nationalism, Globalization and Modernity*, London: Sage.

Gellner, E. (1983) *Nations and Nationalism*, Oxford: Blackwell.

Greek Helsinki Monitor and Minority Rights Group (1998) *Greece Against its Macedonian Minority: The 'Rainbow' Trial*, Athens: ETEPE.

Guibernau, M. (2004) 'Anthony D Smith on nations and national identity: a critical assessment', *Nations and Nationalism*, 10: 1–2, 125–142.

Habermas, J. (1992) 'Citizenship and national identity: some reflections on the future of Europe', *Praxis International*, 12(1)

Hastings, A. (1997) *The Construction of Nationhood: Ethnicity, Religion and Nationalism*, Cambridge; Cambridge University Press.

Hobsbawm, E.J. (1990) *Nations and Nationalism Since 1780. Programme, Myth, Reality*, Cambridge: Cambridge University Press.

Journal of Refugee Studies (1991) *The Odyssey of Pontic Greeks*, Special Issue, 4(4).

Karakasidou, A. (1993) 'Politicizing culture: negating ethnic identity in Greek Macedonia', *Journal of Modern Greek Studies*, 11: 1–28.

Karakasidou, A. (1997) *Fields of Wheat, Hills of Blood*, Chicago, IL: Chicago University Press.

Kedourie, E. (1992) *Nationalism*, Oxford: Blackwell.

Kendrotis, K. (1995) 'Το μεταναστευτικό ζήτημα στην εξωτερική πολιτική των Βαλκανικών κρατών' (The immigration issue in the policy of foreign affairs of Balkan States), *Τετράδια Πολιτικού Διαλόγου, Ερυυνας και Κριτικής*: 36–37.

King, R., Iosifides, T. and Myrivili, L. (1998) 'A migrant's story: from Albania to Athens', *Journal of Ethnic and Migration Studies*, 24(1): 159–175.

Kitromilides, P. (1983) 'Το Ελληνικό κράτος ως εθνικό κέντρο' (The Greek state as national centre), in D. Tsaousis (ed.) *Ελληνισμός-Ελληνικότητα: Ιδεολογικοί και Βιωματικοί Αξονες της Νεοελληνικής Κοινωνίας* (Hellenism and Greekness: Ideological and Biographical Axes of Modern Greek Society), Athens: Estia.

Kitromilides, P. (1990) 'Imagined communities and the origins of the national question in the Balkans', in M. Blinkhorn and T. Veremis (eds) *Modern Greece: Nationalism and Nationality*, Athens: ELIAMEP.

Kokosalakis, N. (2003) 'Nation and Europe: the views and attitudes of lay people in Greece (a qualitative analysis)', Athens, Panteion University, available to download from http://www.iue.it/RSCAS/Research/EURONAT/Projects.shtml.

Martis, N. (1984) *The Falsification of the Macedonian History*, Athens: Evroekdotiki.

Mavrogordatos, G. (1983) 'To elliniko kratos os ethniko kentro', in D. Tsaousis (ed.) *Ελληνισμός-Ελληνικότητα: Ιδεολογικοί και Βιωματικοί Αξονες της Νεοελληνικής*

Κοινωνίας (Hellenism and Greekness: Ideological and Biographical Axes of Modern Greek Society), Athens: Estia (in Greek).

Mikrakis, A. and Triandafyllidou, A. (1994) 'Greece: the "others" within', *Social Science Information*, 33(4): 787–805.

Nimni, E. (1991) *Marxism and Nationalism*, London: Pluto Press.

Pavlou, M. (2001) 'Ρατσιστικός λόγος και μετανάστες στον Τύπο μιας υποψήφιας "μητρόπολης": Οι λαθρέμποροι του φόβου' (Racist discourse and immigrants in the press of a candidate "metropolis": the contraband merchants of fear). in A. Marvakis, D. Parsanoglou and M. Pavlou (eds) *Μετανάστες στην Ελλάδα* (Immigrants in Greece), Athens: Ellinika Grammata.

Renan, E. (1990) 'What is a nation?', translation by M Thom of 'Qu'est-ce qu'une nation?', in H. Bhabha (ed.) *Nation and Narration*, London: Routledge), pp. 8–22.

Roudometof, V. (1996) 'Nationalism and identity politics in the Balkans: Greece and the Macedonian question', *Journal of Modern Greek Studies*, 14: 253–301.

Seton Watson, H. (1977) *Nations and States*, London: Methuen.

Skopetea, E. (1999) *Fallmerayer: Tricks of the Rival Awe*, Athens: Themelio (in Greek).

Smith, A.D. (1986) *The Ethnic Origins of Nations*, Oxford: Blackwell.

Smith, A.D. (1991) *National Identity*, Harmondsworth: Penguin.

Smith, A.D. (1998) *Nationalism and Modernism*, London: Routledge.

Smith, A.D. (2002) 'When is a nation', *Geopolitics*, 7(2): 5–32.

Triandafyllidou, A. (1998) 'Οι "άλλοι" ανάμεσα μας – Ελληνική εθνική ταυτότητα και στασεις προς τους μετανάστες' (The 'others' among us – Greek national identity and attitudes towards immigrants), in *Κοινωνικές Ανισότητες και Κοινωνικός Αποκλεισμός* (Social Inequalities and Social Exclusion), Proceedings of the Sixth Annual Conference of the Saki Karagiorga Foundation, Athens: Exantas.

Triandafyllidou, A. (2000) 'The political discourse on immigration in Southern Europe: a critical analysis', *Journal of Community and Applied Social Psychology*, 10(5): 373–389.

Triandafyllidou, A. (2001) *Immigrants and National Identity in Europe*, London: Routledge.

Triandafyllidou, A. and Mikrakis, A. (1995) 'Greece: a ghost wanders through the capital', in B. Baumgartl and A. Favell (eds) *The New Xenophobia in Europe*, London: Kluwer International Law, pp. 165–179.

Triandafyllidou, A. (2002) *Negotiating Nationhood in a Changing Europe: Views from the Press*, Ceredigion, Wales and Washington D.C.: The Edwin Mellen Press

Triandafyllidou, A. and Paraskevopoulou, A. (2002) 'When is the Greek nation? The role of enemies and minorities', *Geopolitics*, 7(2): 75–98.

Triandafyllidou, A. and Veikou, M. (2002) 'The hierarchy of Greekness. ethnic and national identity considerations in Greek immigration policy', *Ethnicities*, 2(2): 189–208.

Triandafyllidou, A., Mikrakis, A. and Calloni, M. (1997) 'New Greek nationalism', *Sociological Research Online*, 2(1): www.socresonline.org.uk/2/1/7.html.

Tsaousis, D. (ed.) (1983) *Ελληνισμός-Ελληνικότητα: Ιδεολογικοί και Βιωματικοί Άξονες της Νεοελληνικής Κοινωνίας* (Hellenism and Greekness: Ideological and Biographical Axes of Modern Greek Society), Athens: Estia, In Greek.

Tsoukalas, C. (1993) 'Greek national identity in an integrated Europe and a changing world order', in H. Psomiades and S. Thomadakis (eds) *Greece, the New Europe and the Changing International Order*, New York: Pella.

Uzelac, G. (1999) 'Perceptions of national identity', *Canadian Review of Studies on Ethnicity and Nationalism*, 26(2): 123–138.

Veikou, M., (2001), 'Η εττιτελεστική κατασκευή της εθνοτικής ταυτότητας' (Performing ethnic identity), in A. Marvakis, D. Parsanoglou, M. Pavlou (eds.) *Μετανάστες στην Ελλάδα* (Immigrants in Greece). Athens: Ellinika Grammata, in Greek, pp. 305–327.

Veremis, T. (1983) 'Κράτος και Εθνος στην Ελλάδα: 1821–1912' (State and Nation in Greece: 1821–1912), in D. Tsaousis (ed.) *Ελληνισμός-Ελληνικότητα: Ιδεολογικοί και Βιωματικοί Αξονες της Νεοελληνικής Κοινωνίας* (Hellenism and Greekness: Ideological and Biographical Axes of Modern Greek Society), Athens: Estia.

Veremis, T. (1990) 'From the national state to the stateless nation, 1821–1910', in M. Blinkhorn and T. Veremis (eds) *Modern Greece: Nationalism and Nationality*, Athens: Eliamep.

10 Nationalism and the politics of ethnicity in Fiji

Critical perspectives on primordialism, modernism and ethno-symbolism

Stephanie Lawson

Introduction

Nationalism in the Republic of the Fiji Islands is almost invariably associated with the political claims of indigenous Fijians, and what seems to be an ongoing saga of 'ethnic' conflict between members of this group and those whose ancestors originated in India. Those studies which focus most specifically on the issue of nationalism and ethnic politics in Fiji generally fall into two broad categories. First, there are those which have tended to take the ethnic aspects of political conflict in Fiji, as well as many of the specific claims advanced by indigenous nationalist leaders, at face value. This includes accepting that the military coup d'état of 1987, as well as a civilian coup in 2000, really were 'all about' a serious conflict of interests between indigenous Fijians and the immigrant community of Indo-Fijians. This position reflects, more or less, an endorsement of primordialist approaches to such issues. The second broad body of literature, while acknowledging the important role of ethnicity, has not accepted the ethnic conflict model as the prime, let alone the sole, explanation for Fiji's political problems. In addition to viewing ethnicity more in situational, relational and instrumental terms, some studies have also attempted to look beyond the ethnic dimension at other relevant factors. And whereas this approach attracted less support at the time of the 1987 coup, subsequent developments in Fiji have shown that analyses concentrating too narrowly on the ethnic dimension really do miss the mark when it comes to a more satisfactory political analysis.

Assessments of the events of May 2000, including those published in the popular media, have tended to be more nuanced and critical, and much less inclined to accept a simplistic primordialist 'ethnic' explanation than many of those which emerged with the events of 1987. This has been helped considerably by the poor personal profile of the May 2000 coup leader, George Speight. Whereas the 1987 coup leader Sitiveni Rabuka, the third-ranking officer of the Royal Fiji Military Forces, was able to present himself more convincingly as being motivated by concerns for the rights and interests of indigenous Fijians (even though this was really quite disingenuous), George Speight could not. Despite his frequently stated concerns for the plight of indigenous Fijians in the face of the 'Indian threat' embodied in the person of the elected Prime Minister and his government, Speight was quite clearly someone with highly dubious credentials and motives. He was wanted in Australia for fraud and due to face extortion charges in a Fijian court. None the less, demonstrations by indigenous Fijian nationalists which followed the Speight coup did seem to lend credence to the ethnic conflict model.

Although the study of politics in Fiji clearly entails the study of ethnicity and nationalism in context, insufficient attention has been paid to how well – or how poorly – various theoretical approaches to the study of nations, nationalism and ethnicity fare in explaining politics in Fiji.[1] The main purpose of this chapter is to remedy this to some extent by critically examining, in the context of Fiji's political history, both primordialist and modernist approaches to the study of nationalism and ethnicity, as well as the more recent ethno-symbolist approach. In so doing, I shall make a case, based on Fiji's experience, for the importance of situational and relational aspects of national/ethnic identity, and how these feed into the particular kind of ethnic nationalism that has been a feature of Fiji's politics for many years. I also pay special attention to the concept of 'nation' and its close association with 'indigenousness', since it is the latter concept which has grounded the claims of ethnic Fijian nationalism and given it such a strong normative force.

Primordialism, modernism and ethno-symbolism

Primordialism, modernism and ethno-symbolism do not exhaust approaches to the study of nations, nationalism and ethnicity, but they have tended to dominate contemporary discussions of these intertwined topics. Each of the approaches turns primarily on the question of '*when* is the nation?' This question also feeds into a whole range of additional questions and issues, including the extent to which ethnic (or national or cultural) identity/difference is, *in itself*, the cause of conflict. Primordialism, in particular, has featured either implicitly or explicitly as the conceptual underpinning for studies which take ethnic identity or ethnic difference *per se* as the primary cause of political conflict in Fiji and as the driving force behind indigenous Fijian nationalism. As we shall see, in the case of Fiji at least, primordialist perspectives have actually aided and abetted the normative claims of ethnic identity expressed in terms of indigenousness over and above other claims or considerations. Indeed, the articulation of a 'politics of primordialism' through Fijian nationalism has resulted in something of a self-fulfilling prophecy. I return to this issue later. In the meantime, the purpose of this section is to cover some fairly well worn ground with respect to understandings of primordialism as well as modernism and ethno-symbolism, but with a view to generating some insights into their utility in analysing the case of Fiji. This exercise has implications, in turn, for the more general utility of these approaches in the analysis of nationalism and ethnic conflict.

Primordialism generally depicts the 'nation' in terms which highlight robust qualities of longevity, relatedness, constancy and emotional attachment with respect to a particular group. The group is defined, and differentiated from other human groups, by reference to an array of factors which usually includes not only a shared history but also a common culture (including language and religion, art and artefacts), territorial affiliation and a repertoire of myths (including myths of origin), rituals and symbols, all of which combine to provide a common identity. In addition, a primordialist approach would regard the tendency to form such groups, and to relate to them with a deep emotional attachment, as ultimately embedded in human nature and therefore as something which is so much part of our psyche as to make it virtually inescapable. In this sense the nation is a universal, perennial phenomenon, and its existence in one form or another is essentially constant through time and space. 'When' is the nation is answered simply by 'forever and ever, amen'. It is but a short step to then assert that nations defined in this way are the 'natural' units for *political* as well as social/cultural organisation. Moreover, this conception resonates with widespread, popular conceptions of the nation as seen through the prism of nationalism. John Hutchinson notes the 'pervasive acceptance of the assumption of nationalism that nations are facts of nature that have differentiated humanity into distinctive cultural communities, each of which has its own territorial habitat and capacities for self-government' (Hutchinson 1994: 1).

The understanding of 'nation' outlined above is almost indistinguishable from 'ethnic group', and indeed a primordialist approach does emphasise certain qualities of nationhood or 'nation-ness' precisely in terms of ethnicity – as distinct from other possible forms such as the civic nation which we shall come to later. If there is any difference between the categories of *ethnos* and nation, this is to be found in the political dimension. For whereas an ethnic group, defined largely in terms of certain common cultural characteristics and heritage, may or may not seek political autonomy as a means of preserving, enhancing or asserting its identity, a 'nation' is an entity that almost by definition represents itself as deserving or requiring, in a normative sense, some form of political autonomy. The contemporary world abounds with examples of such groups whose demands range from a measure of sub-state autonomy to a separate, independent sovereign state. Where an ethnic group develops a political agenda that includes a demand for full-scale autonomy, and which therefore regards itself as a 'nation' more or less in waiting, this is often termed 'ethnic nationalism'. However, this is not the only form of ethnic nationalism. In the case of Fiji, ethnic nationalism among indigenous Fijians has generally taken the form of a demand for absolute political dominance within an existing multi-ethnic state, although some of the more extreme, exclusivist indigenous nationalists have actually called for Fiji to be largely 'cleansed' of ethnic others (and especially Indians) in order to create a more ethnically pure Fijian state that actually accords with the ideal embodied in the term 'nation-state'.

If the primordialist approach to the concept of 'nation' and its perennial qualities has an opposite category, it is the modernist approach. In fact, the latter arose as a very direct, critical response to national historiographies steeped in a celebratory primordialism characterised by anachronism, romanticisation and essentialism. In contrast, modernists see the nation as a product of modernity itself, a phenomenon which includes (but is obviously not limited to) the emergence of the sovereign state system in Europe and the politically attuned myth-making that has accompanied it – that is, the political ideology of nationalism. To use the language of contemporary historic contextualism, one may say that nations and nationalism emerged as historically, culturally and geographically contingent constructs with a specificity rooted in the emergence of European modernity. Nations are therefore a comparatively recent phenomenon, at least in the specific form that they have taken in pursuit of political goals. Since modernists discern a more or less definite starting point for nations and nationalism in European history with a subsequent expansion throughout the rest of the globe, modernism may be likened to a 'big bang' theory whereas primordialism represents a classic steady state model while ethno-symbolism, as we shall see below, synthesises aspects of both.

From this point on, however, modernists may diverge or disagree over any number of issues, including how the basic categories – 'modernity', 'nationalism', the 'nation' and so on – are actually defined, how they relate to the category of ethnicity, what role industrialisation, colonialism and elite interests has played in their development, whether nations and nationalism are a 'mass' phenomenon and so on. There is also no agreement as to the future of nations and nationalism. The resolution of these particular problems and issues is well beyond the scope of the present discussion. What is useful about the modernist approach for the subject matter of this chapter is that it generally emphasises the role of contingency and provides more scope for constructivist perspectives which highlight the situational, relational and instrumental aspects of the indigenous Fijian 'nation', the ethnic/indigenous basis of 'its' identity, and how these are manifest in contemporary Fijian nationalism.

The third approach, ethno-symbolism, has been worked out in response to both primordialism and modernism. Its major proponent, Anthony D. Smith, sees it as complementing certain aspects of modernism while rejecting the modernist insistence that nations are both recent in time and novel in conception and structure. Ethno-symbolism therefore joins with primordialism in locating the origins of nations (and ethnic groups) in the depths of the pre-modern past, and so endorses their perennial presence in history. But it joins as well with the modernists in identifying national*ism* with developments in the not-so-distant past. The ethno-symbolic approach, as explained by Smith, also lays particular emphasis on the subjective elements of attachment to nations and ethnic groups by their members, as well as the institutionalisation of these elements in various ways – recorded myths, memories, traditions, symbols, art, music, literature, law, ritual and so on – and it is these institutionalised expressions of collective identity that provide evidence for the 'pedigrees of particular nations or different types of nations' (Smith 2002: 29–30). Due attention to these, it is suggested, will deter the scholar of nations and nationalism from seeking refuge in 'a one-sided and ethnocentric "modern western" version of the concept of nation' (ibid.: 30).

Leaving aside Smith's definition of the 'modern western nation' (which seems to blur the categories of state and nation) (ibid.: 7), the 'ethnic form' of the modern nation is depicted as a variant which locates the nation in a historic homeland and defines it in terms of its genealogical myths, vernacular public culture, nativist history and popular mobilisation (ibid.: 16). Smith is concerned to develop a definition of the nation that pays due attention to these factors – factors which are not simply a product of modernity. This leads to a definition of the nation 'as a named and self-defined community whose members cultivate common myths, memories, symbols and values, possess and disseminate a distinctive public culture, reside in and identify with an historic homeland, and create and disseminate common laws and shared customs' (Smith, Chapter 10, this volume). Smith also poses the question:

> if nations are not always the result of nationalism (and modernity), then what are the processes that help to make nations? In other words, in addition to the historical and rather linear question, 'when is *the* nation?', an ethno-symbolist approach requires that we ask a more general sociological question, 'when is *a* nation'?
>
> (Smith 2002: 16)

As we shall see, the description of the ethnic national form outlined by Smith does indeed describe key features of the Fijian nation as imagined by contemporary Fijian nationalists. However, no such entity as the 'Fijian nation' as described in the definition of 'nation' above existed before the late nineteenth century when the islands came under colonial control. Rather, it does seem that it was the processes of modern state formation, along with the ideology of Fijian national-*ism*, that brought the subjective elements together. Moreover, Fijian nationalism has been formulated very specifically with political control of the state as its prime objective, and against assumed Indo-Fijian interests, and has so far trumped other possible conceptions of 'a nation' at a practical level. The very fact that alternative conceptions are possible also highlights the fact that Fijian national/ethnic identity is situational, relational and instrumental. While the relevance of these aspects of identity are not excluded from analysis by an ethno-symbolist approach which is, after all, interested in deeply subjective factors from a sociological perspective, they do not seem to figure prominently. This is quite apart from the fact that the subjective elements often referred to by various Fijian nationalists do not add up to a coherent and uncontested repertoire.

What different nationalist discourses do converge on is a collective sense of indigenousness which carries with it certain superior rights, and a concomitant rejection of Indo-Fijian political legitimacy and status on terms equal to that of indigenous Fijians. It seems, then, that although the ethno-symbolist approach may be right to emphasise the importance of pre-modern elements, the modernist approach provides a more satisfactory account of the particular case of how the 'Fijian nation' came into being. The case study that follows will therefore concentrate, for the most part, on the period immediately prior to colonisation as well as the colonial period to illustrate how the Fijian nation took shape as Fiji itself became a unified political entity.

Nation, state and nationalism in Fiji: a case study

The 520 islands which make up the contemporary state of Fiji are home to approximately 720,000 people. Around 52 per cent are indigenous Fijians, while 43 per cent are of Indian origin with the remainder made up of smaller minorities including Europeans, part-Europeans, Chinese and other Pacific Islanders. The elected governments that were overthrown in coups d'état in 1987 and 2000 were made up of coalitions, significant elements of which were parties supported by Indo-Fijians. Neither government, however, was by any means controlled exclusively by Indo-Fijian leaders and indeed the Prime Minister displaced in 1987 was an indigenous Fijian. None the less, both coups were ostensibly carried out in the name of indigenous Fijian rights and interests which were portrayed by Fijian nationalists as being under grave threat from an 'Indian' government. Indeed, nationalist rhetoric has consistently portrayed the two groups as possessing opposed and irreconcilable interests, but with indigenous Fijians obviously enjoying superior rights.

The ancestors of the indigenous Fijians are thought to have commenced settling the islands about 3,000 years ago with subsequent waves of immigration continuing up until the time of colonisation in 1874. The earliest arrivals were probably the same people who went on to settle in Tonga and Samoa – the ancestral Polynesians. In Fiji, however, the later migrations produced a mixed population with Melanesian characteristics, thereby contributing to physical, cultural and linguistic diversity throughout the islands (see France 1969: 4–5, 8; Routledge 1985: 21). By the time European explorers and traders came into contact with the islands, known collectively as 'Viti' (from which the name 'Fiji' derives), socio-political organisation within the group consisted of very disparate entities. Indeed, there is a mass of anthropological evidence to support the presence of significant ethnic diversity among the people of the islands at the time of European contact, at least some of which may be attributed to different origins or waves of migration (see e.g. Hocart 1952).

In addition to ethnic diversity, a 'problem' confronting those searching for a common creation myth, or myth of origin, has been that they are unable to find any evidence to support one. The legendary 'Degei' who some Fijians regarded as the spirit figure responsible for spreading Fijians throughout the islands from a single point, was clearly unknown outside of his more or less immediate locale in Viti Levu. The well known recorder of events and oral traditions in pre-colonial Fiji, the Reverend Thomas Williams, noted by 1860 that he 'had sought in vain for a single ray of tradition' concerning the origin of Fijians (quoted in Gravelle 1979: 6). And at the time of a colonial Lands Commission, some fifty diverse legends were recorded, none of which mentioned Degei. Even more telling is that the best-known 'traditional' legend concerning Fijian origins appeared in 1892 when a local Fijian paper, *Na Mata*, actually ran a competition to discover the origins of Fijians. The winner described Fijians as having come originally from Thebes, and who then travelled up the Nile to Tanganyiki from where they made their way to Fiji (ibid.: 7). Despite the lack of any unifying structures in terms of myths, symbols, language or socio-political arrangements, however, it was not long after European contact that the idea of Fiji as constituting a single 'national' political entity gained ground.

The largest and most powerful native communities were located in the east where relatively large-scale confederacies called *matanitu* had been established. Headed by paramount chiefs, these were characterised by hierarchical socio-political structures usually associated (in anthropological terms) with Polynesian forms which contrasted quite markedly with arrangements in the central and western regions where much smaller scale and less stratified units were found and which have often been described as more Melanesian in character (Norton 1977: 54; Durutalo 1985: 76). In the period leading up to colonisation, the most important of the chiefly figures in the east were Cakobau who controlled an important region around the south-east of the main island of Viti Levu from the island of Bau. The other important paramount chief was Ma'afu, a Tongan who had colonised the Lau area of eastern Fiji. The Lau group of islands formed a basis for the Tovata confederacy while Cakobau's stronghold of Bau dominated the Kubuna confederacy, and a third confederacy, Burebasaga, controlled the south-western region. As noted above, larger scale confederacies of this nature did not exist in the western areas.

The presence of Europeans inevitably impacted significantly on many aspects of politics and economy in the islands, but especially in the east where European missionaries, traders and some settlers had become established by the mid-nineteenth century. The islands of Fiji also assumed greater strategic importance as plans for the Panama Canal, which would mean much more traffic across the Pacific from Panama to Australia, were being drawn up. This led to a flurry of diplomatic activity, and treaties were soon established between some of the paramount chiefs and agents acting for France, Great Britain and the USA (Derrick 1950: 156). But European contact also brought some major difficulties, especially for the chief Cakobau, who found himself at the centre of a dispute involving alleged outrages against a number of Americans by some native people. By this time, Cakobau had come to be known as Tui Viti – 'King of Fiji' – a title which had not previously existed and which was obviously not recognised throughout the islands (and which is not in use today). It was a largely European invention, and one which the Americans found useful in pressing their claims for compensation against an individual who held ostensible authority and responsibility. In addition to these problems, Cakobau was facing challenges to his authority from his arch rival, Ma'afu of Lau.

By 1858, the first British consul had arrived, and Cakobau found himself persuaded that he might resolve all his difficulties by ceding the whole of the island group to the British Crown, although his 'authority' to do so simply did not exist. The first offer of cession was, in any case, turned down. With the aid of various native and European allies, Cakobau then looked to alternative schemes, including one in 1865 which envisaged a confederation of certain chiefs acting as a central government for the whole island group. But it was almost completely ineffective and survived for just a year. One analysis points out that the confederation was not representative of the western area of Fiji, and its authority in the east was insecure. . . . The chiefs who went . . . were not traditionally allies and were too much preoccupied with the affairs of their own chiefdoms to pay too much attention to an introduced nationalism. The diversity of . . . interests which had always characterised events in Fiji was too powerful, and there was, in 1865, no reason evident to the chiefs why they should subordinate these to a national good. The first attempt to create a political unity out of the social and cultural diversity came to nothing.

(France 1969: 74)

Further offers of cession were made to Germany and the USA, but were declined. In 1871 another type of 'national' government was set up involving Cakobau and a group of European entrepreneurs, but this failed too. Increasing problems with law and order, engendered largely by the impact of European activity in the region which included trade in goods as well as labour and land, eventually saw another offer of cession to the British Crown accepted. This followed a report by the then Secretary of State for the Colonies, the Earl of Kimberley, outlining various courses of action open to the British, one of which was: 'To assume territorial sovereignty over the islands and, as a necessary consequence, to constitute within them a form of colonial government' (Parliament of Great Britain, April 1874: 5). A further report by Lord Carnarvon, now responsible for colonies in the Disraeli government, delivered the final – and now frequently quoted – recommendation that a crown colony 'of a rather severe type' be established in Fiji (Parliament of Great Britain, 17 July 1874, col. 182). And so, on 10 October 1974, Cakobau and eleven other high chiefs – including Ma'afu but excluding all but one western chief – signed an unconditional deed of cession to the British Crown. Fiji's first substantive Governor, Sir Arthur Hamilton Gordon (later Lord Stanmore), was installed on 1 September 1875. Thus began the period in which the islands of Fiji, and the people settled there, were formally brought together under a single sovereign power.

There was, however, no real sense in which the native people formed a 'Fijian nation' at this time. Diversity in terms of linguistic and other markers of cultural identity was a prominent feature at the time of cession, and there was no political unity to speak of either. For while the eastern parts of the islands, led by their paramount chiefs, had obviously accepted colonial rule and were host to the initial 'capital' of Levuka on the island of Ovalau, the people of much of the western and central area had not. In fact, events were soon to show just how much the people of these latter regions regarded themselves as politically separate, since Gordon found it necessary to wage a war of 'pacification' on these unwilling colonial subjects, assisted by native troops from the east. As a result of this, and the other factors outlined above which made eastern Fijians the logical allies of the colonising power, eastern Fijians came to dominate that part of the colonial administration concerned with native affairs. Moreover, it was eastern socio-political structures, particularly those of Bau (see Groves 1963), that were adopted as the basis of the colonial construction of the 'Fijian way' and all the orthodoxies that were to be developed in its name throughout the colonial era and into the post-independence period (see Lawson 1991).

The essential aspects of 'a Fijian way of life', which Gordon was intent on preserving as something of a living museum of anthropology, were standardised around several key structures. These included the Native Administration (later renamed the Fijian Administration) which, for the purpose of governing the local population, divided the country into twelve provinces with a chief appointed as governor for each one and various other chiefs at district and village level. Alongside this was a system of deliberative bodies, the highest of which was the *Bose Vaka Turanga* – known also as the Council (or sometimes Great Council) of Chiefs which served as the national apex of the new native system. It is generally agreed that this body, in particular, had no predecessor at all. One author says that it arose in an *ad hoc* manner on the occasion of Gordon's installation as 'supreme chief' – representing Queen Victoria – when chiefs gathered from different parts of the island. Thereafter it became an annual event and, when vested with certain authority, came to represent a 'new national element' grafted on to existing traditional structures (Legge 1958: 209). This body, however, came to play a central role in politics as the pre-eminent institution claiming to embody a singular version of Fijian tradition and, since independence, has been constitutionally entrenched as a symbol of indigenous Fijian identity and political pre-eminence alongside parliamentary institutions.

The creation of a Fiji nation in the colonial state also required that different languages, land tenure and kinship systems be reduced to a single, uniform standard. With respect to language, the Bauan dialect presented itself as the obvious choice for a common language for Fijians since it had been adopted by missionaries in the east as the language for biblical translation and therefore for initial literacy. Thus the 'Fijian language', like many other national languages around the world, derives from just one of the languages spoken by the inhabitants of the space which was to become a nation-state. There are some particularly interesting historical attitudes to the adoption of the Bauan dialect as the 'Fijian language'. A study of Fijian dialects, for example, notes that 'there once existed the feeling that the non-Bauan dialects were somehow impure or inferior to Bauan' (Schutz 1963: 254).

But the adoption of a uniform land tenure system presented the greatest challenge. The system that was eventually adopted vested ownership of native land in kinship groups known as *mataqali*, although this particular unit was not recognised throughout the islands, nor was it connected more than very tenuously with a notion of land 'ownership'. One Fijian chief at the time is reported as saying that: 'The recording of mataqali boundaries is a wholly European ideal . . . it is not correct to write down the mataqali boundaries, in accordance with European practice' (Ratu Savenica Seniloli quoted in Macnaught 1982: 144). It was further decreed that native land was inalienable (which it had not been previously) and therefore could not be sold.[2] More generally, the land issue has become linked inextricably with a 'doctrine of Fijian paramountcy'. This developed at the time of Gordon, and was initially part of his vision of preserving the 'Fijian way of life' against incursions by Europeans. But it came to acquire its present political salience in the presence of another immigrant population, the people now known as Fiji Indians or Indo-Fijians.

Colonies like Fiji were not acquired because of the economic benefits they might bring to the British government. In fact, such colonies were more of a financial liability, and one of Gordon's prime responsibilities was to establish a sound economic basis for the new colony. Fiji was ideal for the development of sugar plantations, and native ownership under the land tenure system by no means precluded leases for plantation (and other) purposes. Moreover, there was Crown land (which had no official *mataqali* owners) as well as some of the best agricultural land alienated to Europeans before colonisation. Some of this had been returned to native ownership, but tracts amounting to 17 per cent of land in the islands remained in private ownership.

Land was therefore available for plantations, but preserving the Fijian way of life also meant prohibiting the use of indigenous labour. Ordinary or 'commoner' Fijians were required to remain in their villages under the control of chiefs. The issue of cheap labour was therefore resolved via the importation of indentured 'coolies' from India. Over a period of almost forty years some 60,000 labourers were transported to the islands, about two-thirds of whom remained as 'free settlers'. The presence of a large immigrant population was to become another factor contributing to a sense of Fijian uniformity, but, like Fijians, Indo-Fijians did not constitute a homogeneous social/cultural entity. Most were Hindu, but subscribed to different schools of practice, while Muslims and Christian Indians retained a distinctive identity. Place of origin in India was another differentiating factor. In later years many Indo-Fijians remained on the land, mostly growing sugar on leased smallholdings. Others moved to urban areas and engaged in trades, professions and small businesses. The relative success of Indo-Fijians in these latter activities, in particular, has led to a perception that they are an advantaged group and this has fuelled anti-Indian nationalist rhetoric. This is despite the fact that poverty afflicts many Indo-Fijians as well as ordinary Fijians in both urban and rural areas.

Despite evident social and cultural cleavages within the various population groups, political uniformity on the basis of broad racial or communal identity was reinforced through various aspects of colonial rule. The separate native administration was augmented by rules which kept Indo-Fijians strictly segregated from indigenous Fijians. It was actually an offence for an Indo-Fijian to enter a native village – or for the villagers to harbour such a person. This gave rise to a system akin to apartheid, with separate schools and other social facilities being set up to cater for the different 'races' in the colony. All this was reinforced by the method of representation in the colonial legislature where there were racially designated seats and electorates for Europeans and Indo-Fijians. Fijian representatives were chosen by the Governor from a list submitted by the Council of Chiefs (and all nominees were themselves chiefs), and neither ordinary Fijians, nor women from any group, were enfranchised until the early 1960s. Indo-Fijians objected to racial or communal representation (as it became known) from the start, but representation on this basis was retained as a key feature of the political system throughout the colonial period and beyond. To this day, communal representation on the basis of race remains enshrined in the constitution alongside electorates which allow for 'cross-voting' on a non-communal basis.

I mentioned above a 'doctrine of Fijian paramountcy' which developed as an orthodoxy from Gordon's time. It reflected not only his policy of protecting native interests, but also the concerns of the leading chiefs to preserve their status. The doctrine holds that the rights and interests of Fijians with respect to land and customary practices are inalienable as well as paramount over any other claims. Reference is frequently made to the Deed of Cession to support the doctrine, but there is actually nothing in it which specifically supports claims of indigenous paramountcy. It seems to have initially developed in opposition to perceived threats from European settlers, but over time the threat perception shifted and it became a rallying cry in opposition to Indo-Fijian claims for greater political equality. Interestingly, the doctrine came to be promoted by many Europeans in the colony who, for reasons of expediency, aligned themselves politically with indigenous Fijian leaders as the number of Indians in the colony increased. It was therefore a European member of the legislature who moved, in 1946, a motion formally recognising the paramountcy doctrine. The original motion called for the Deed of Cession to be recognised as assuring that 'the interests of the Fijian race are safeguarded and a guarantee be given that Fiji is to be preserved and kept as a Fijian country for all time' (Legislative Council of Fiji, 16 July 1946: 163). The motion was subsequently amended, following protests from Indo-Fijian members against whom it was directed, to read more simply that: '[I]n the opinion of this Council the Government and the non-Fijian inhabitants of this Colony stand by the Deed of Cession and shall consider that document a Charter of the Fijian people' (ibid.: 214). Although the language here is less specific in its intention than the original motion, it is none the less clear in conveying the message that Indo-Fijian interests were subordinate to those of the indigenous population which, by this time, were clearly constituted by the colonial state as an undifferentiated whole in relation to other communal groups in general, and Indo-Fijians in particular.

As I have argued elsewhere, the doctrine of paramountcy underpins the special provisions relating to Fijians that have featured in all three post-independence constitutions and, most importantly, constitutes the foundational principle from which Fijian nationalist claims proceed (Lawson 2004). This has logically required the political subordination of Indo-Fijians. Thus, although many of the early paternalistic policies were well intentioned as far as native Fijians were concerned, one cannot say the same about policy towards Indo-Fijians. Although the latter were brought in to work the land, and encouraged to stay in Fiji after indenture to support the economy with their labour and skills, little thought was given to how future generations might be accommodated. Today, any notion that Indo-Fijians may have 'rights' with respect to land is completely anathema to nationalists. Indeed, land – the *vanua* – is regarded as virtually sacred and, together with the chiefly system, is often said to embody the very essence of Fijianness. Even those nationalists critical of the chiefly system today none the less regard the *vanua* as a hallowed symbol of identity and as an important factor in legitimating Fijian predominance. The name *taukei* has been used in relation to various Fijian nationalist movements and parties and means, literally, 'owners' (of the land).

Much of the evidence suggests, however, that land only acquired such a strong symbolic dimension during the colonial period, and in the context of political and economic developments which had much to do with the issue of European settlement as well as chiefly power and control in the new colonial state. As we have seen, the notion that indigenous Fijian units called *mataqali* had owned certain tracts of land since 'time immemorial' does not hold; nor does the idea that land was completely inalienable. Evidence adduced during the process of fixing a uniform land tenure system in the early colonial period suggests not only that tenure practices varied significantly throughout Fiji, but that relationships between people and the land was much more fluid and flexible (see France 1969; Lawson 1991; Ward 1995). Furthermore, not every square inch of land in Fiji had an 'owner', whether in the form of a *mataqali* group or something else. And although the alienation of land to European settlers in the pre-colonial period may now be regarded as morally objectionable, it was a practice that Fijian chiefs at the time participated in actively. To suggest that Fijians of the time had no understanding at all of what they were doing in selling or trading land, and were merely dupes of more wily Europeans, is patronising in the extreme. That issue aside, the evidence regarding a rigid doctrine of the inalienability of land as well as the notion that it was a sacred symbol of identity were all produced in the processes of colonial state formation.

In all these developments, little attention has been paid to how Indo-Fijian farmers and rural communities might relate to land in cultural terms. Carens, for example, has said that the concern of Indo-Fijians with the land is economic *rather than* cultural (Carens 1992). One objection to this view is that economic concerns are hardly unimportant when it comes to fairly basic issues of survival. Of course for Fijians, too, the relationship is also very much a question of economics. Apart from Fijian village communities whose way of life is largely one of subsistence on their land, other Fijians who control land with a high economic value (for example, the land leased for tourist resorts on the west coast of Viti Levu) could hardly deny that the economic benefits brought to their communities are important. That the last coup was as much about the exploitation of valuable plantation timber as anything else also underscores the salience of economic *rather than* cultural factors.[3] Furthermore, an emphasis on the cultural rights that go with indigenousness should not automatically negate the claims that groups such as Indo-Fijians might make in terms of their own 'culture'. As I have argued elsewhere, after four or more generations on the land one would be hard put to argue that Indo-Fijian farmers have no 'cultural' attachments to it (Lawson 2004).

This raises more general issues to do with the specific rights that may be attached to indigenousness on the one hand, and the rights and interests of later settlers on the other. There is not the space here to deal with this issue in any great detail, but it has of course become an extremely important one in a number of countries and is at the heart of the themes of this volume. In Fiji, it is precisely the 'indigenousness' of one group *vis-à-vis* the 'alien' status of another that is at issue. A recent study by Jeff J. Corntassel of definitional standards for indigenousness notes the contribution made by instrumental approaches to ethnic/indigenous identity to highlighting the importance of context – that is, the specific situations in which such identities have become politically salient in the recent past – but goes on to argue that while this approach has merits, it does not accurately depict indigenous nations 'who have existed for 10,000 years or more on their home-lands'. And, quoting nationalism theorist Umut Özkirimli, Corntassel goes on to say that these first nations clearly do not fit the instrumentalist scheme of being 'the products of developments of the last two centuries' (Corntassel 2003: 84).

Although one can hardly disagree with the assertion that the contemporary groups called first nations are by and large descended directly from people who were unquestionably occupying certain lands well before European (and other) people arrived in the past few hundred years, and who may have powerful moral arguments to back up certain claims to land and other goods, other aspects of the claim are arguable. The very notion of indigenousness, the particular collective identities that such a notion now attaches to and, most importantly, the moral claims that arise from them in the present, are quite certainly the product of settlement by later people (mostly, but not always, Europeans) and the political institutions – including colonial and then sovereign states – that were created in the ensuing period. Moreover, the claims arising from indigenousness itself are very much part of the general human rights discourse that has emerged over the past half century.

Conclusion

The historical record shows that the ingredients of nation-ness – which must at the very minimum include a common sense of Fijian identity at elite level, if not among members of the population at large – were not in evidence at any time before the establishment of a colonial state. Political (and other forms) of identity certainly existed, but these would have been constructed in relation to Fijian 'others' as well as in relation to Europeans, other Pacific islanders and so on. The act of cession was a landmark because it brought together a number of Fijian chiefs (one of whom was actually Tongan) in the execution of a significant politi-cal act which more or less created the Fijian nation *ab initio*. As we have seen, these chiefs purported to act on behalf of all the people(s) of the island group but in fact, those of the central and western areas had not acceded and subse-quently required pacification. After this, the 'Fijian nation' took form through various colonial institutions, including the Great Council of Chiefs, the Native Administration, the uniform tenure system and, not least, the doctrine of Fijian paramountcy which acted as a powerful unifying discourse.

Initially, a common Fijian identity, such as it was, developed largely in relation to the British/European presence, but with the arrival of Indian labourers in the colony an additional relational and situational element was added. As the number of immigrants grew, so did the political 'threat' against which a common Fijian identity could be discursively constructed. Politics in the independence period, from 1970 to the present time, has been characterised by the full-blown development of Fijian nationalist politics seeking control of the new sovereign state.[4] In this context, the claims on behalf of an indigenous Fijian nation with superior entitlements to the exercise of sovereign power have been used to justify two coups against elected governments and, for a period, a form of political apartheid in which Indo-Fijians were relegated to second-class status.[5] This has resulted in major social and economic disruption not simply for Indo-Fijians but for most ordinary Fijians too – 'the Fijian nation' – on whose behalf the coups have ostensibly been carried out.

Another point to note is that although certain aspects of material culture may be described as 'Fijian' rather than 'Indian' – and vice versa – and may therefore be seen in some sense as 'ethnic symbols', it is difficult to assert that they functioned to underscore a sense of separate Fijian ethnic identity until such times as 'Fijianness' itself as a distinct identity developed in the particular historical circumstances of the colonial period. Furthermore, many aspects of material culture, such as bark cloth-making, weaving, bodily decoration and so on, as well as ceremonial practices and kinship customs, are shared by other Pacific islanders. Of course, material culture will exhibit many variations according to locale, but these variations are no less extensive within the islands of Fiji as between these and other island groups. This is not to say that material culture(s) or ceremonial practices derived from the various ethnic pasts of inidigenous Fijians have no relevance to important aspects of Fijian identity in the current period, but it is difficult to see how they could be used to demonstrate the presence of a 'Fijian nation' in the pre-colonial period. Similarly, although popular legends (retailed mainly for the benefit of tourists) tell a story of descent from the spirit figure Degei, the evidence shows that this myth was originally limited to a very specific locale on the main island of Viti Levu.

The main focus of the discussion, however, has been on the 'ethnic symbols' which Fijian nationalists have tended to rally around most strongly. To date, these have been the chiefly system (as incorporated into the official Fijian Administration and various constitutional devices both before and after independence), together with the notion of the inalienability of land. Christianity has also been an extremely important institution in the construction of the Fijian identity, but it is clear that none of these could have underpinned any sense of nation-ness before the advent of the colonial state. The 'chiefly system' varied significantly throughout Fiji in the pre-colonial period to the extent that one can really only speak of 'systems' in the plural. Nor is it possible to argue that any of these systems were unique to Fiji. Indeed, as mentioned above, those in the east have frequently been compared (at least in conventional anthropological terms) with Polynesian systems elsewhere, and those of the central and western regions with Melanesian systems. This is apart from the fact that chiefly systems are now under attack by some nationalists whose major claims about the 'nation' are based on a notion of indigenousness which rests not on any cultural symbols but on a narrow racialist view of biological descent. With respect to land tenure systems, these were also highly variable and did not necessarily entail sacredness or inalienability. Together with Christianity, their status as differentiating symbols of ethnic identity can therefore best be interpreted through a modernist lens. This does not mean that ethno-symbolism is not relevant to other cases, nor that the modernist approach provides a satisfactory account of the emergence of 'nations' in general. In the case of Fiji, however, both 'nation' and 'nationalism' are very much products of the modern state-making process.

Notes

1 This includes my own previous analyses.
2 For detailed studies of the land issue see France (1969) and Ward (1995).
3 The election of the new government had cost Speight the chairmanship of a major timber corporation given to him by the previous government, and had therefore blocked him from managing a multi-million dollar timber deal. This is regarded as a major personal motivation for the coup leader (see Keith-Reid 2000: 30).
4 For details see Lawson (2004).
5 This refers to the period following the first coup in 1987 until the promulgation of the 1997 constitution which restored the political status of Indo-Fijians to something approximating parity with other communal groups.

References

Carens, J. (1992) *Democracy and Respect for Difference: The Case of Fiji*, published as 25(3 and 4), *University of Michigan Journal of Law Reform*.

Corntassel, J.J. (2003) 'Who is Indigenous? "Peoplehood" and Ethnonationalist Approaches to Rearticulating Indigenous Identity', *Nationalism and Ethnic Politics*, 9(1).

Derrick, R.A. (1950) *A History of Fiji* (rev. edn), Suva, Government Press.

Durutalo, S. (1985) 'Internal Colonialism and Unequal Political Development in Fiji: The Case of Western Viti Levu', unpublished MA thesis, University of the South Pacific.

France, P. (1969) *The Charter of the Land*, Melbourne, Oxford University Press.

Gravelle, K. (1979) *Fiji's Times: A History of Fiji*, Suva, Fiji Times Ltd.

Groves, M. (1963) 'The Nature of Fijian Society', *Journal of the Polynesian Society*, 72(3), pp. 272–291.

Hocart, A.M. (1952) *The Northern States of Fiji*, London, Royal Anthropological Institute of Great Britain.

Hutchinson, J. (1994) *Modern Nationalism*, London, Fontana.

Keith-Reid, R. (2000) 'How Speight Pushed Too Far', *Islands Business*, August.

Lawson, S. (1991) *The Failure of Democratic Politics in Fiji*, Oxford, Clarendon Press.

Lawson, S. (1996) *Tradition Versus Democracy in the South Pacific: Fiji, Tonga and Western Samoa*, Cambridge, Cambridge University Press.

Lawson, S. (2004) 'Nationalism Versus Constitutionalism in Fiji', *Nations and Nationalism*, 10(4), pp. 519–538.

Legge, J.D. (1958) *Britain in Fiji 1858–1880*, London, Macmillan.

Legislative Council of Fiji (16 July 1946) *Debates*.

Macnaught, T.J. (1982) *The Fijian Colonial Experience: A Study of the Neotraditional Order under*

British Colonial Rule Prior to World War II, Canberra, Australian National University Press.

Norton, R. (1977) *Race and Politics in Fiji*, St Lucia, University of Queensland Press.

Parliament of Great Britain (April 1874), Cmd. 983.

Parliament of Great Britain (17 July 1874) *Debates* (House of Lords).

Routledge, D. (1985) *Matanitu: The Struggle for Power in Early Fiji*, Suva, Institute of Pacific Studies.

Schutz, A.J. (1963) 'Sources for the Study of Fijian Dialects', *Journal of the Polynesian Society*, 72(3), pp. 254–260.

Smith, A.D. (2002) 'When is a Nation', *Geopolitics*, 7(2).

Ward, R.G. (1995) 'Land, Law and Custom: Diverging Realities in Fiji', in R.G. Ward and E. Kingdon (eds), *Land, Custom and Practice in the South Pacific*, Cambridge, Cambridge University Press.

Conclusion

So, when is the nation?

Gordana Uzelac and Atsuko Ichijo

It is often said: 'Looking at a tin can from one perspective some people see a square and some see a circle.' The conclusion of this analogy seems obvious. In order to investigate what the object in question is, one has to observe it from different perspectives. But how many perspectives are necessary to give us the true picture?

Here, the question of 'When is the nation?' is observed from three distinctive perspectives: modernism, primordialism and ethno-symbolism. The *differentia specifica* of these perspectives is seemingly their answer to the question. The theories that claim nations have emerged in antiquity are labelled as primordialist. Those that locate the process of the nation-formation in the medieval period through the transformation of ethnic groups are called ethno-symbolist. Finally, those theories that claim the nation to be entirely a modern phenomenon are marked as modernist. So, what is the purpose of a debate that brings these three perspectives together to discuss the issue that clearly separates them from each other?

We are by training, and by choice, sociologists, and we do not intend to apologise for that. We have undertaken the challenging task to organise the conference, to set its format and, ultimately, to answer the above question as sociologists. Therefore, we admit from the outset our professional bias in examining issues of nations and nationalism (see Introduction to this volume).

Those who are familiar with the state of current debate could not have hoped for any reconciliation of the three perspectives at a single conference. Neither could they have hoped for the formation of one 'true perspective' that would finally resolve the mystery of the national phenomena. We will argue in this conclusion that such a general theory of nations and nationalism that could subsume these different perspectives is not only impossible but also undesirable.

The question 'When' is obviously not about a date. Not a single participant has suggested that he or she is able to date the emergence of the nation. The reason for that is not the lack of historical data or willingness to commit to a specific historical moment as the crucial moment for the nation's birth. One point around which some consensus exists is that the emergence of the nation is a result of a set of social processes. Therefore, a search for the answer to the question 'when is the nation' is a search for sufficient and necessary conditions for social change which transformed a society in such a way that the resulting product deserves a new name – the nation.

One could hence argue that any theory of nation-formation requires an identification of, first, relevant processes of social change, and, second, a set of characteristics of the transformed society that marks the end of transition period. The first requirement addresses the issue of how society changes and the second issue offers a definition of the nation.

The debate presented in this book, as, indeed, in numerous works of our contributors, demonstrates that *differentia specifica* is not their temporal definition of the nation – primordial, medieval or modern – but the selection of social processes signified as necessary and sufficient for the formation of the nation. Even theoreticians that have been seen as primordialists would agree with this approach. While the organic nationalists might hold that nations are part of human nature, both Grosby and van den Berghe observe the transformation of previous social groups into nations through certain sets of social processes. Hence we can read about the social changes that occurred as a consequence of politicisation of ethnicity or religion, myth- and memory-making, territorialisation, spread of public culture, legal standardisation, industrialisation, consolidation of modern state, urbanisation, secularisation, inventions of traditions, development of print capitalism, standardisation of culture and so on. None of the main theorists of nations and nationalism bases his or her theory on a single social process.

The reason for this is obvious. Even the broadest social processes, such as industrialisation, cannot offer sufficient explanation for the dramatic changes that society has to undertake in order to acquire a new form. However significant a structural change of society may be, it fails to explain the changes of its culture or agency. However drastically the culture of society changes, it cannot by itself explain its impact upon the existing social institutions or behaviours and belief systems of agency.

The current sociological theories of social change clearly point to a consensus that a change of a society cannot be explained by concentrating on a single aspect of social life. Hence Jeffrey Alexander (1987) and Randall Collins (1981) call for integration of micro and macro approaches, while Anthony Giddens (1984) and Margaret Archer (1988) stress the necessity for an agency and structure integration.

The nation, theorists would agree, is a form of social community. Social processes that formed its structure are examined by John Breuilly and Steven Grosby in this volume. For Breuilly, the process of the formation of a modern state assumes processes of territorialisation, centralisation of power and others, and hence firmly emphasises the role of institutions in the formation of the nation-state. At the same time Breuilly's approach denies the active role of agency by mainly explaining it as 'subjects of the rule'. The impact of culture upon society is deemed as an unreliable analytical tool and hence is dismissed from the discussion.

Steven Grosby observes the formation of the nation within the process of institutionalisation of territorial kinship. The nation is a bounded community, where its boundaries are not only geographically determined but also sealed by the extent of a belief system. One may argue that this process could take place only once the fact of kin relations is transformed into a myth, a myth well supported by the main social institutions, especially religious ones.

The role of agency is strongly emphasised by Eric Hobsbawm, Pierre L. van den Berghe and Walker Connor. Agency in Hobsbawm's approach is seen as undetermined and unconditioned by the existing social structure or culture. As such it is open for labelling as constructionist theory. The rise of the nation in modernity is conditioned by a collapse of previous structures and culture. A new form of community is invented by a select few with the purpose of creating a new equilibrium in a modernity-stricken society.

Pierre L. van den Berghe emphasises rightly that humans as social beings are those who create and then transform and maintain a specific set of relations known as social structure and cultural system such as kinship, the family, tribe, ethny and, hence, the nation. Van den Berghe sees these social forms as 'evolutionary stable strategies' which secure human survival. Hence, the main rationale behind the creation and maintenance of these social forms is found neither in human free will nor in the 'nature' of social structure and culture, but in the internal driving force of genes.

Walker Connor sees the nation formed mainly by a set of agency's beliefs – the belief in common ancestry – and disregards the importance of social structure. What this approach lacks in its explanation are social processes that change one's belief system.

It has to be admitted that in this volume Anthony D. Smith attempts to move beyond cultural determinism, a position he has been accused of so many times. In an attempt to determine a genealogy of nations, Smith moves from his previous method of searching for constituent elements of the nation (name, homeland, myth-symbol complex, public culture), to identifying a set of processes that, eventually, will characterise a social community as a nation. It is not the end-product of social change that marks the birth of the nation, but the change itself. The five identified processes that Smith defines as sufficient and necessary for nation-formation may now be seen as processes of institutionalisation of distinctive culture. In this concept the role of agency is assumed but not explained. The *making* of national myth and memory or the *creation* and *dissemination* of a distinctive public culture and laws, for example, require an agency that will undertake this making, creation and dissemination. Yet Smith's account cannot be termed as constructionism, since he sees agency's actions as being conditioned by previous social structures and cultures.

As was demonstrated, the six scholars offer us quite distinctive perspectives on processes of the formation of the nation. The social processes marked as crucial are of a different level of generalisation and complexity. Nevertheless, current literature often places them within the same schools of thought. So, what would be the common ground for their comparison? What categorises these different approaches into a single perspective is obviously not their methodological framework for explaining the process of social change that, as sociological theories remind us, necessarily takes place on levels of structure, culture and agency. After all, some modernist theories are labelled as structuralist or functionalist and some as constructionist; some see the nation as created 'from above' and some 'from below'.

One clear distinction between these approaches is the nature of the selected social processes. While primordialists and ethno-symbolists tend to base their explanations of nation-formation on historically continuous processes, modernists choose those that are discontinuous. For this reason the former concentrates on the issue of persistence of nations, while the latter focuses on their novelty.

For example, Smith's earlier explanations of the process of nation-formation (e.g. 1986, 1991) have been seen as, to paraphrase Gellner, 'modernism plus navels'. This process of nation-formation, Smith has agued, has occurred over time through triple revolutions: the division of labour, a revolution in the control of administration, and a revolution in cultural co-ordination (Smith 1986: 131). Even the choice of terms – 'revolutions' – signifies radical break with previous stages of social development. Regardless of the fact that Smith sees nations as 'continuations' of earlier ethnic groups, the new phenomenon – the nation – could not but be seen as modern(ish). Twenty years (and books) later the notion of revolutions is lost. Now, the insistence on social processes allows Smith to leave the periodisation of the emergence of the nation more vaguely defined, and, at the same time, to see them as older than modernity.

In contrast, Breuilly's insistence on equating the development of the nation with the development of the modern state evokes those processes that are radically 'new' and specific for a certain stage of social history. The emphasis here is not on 'what is continuous' but 'what is different', so that the nation may be explained as a new form of social organisation. One could assume that Breuilly could easily agree with Smith that the process of territorialisation has started way before the age of modernity, as have the processes of legal standardisation or dissemination of public culture. But the two theorists offer different answers on the *conditional* question of 'when is the nation'.

An attempt to delineate a clear set of conditions for the existence of the nation brings us to the problem of defining the phenomenon. Out of the three chapters that presume to represent the three main approaches to the study of nations and nationalism, Grosby is the only one who defines nation in the 'essentialist' way by placing it 'within the continuum of forms of kinship'. Its *differentia specifica* is territorial delimitation. Yet one can easily list other forms of social communities that could fit this definition (city-state, religious community) and hence doubt the discriminatory potency of such a definition.

On the other hand, Breuilly accepts Smith's newly redefined definition of the nation as 'a named and self-defined community whose members cultivate common myths, memories, symbols and values, possess and disseminate a distinctive public culture, reside in and identify with a historic homeland, and create and disseminate common laws and shared customs' (Smith, Chapter 5, p. 98). Smith's definition may easily be seen as a form of operational definition, where all variables, perceived as sufficient and necessary, are stated. When Breuilly attempts to apply this definition in a specific case of England, he arrives at different conclusions from Smith, claiming modern origins of the English nation. The reason why Smith's definition may be used to prove opposing arguments is its unclear statement on the *relationships* between those variables.

The conditional form of 'when is the nation?' question asks at which point of these processes of social change we may claim that the nation is formed. What are the necessary and sufficient results of these changes a society has to experience in order to be marked as a nation? Smith (Chapter 5) claims that '[w]hen we can show that a community exhibits a sufficient development of these processes, and that they combine and reinforce one another, then there is a *prima facie* case for designating it a "nation"'. Breuilly (Chapter 1) 'think[s] that the importance is when the nation is used'. Connor (Chapter 2) says that we have 'got to establish [whether the] sense of identity goes beyond a relatively small number of people at the top'.

It is obvious that when set out like this the conditions are not clearly defined. What is 'a sufficient development'? 'When the nation is used' by whom? How far 'beyond a relatively small number of people at the top' should this identity go in order that a group may now be labelled as a nation?

The space for a meaningful comparison is further limited by Smith's introduction of the distinction between nations and 'modern nations'. Now one may conclude that these theories or, as Smith insists, approaches are not dealing with the same social phenomenon. It also contributes to the proverbial terminological confusion in the field of ethnicity and nationalism. Not only is current literature on nations and nationalism characterised by a conflation between terms such as 'ethnic groups' and 'nations', and 'nations' and 'nation-states', but we now also require a clarification of terminological differences between 'ethnic groups' and 'non-modern nations'.

Most of the theorists discussed above would agree that the nation, whether created or re-created, has acquired new forms in the age of modernity. Most of the theories concur that nationalism, as an ideology or political movement, could easily be seen as a modern phenomenon. However, this apparent consensus does not bring us closer to understanding the processes of nation-formation. The reason for this is the obvious difference between methodological frameworks applied by these approaches. Could sociological perspectives help us with a systematisation of the theories of nations and nationalism?

The current sociological debate has already provided clear criticism of 'one-way theorising' that conflates structure, culture and agency. Theories that deny their independence as different strata of social reality, and assume either structure, culture or agency to be pure epiphenomena and hence entirely determined by other spheres of social life, are seen as, in Margaret Archer's (1988) words, upward or downward conflations. From a sociological perspective the process of social change necessarily occurs on all three levels of social life. The question is 'how it occurs?' While the main proponent of social change is agency, every agency acts within an existing social structure and culture. But these structures and cultures do not determine agency's action, but condition them. An analytical separation of structure, culture and agency of a society undergoing change could enable us to examine their interplay and hence explain changes that occur in all three spheres of social reality.

Theories of nations and nationalism in general, and the approaches presented in this volume more specifically, already offer us a rich analysis of the main structural, cultural and agential changes that occur in the process of nation-formation. Among others, Breuilly's analysis points to the changes of social structure; Smith and Grosby's to the changes on the cultural level; van den Berghe, Hobsbawn and Connor's to the role of agency. Can we expect their synthesis?

We would argue that, at this point of debate, such a synthesis is not only impossible but also undesirable. The approaches examined in this volume serve as building blocks of case study analyses. The second part of this volume witnesses this point. Krishan Kumar, Susan-Mary Grant, Anna Triandafyllidou and Stephanie Lawson, apply different approaches in order to obtain a better understanding of the processes of social change that result in the formation of particular nations.

One of the most debated case studies – the case of the formation of English nation – has been addressed in this volume by both Kumar and Breuilly. Both authors argue that the English nation is a modern phenomenon. Indeed, a thorough historical analysis seems to confirm their views. However, Liah Greenfeld (1992) and Adrian Hastings (1997) have used the same case study to demonstrate that the English nation was born much earlier: according to Hastings in the fourteenth and according to Greenfeld in the sixteenth century. The reason for such a different dating of the English nation lies in the authors' different understanding of the processes that are necessary and sufficient for the formation of the nation. While both Kumar and Breuilly insist on nations to be mass phenomena in the full meaning of the word, Hastings and Greenfeld are content with tracing notions of the nation among a narrower circle of a mainly political and cultural elite. Because of this definitional difference, the time span allocated for the birth of the English nation now spans five to six centuries. Yet, if nation-formation is understood as a process, would it not be of crucial importance to understand how an elite concept became a mass phenomenon?

The case studies presented in this and many other volumes are used for both verification and falsification of the existing theories of nations and nationalism. There is not a single case where this process is fully explained from a single perspective. These debates are forcing us to consider other perspectives and to reconsider our own. So long as these debates exist, not a single perspective will assume the position of a dominant paradigm, yet every step will bring us closer to understanding a phenomenon that continues to play a crucial role in shaping our lives – the nation. We hope that this debate has been a right step in that direction.

References

Alexander, J.C. and Bernhard, G. (1987) 'From Reduction to Linkage: The Long View of the Micro-Macro Link', in J.C. Alexander *et al.* (eds) *The Micro–Macro Link*. Berkeley: University of California Press, pp. 1–42.

Archer, M. (1988) *Culture and Agency: The Place of Culture in Social Theory*. Cambridge: Cambridge University Press.

Collins, R. (1981) 'On the Microfoundations of Macrosociology', *American Journal of Sociology*, 86: 984–1014.

Giddens, A. (1984) *The Constitution of Society: Outline of the Theory of Stracturation*. Berkeley: University of California Press.

Greenfield, L. (1992) *Nationalism: Five Roads to Modernity*. Cambridge, MA, and London: Harvard University Press.

Hastings, A. (1997) *The Construction of Nationhood*. Cambridge: Cambridge University Press.

Smith, A.D. (1986) *Ethnic Origins of Nations*. London: Blackwell.

Smith, A.D. (1991) *National Identity*. Harmondsworth: Penguin.

Index